MAJESTY AT SEA

The Four~Stackers by John H. Shaum Jr & William H. Flayhart III

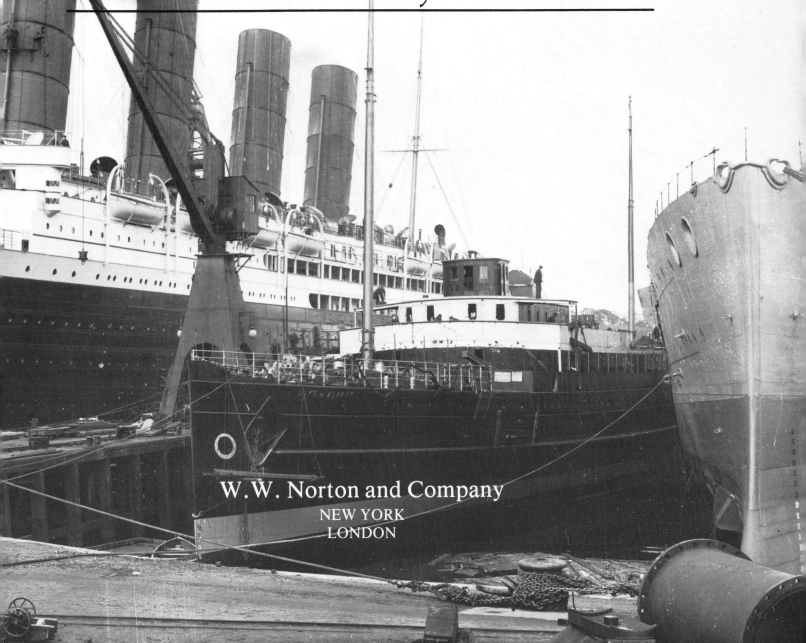

W.W. Norton and Company

NEW YORK
LONDON

First American edition 1981

ISBN 0-393-01527-0

Title pages

*July 29 1907 was a dreary, grey day on the Clyde.
But the* Lusitania, *resplendent in her fresh paint,
towers magnificently over other ships in Brown's yard.
She is preparing to embark on her trials*
(Scottish Record Office).

Text photoset in 11 pt Plantin
by Manuset Limited, Baldock, Herts.
Printed in Great Britain on 135 gsm Fineblade coated
cartridge by Lowe & Brydone Limited, Leeds,
and bound by Norton Bridge Bookbinders Limited,
Stotfold, Herts, for the publishers,
W.W. Norton and Company, Inc.,
500 Fifth Avenue, New York 10110

Contents

Foreword by Walter Lord

What was the Golden Age of ocean travel? Was it from 1871, when the first *Oceanic* revolutionised passenger ships, to 1974, when the *France* (last of the true breed) was withdrawn from service? Was it from 1907, when the *Lusitania* and *Mauretania* set a new modern standard, to 1967, when the *Queen Mary* and *Queen Elizabeth* saluted each other in mid-Atlantic, never to pass again?

Steamship buffs could argue endlessly over the question, but a good case can be made that the age really ran from 1897 to 1949—the era of those great, majestic four-funneled liners that drew attention wherever they went. It was on September 19 1897 that the new German express steamer *Kaiser Wilhelm der Grosse* left Bremen on her maiden voyage to New York. Describing her arrival on the 26th, the newspaper *Tribune* reported in awe, 'Her four yellow funnels towered as high as the highest building in town'.

Some 52 years later, the Cunard Liner *Aquitania* arrived in Southampton from Halifax, Nova Scotia, on December 1 1949. When the bridge signalled 'Finished with engines', the last four-funneled liner was gone.

Altogether, 14 of these noble vessels were built—12 for the North Atlantic run, two for the Southampton-Cape Town trade. This book is about them all, their triumphs and their tragedies. Like true aristocrats, they often made the news—sometimes by playing a part, at other times just by being present. Some of the events are familiar to us, like the incredible night the *Titanic* went down. Other incidents are fascinating but long-forgotten. Nothing could be more astonishing than the *Kronprinz Wilhelm*'s feat of steaming 20 knots *in reverse* to avoid an ambush during her commerce-raiding days in World War 1.

What is it that is so special about four smokestacks? Other ships made history too. Other ships were larger, faster, even more luxurious. Social historians have suggested that the immigrant trade believed that the more funnels, the better the ship; so the builders were happy to oblige. But seasoned travellers, too, thrilled to the sight of those mighty stacks.

The mind goes back to a westbound crossing of the old *Mauretania* in 1932. On the fourth day out an eager 14-year-old climbed to the Sun Deck, went all the way forward on the starboard side and, leaning against the Fourth Officer's cabin, took a picture from the one spot on the whole ship where a passenger could face aft and photograph at least part of all four funnels. The result appears on page 102 of this book—and I still consider it the most satisfying picture I have ever taken.

Looking at it recently, I was struck by the disparity between the small figure playing deck tennis and the huge funnels towering overhead. It wouldn't be that way today. Now, there would be acres of sports deck and maybe one tiny funnel tucked out of the way.

The thought occurs that this contrast might hold the key to what made these old liners unique. Today's cruise ship stands for frills and play . . . luaus and lido decks. The old four-stackers, with their emphasis on power over deck tennis, brooked no nonsense. They had a stern majesty that won the admiration of all who sailed on them, as well as the respect—even awe—that casual bystanders are likely to shower on passing royalty.

This splendid book catches these steamers in all their regal glory, and it is eminently fitting that Messrs Flayhart and Shaum have chosen the title, *Majesty at Sea*.

May 1981

Introduction

Few subjects captivate the minds of individuals more than tales of the sea, famous ships and the men who sailed them. In the years between 1897 and 1950, the most majestic maritime visions which thrilled or terrified individuals crossing the Atlantic were the great four-funnel passenger liners flying the German, British or French flags. Initially conceived as the slowest vessels with the smallest power plants capable of sustaining the next leap forward in transatlantic transportation, the four-funnel greyhounds represented a pinnacle of marine technology and architecture. They were the penultimate products of the great German, British and French shipbuilding yards at the turn of the century and were the maritime symbols of what often is referred to as the 'Gilded Age'. In all there would be fourteen ships graced by four funnels, but not all would have power plants requiring such smoke stacks since what 'necessity' dictated at the turn of the century, 'fashion' would demand slightly later. Nonetheless, the thought of an *Olympic* or an *Aquitania* with three funnels causes one to shudder at the marring of two of the most symmetrically beautiful creations of the shipbuilders' art.

The first vessel was Norddeutscher Lloyd's *Kaiser Wilhelm der Grosse* which was the 'ship of the year' in 1897 as the largest and fastest steamship in the world. She was conceived as the first of a series of vessels by the Bremen-based line which would herald the coming of age of Northern Germany as a first rank industrial power, and establish NDL's dominance on the North Atlantic. The reaction within Germany was predominantly pride in the achievement, modified by a degree of envy on the part of the Hamburg-America Line. The competitive psychology of shipowners caused HAPAG to order the *Deutschland* over the objections of the distinguished Albert Ballin who foresaw a

haemorrhage of red ink in his neat account ledgers. The *Deutschland* proved a record-breaker but also too delicate a vessel, prone to over-straining her machinery on the rugged North Atlantic run. The HAPAG liner would have no comparable running mates, while Norddeutscher Lloyd went on to complete a quartet of greyhounds for its first class service.

The British response to the German capture of the North Atlantic speed records involved considerable debate but no immediate ship orders since economic conditions could not justify the building of high-powered tonnage. Furthermore, the early 1900s saw the acquisition of White Star by the International Mercantile Marine and the continuation of that concern's commitment to huge medium-speed vessels. The combination of the technological advance involved in the invention and successful testing of turbines with the threat that the British flag might disappear from the first class North Atlantic run finally brought acceptable financial terms for the Cunard Line to order the *Lusitania* and *Mauretania*. The Cunard speed-queens swept the record book and re-established British prestige on the Atlantic. Within Britain the Cunard achievement made it redundant for White Star to make an attempt on the record even if the Ismays had wanted to, and White Star went to Harland & Wolff for a huge trio of 40,000-ton super liners as the foundation of their first class service. The *Olympic* trio was designed to the highest possible standards of luxury in the best tradition of the 'Gilded Age', and the reception of the *Olympic* in 1911 involved a symphony of superlatives. That her sisters, the *Titanic* and *Britannic*, never completed a successful crossing in the service for which they were intended remains one of the most poignant and tragic tales of the North Atlantic. Cunard would complete its trio with the great *Aquitania* in order to have the requisite number of big ships for the weekly first class service.

Across the Channel in France the building philosophy of the Compagnie Générale Transatlantique placed emphasis upon a continuous series of new vessels to attract the first class travelling public and that portion of humanity always intent upon the newest attraction. Accordingly, the French Line periodically ordered a single new first class unit with no particular concern for having a uniform fleet. The vessel of the era for France would be the glorious *France* of 1912. A masterpiece of Gallic technology and decorative art, the *France* was the largest ship built in France at that time and the first large turbine-driven vessel from a Continental yard.

Sometimes it is forgotten that the North Atlantic serves a multitude of sea routes besides the famous Europe-North America run. The first class service of the Union-Castle Line from Southampton to South Africa frequently saw the construction of noteworthy ships and the four-funnel *Arundel Castle* and *Windsor Castle* which round out the age of the four-stackers were no exception. At the time they were the largest ships in service on the important South African run and both experienced famous careers. Ultimately though, before World War 2 the *Windsor Castle* and *Arundel Castle* would be reconditioned with two funnels and be just as beautiful with two crowning glories as they had been majestic with four.

The four-funnel liners truly represented and reflected their times. In technology these great ships embodied the most advanced engineering achievements of their day with power plants that were second to none on land or sea. As works of art no effort was spared and no expense hesitated at in order to create an atmosphere of opulence and grandeur. The stated desire was to overwhelm the passenger and to make even the millionaires who annually shifted their families across the Atlantic feel more comfortable than at home. Four towering uptakes for the furnaces vividly underlined the image of awesome power, and four perfectly spaced funnels impressed the beholder with the dignity and grace of a royal creation when man endeavoured to excel and surpass all previous human achievement to create 'Majesty at Sea'.

1 Norddeutscher Lloyd

Norddeutscher Lloyd (NDL) of Bremen held a proud place in the ranks of the transatlantic steamship lines during the second half of the 19th century. Founded in 1857, the line's development paralleled that of the economy of Northern Europe and was stimulated by the political unification of Germany after 1870. The constant rivalry with the senior Hamburg America Line (HAPAG) of Hamburg in part provided the stimulus for NDL to order in 1896 a vessel larger and faster than any yet seen on the Atlantic. The growth of the industrial revolution within Imperial Germany made it possible to place the order domestically with the contract going to the Vulcan Yard of Stettin. The keel of the 14,000-ton liner was laid in 1896 and the formal launching occurred on May 3 1897 in the presence of His Imperial Majesty Kaiser Wilhelm II. Appropriately, the premier unit of the German Merchant Marine was christened *Kaiser Wilhelm der Grosse* in honour of the Kaiser's grandfather and the first German Emperor, Wilhelm I.

Norddeutscher Lloyd was anxious to place the new liner in service as quickly as possible. The first sailing was scheduled for September 15 and all cabins sold when unforeseen elements intervened. The *Kaiser Wilhelm der Grosse* was delayed and did not leave the yard until August 29. She made the 600 mile run from the builders to her home port in good time but, as she was navigating upstream to Bremen, she stranded in the Kaiserfahrt because of low water. Tides came and went for a week until she finally slipped free on September 7, although low water still made it impossible for her to proceed to her berth. A September 15 departure was now out of the question and in spite of frantic provisioning and coaling she was not ready to leave until September 19 when she passed the Weser Lightship at 7.10 pm.

Wherever the *Kaiser Wilhelm der Grosse* steamed she caused a sensation and many people travelled down from London to Southampton just to see the new German monarch. She made the fastest run on record from Bremen to Southampton in 19 hours 10 minutes, and was greeted at her first foreign port by crowds cheering, bands playing and handkerchiefs waving. Following hurried ceremonies of welcome the *Kaiser Wilhelm der Grosse* slipped down Southampton Water with 543 passengers in first and second class plus 213 in steerage to begin the first of many high-speed runs to America. Summoning everything at her command the largest liner in the world slammed westward manned by a crew determined to capture the fabled 'Blue Riband'. Daily mileage began to build up: 208, 531, 495, 512, 554, 564, culminating in a 186-mile dash to the Sandy Hook Lightship. The average speed was a superb 21.39 knots over 3,050 nautical miles which were covered in 5 days 22 hours 45 minutes and represented a record for the Southampton-New York run.

The overall claim of a 'Blue Riband' was specifically disputed by the Cunard Line as, in October 1894, the *Lucania* had crossed from Queenstown to Sandy Hook on a course of 2,779 miles in 5 days 7 hours 23 minutes at an average of 21.81 knots, which was unquestionably faster. It should be noted that, at this time, some authorities regarded a 'Blue Riband' passage as involving the shortest elapsed time, while others saw it as the fastest crossing speed regardless of time. Ultimately agreement would be reached that the ship's speed was the determining factor, but this was not universally accepted as late as 1897 on the Continent or in America. For the moment NDL had to be content with having made the fastest maiden voyage, but any disappointment they may have felt was short-lived as, on their third

The Kaiser Wilhelm der Grosse *in two superb portraits by the marine photographer A. Loeffler of New York. The starboard view was taken in 1897 and the port view in 1900* (Library of Congress).

Norddeutscher Lloyd

homeward voyage in November 1897, she averaged 22.35 knots between Sandy Hook and the Needles, the 3,062 mile track being completed in 5 days 17 hours 8 minutes with daily runs of 401, 520, 510, 528, 525, 507 and 71. The *Kaiser Wilhelm der Grosse* thus became the fastest as well as the largest liner in the world, and gave unlimited satisfaction to the German people, signifying as she did another major step forward in national development at a time when such accomplishments were enormously important. The complete triumph had to wait until March-April 1898 when the liner gained the westbound record as well by a passage of 5 days 20 hours from the Needles to Sandy Hook at an average speed of 22.29 knots over a course of 3,120 miles. The *Kaiser Wilhelm der Grosse* was the first non-British built record-breaker in 40 years and was regarded with justification as a masterpiece of German science, art and industry.

The most striking aspect of the external appearance of the new German record-breaker were the four towering funnels arranged in pairs. Apart from the *Great Eastern,* no regular transatlantic liner before the *Kaiser Wilhelm der Grosse* had possessed so many crowning glories. Her stacks were 12 ft 2 in in diameter and towered an impressive 106 ft above the waterline. In the future many unsophisticated travellers would rate the size, safety and speed of vessels by the number of stacks and some steamship lines would fit 'dummy' funnels for prestige purposes even on the largest vessels. On the *Kaiser Wilhelm der Grosse* the funnel arrangement was purely functional, permitting appropriate draught from the boilers and at the same time eliminating funnel casings from the large first class dining saloon amidships because of the pairing of the uptakes fore and aft. As the largest liner in service her dimensions were significant: length overall 648 ft; beam 66 ft; depth of hull 43 ft; gross tonnage 14,349.

The machinery of the new greyhound consisted of four-cylinder, four-crank, triple-expansion engines. The diameters of the cylinders were impressive: High Pressure 52 in; Intermediate 89¾ in; and two Low Pressure, 96½ in. The stroke was 69 in. The liner was driven by two three-bladed, bronze propellers 22 ft 3¾ in in diameter which weighed 26 tons and had a pitch of 32 ft 8 in. The hull was divided into 18 watertight compartments and the vessel was given a double cellular bottom which proved its value from the very beginning during the stranding in the Kaiserfahrt. There were 12 double-ended boilers in four groups with three boilers feeding

Abstract of Log.

Imperial German and U.S. Mail twin-screw steamship *Kaiser Wilhelm der Grosse*, Captain H. Engelbart.

Passed Sandy Hook Lightship Nov. 23rd 4.47 p.m.
Arrived Needles Lighthouse Nov. 29th, 3.10 p.m., 1897.

Date Nov.	Miles	Lat. N.	Lon. W.	Remarks.
24th	401	41·27	65.12	Overcast; snow squalls; rough sea.
25th	520	44 12	54·2	Cloudy; moderate sea.
26th	513	47.3	42·31	Mostly overcast; moderate sea.
27th	528	49·24	39.48	Cloudy; smooth sea; northerly swell.
28th	525	50·0	16·19	Rain squalls, moderate high W. sea.
29th	507	50·14	3·16	Heavy squalls; very high N.W. sea.
29th	71 to Needles.			Gale from N.W.

Passage—5 days 22 hours 23 min.
Distance, 3,065 miles. Difference in time 4 ,, 50 ,,
Delayed by a burning ship 25 ,,
Time of passage—5 days 17 hours 8 ,,
Average speed, 22·35 knots.

Kaiser Wilhelm der Grosse: *abstract of log, record passage November 24-29 1897.*

each of the four funnels. Sixteen ventilating fans could provide forced draft but since the funnels themselves were 106 ft above the fire grates they were regarded as supplementary equipment. The separation of the boilers into four compartments was intended to insure that no accident by stranding or collision could deprive the engines of all steam. The Krupp Foundry manufactured the nickel steel stafting which was 198 ft long and 24 in in diameter. The bilge pumps could discharge 3,600 tons of water per hour from the ship. Electricity was supplied by four large dynamos placed aft between the twin shafts which lighted the vessel and also provided refrigeration for the kitchens. The *Marine Engineer* noted: 'Altogether, with steering apparatus and sanitary pumps, there are no less than 68 separate engines with 124 cylinders aboard the vessel'.* The ship was manned by a crew of 450.

The boat deck of the *Kaiser Wilhelm der Grosse* extended nearly 400 ft and formed a permanent awning over the passengers' promenade. The 24 lifeboats were carried on this deck while forward were located the chart house, wheel house and officers' quarters. The complete removal of the ship's officers from contact with the passengers while carrying out their navigational duties was regarded as a major safety factor. The four decks below the navigation deck were wholly or largely devoted to passenger accommodation. The promenade deck provided a sheltered walk of 400 ft for the first class passengers. Forward of the promenade was a short waist where the emigrants travelling in steerage could get some air on the spar deck, and forward of that the long slim forecastle swept towards the knifelike bow. Spare

* 'Kaiser Wilhelm der Grosse', *The Marine Engineer,* Vol XIX, January 1 1898, p 378.

Above *One of New York's most famous marine photographers was 'Byron', who captured the exteriors and interiors of many liners. This photograph captures the decor and plush environment of the library on the* Kaiser Wilhelm der Grosse (Museum of the City of New York). **Below** *A portion of the first class dining salon on the* Kaiser Wilhelm der Grosse *by 'Byron'* (Museum of the City of New York).

anchors were secured to the deck on the forecastle and a couple of breakwaters were fitted to assist the quick run-off of heavy seas.

The *Kaiser Wilhelm der Grosse*'s passenger accommodation was of the highest standard in the Continental fashion. Within the promenade deck from fore to aft were located the library, several luxurious suites and the ladies' drawing room. Segregation of the sexes after dinner was observed rigorously making it necessary to have ladies' and gentlemen's public rooms. Therefore, the other major public room on the promenade deck was the men's smoking room which occupied the aft end of the deck and was horseshoe shaped in order to curve around the casing of the fourth funnel. The wall panels were of stamped leather and some bore colour representations of sea scenes.

The largest room on the liner was the main dining saloon stretching the width of the ship and over 100 ft long. Retractable doors could slide out of the fore and aft bulkheads to convert the one large room into five, four of which could seat groups of 20-30. These small dining saloons were named respectively Konigin Luise, Kaiserin Augusta (sic), Moltke and Bismarck. Each of the smaller saloons had different decorations and the main saloon received natural light through a large central skylight of stained glass reinforced with external glass plates. All the first class passengers could be served at one sitting in the main dining saloon.

The elite among the first class passengers occupied a number of suites on the upper deck consisting of sitting room, bedroom and bathroom. The baths had marble washstands and lift-up basins as in the best hotels ashore and were considered the ultimate in luxury. An innovation in the staterooms was the covering of the outer rail of the iron bunks with carpet-type material to make them less frigid to the touch in the morning. Second class passengers were berthed aft and had a promenade on the poop deck. In all, there was accommodation for 400 first, 350 second and 800 steerage. On one occasion in September 1900 the liner docked at Hoboken (New York) with 825 in the first two classes and 658 in steerage for a near capacity complement.

Certain measures were taken during the construction of the *Kaiser Wilhelm der Grosse* to make her useful as a naval auxiliary. The rudder was placed entirely beneath the water in order to prevent easy damage from an enemy. The upper decks were specially strengthened to carry guns with arrangements reportedly made to have armament available for the vessel. Bilge keels fitted to the hull provided additional stability for commercial as well as naval service. Because of the length of the vessel 'supplementary bridges' were constructed half way along the Navigation Deck and then again at the stern in order to assist manoeuvring.

During her first full year of operation the *Kaiser Wilhelm der Grosse* succeeded in increasing her best day's run from 564 miles to 567 and then to 580. On her eighth westward crossing the machinery produced an even 560 miles on three consecutive days and 557 on the fourth. Consistency became a hallmark of the Norddeutscher Lloyd record-breaker and many crossings were at or near record times for the Southampton-New York run. Since the Line had an agreement with the Vulcan Shipyard that the vessel could be returned to them if she failed to perform to expectations these results were deeply gratifying.

The *Kaiser Wilhelm der Grosse* was proving an outstanding performer for her owners even under duress. On May 30 1898, one day out from New York, the port propeller lost a blade causing a slight delay but the crossing still was accomplished in 5 days, 21 hours, 48 minutes. Again, on September 1 1898, a blade was lost off the starboard propeller and in both cases new propellers were put into place on arrival at Bremerhaven. In light of the difficulties experienced by the *Kaiser Wilhelm der Grosse* it was a major relief for the management of Norddeutscher Lloyd when the new 722-ft Kaiser Dry Dock was completed at Bremerhaven in September 1899. The largest stone graving dock outside the British Isles was over 90 ft wide and had a sill 34 ft 8 in below the highwater mark of the Weser in normal tides. The new repair and servicing facilities with four electric cranes ranging up to 120 tons capacity cost approximately £300,000 of which the Imperial Exchequer provided £120,000. The Line took a 25 year lease on the facility at a rent of around £6,000 per year, and with the understanding that vessels other than those of Norddeutscher Lloyd could use the dock.

A series of minor international conflicts in the late 1890s immensely benefited the company. In 1898 the Spanish-American War saw the withdrawal of all vessels of the rival American Line on the Southampton-New York run for six months during the high season. No sooner had the American Line returned to the Atlantic Ferry than the outbreak of the Boer War permitted Norddeutscher Lloyd to increase its percentage of the trade thanks to the removal of a number of Cunard and White Star vessels for troopship duties. The overall position of NDL might have

been even better had not Kaiser Wilhelm II attempted to play international power politics by issuing pro-Boer statements which severely irritated British public opinion and created an atmosphere of Germanophobia. The disruption to competitors in part contributed to the increase in the NDL carrying trade during 1899, but the popularity of the *Kaiser Wilhelm der Grosse* certainly helped as well.

On the Bremen-New York route in 1899 the line carried 17,759 first and second class (collectively referred to as 'cabin' for statistical purposes), up from 15,794 in 1898; and 53,646 steerage, up from 32,205 in 1898. These figures encouraged the line to pursue a construction programme aimed at providing suitable consorts for their record-breaker. Among the unique experiments conducted by Norddeutscher Lloyd in 1900 were some of the earliest ship-to-shore wireless communications. The Marconi outfit was set up in a temporary deckhouse on the *Kaiser Wilhelm der Grosse* and signals exchanged with land-based stations.

Norddeutscher was riding a crest of success and prosperity when, shortly before 4 pm on June 30 1900, disaster struck at the Hoboken piers in New York Harbour. The *Aller* had sailed for Genoa at noon leaving four fine ships of the fleet at their berths: the crack *Kaiser Wilhelm der Grosse;* the new steamers *Main* and *Bremen* and the *Saale* of the Mediterranean Service. A spontaneous explosion among highly inflammable cargo stacked on the piers touched off a violent fire which threatened to consume the entire shoreline and all the liners. Captain Engelbart and the crew of the *Kaiser Wilhelm der Grosse* worked frantically with the aid of tugs to cast off and back her into the North River. The Norddeutscher Lloyd piers were soon an inferno and on several occasions debris set fire to the decks of the record-breaker, but each time quick action extinguished the blaze before it could catch hold. The *Kaiser Wilhelm der Grosse* was singed with much paint burnt off or blistered but she was able to take her assigned sailing on Tuesday, July 3 1900. The other vessels were not so fortunate. The *Saale* of 1887 was towed out into the stream and abandoned to drift on to the Communipaw Flats off Liberty Island and settle on the bottom. The *Bremen* and the *Main* drifted up the river on the incoming tide and grounded off 42nd Street. The three liners were burnt out and the death toll was fearsome because the narrow diameter of the portholes trapped many within the burning ships. The *Saale* lost 109 out of 272, the *Bremen* 12 out of 200 and the *Main* 44 out of 149. In spite of their extensive damage all the ships involved in the disaster were eventually reconditioned, although the *Saale* was sold.

The loss of the *Kaiser Wilhelm der Grosse* in the fire would have been monumental indeed because the arch-rival HAPAG introduced their record-breaking *Deutschland* the next month. The *Deutschland* was a larger and more powerful edition of the NDL ship and took the 'Blue Riband' away from the *Kaiser Wilhelm der Grosse*, but the latter proved a more consistent and comfortable performer. The introduction of the rival prompted NDL to proceed with construction of two additional first class units of the fleet to be named *Kronprinz Wilhelm* and *Kaiser Wilhelm II*. Dominance of the North Atlantic in 1900 clearly seemed to be in German hands for the foreseeable future.

The commercial career of the *Kaiser Wilhelm der Grosse* was highlighted by one major accident. On the evening of November 21 1906 she was leaving Cherbourg and visibility was clear when the inward-bound *Orinoco* of the Royal Mail Steam Packet Company's West Indies service was encountered. The German greyhound approached the slower vessel from starboard and attempted to cross ahead of her at high speed. The *Orinoco* was going faster and the German vessel not as fast as her captain thought. The *Orinoco* reversed engines and put her helm hard to port but a collision was inevitable. Her clipper bow sliced into the forward section of the German liner, tearing a mammoth hole in the starboard side which stretched some 70 ft long and 26 ft high, ending just 3 ft above the waterline. The bow of the *Orinoco* was crumpled and three people drowned while five were crushed to death in the forward cabins of the *Kaiser Wilhelm der Grosse*. Neither vessel was in danger of sinking but their sailings had to be cancelled and passengers transferred to other ships. Following temporary repairs the *Kaiser Wilhelm der Grosse* sailed for Gëestemunde. In the Admiralty Court that examined the accident the German vessel was held to be 100 per cent at fault and the Royal Mail received handsome compensation.

The otherwise charmed life of the oldest German four-stacker was emphasised during an eastbound crossing in October 1907. The *Kaiser Wilhelm der Grosse* was about 1,300 miles from New York when she was struck by an enormous following sea on October 25. The stern was lifted high in the air and the normally submerged rudder was ripped off. The ship shuddered but kept going since the propellers were not damaged. Captain Pollack assessed the situation and elected to continue on course and declined assistance

from no less than 21 vessels. The *Kaiser Wilhelm der Grosse* steamed on maintaining a speed in excess of 18 knots for the whole crossing. Steering the big liner was accomplished by judicious use of the twin screws. On one day following the loss of the rudder she logged 416 miles—a truly marvellous achievement. Captain Pollack never left the bridge until the Scilly Isles were abeam and then only briefly. When the German Emperor was informed of this outstanding navigational and engineering feat he lost no time in decorating the Master.

As the years passed the *Kaiser Wilhelm der Grosse* seemed to grow slightly faster. She sailed from Southampton at 11.40 am on Wednesday, August 31 1910, and was off Fire Island, New York, at 3 am on Tuesday, September 6, having averaged 22.18 knots for the crossing and beating by nine hours the *Deutschland* which had sailed the same day. Prominent figures still travelled on the *Kaiser Wilhelm der Grosse* even if larger and faster vessels were available. One reason undoubtedly was that with the commissioning of a fourth major liner, the *Kronprinzessin Cecilie* in 1907, Norddeutscher Lloyd possessed the best-balanced express fleet in service. The years between 1910 and 1914 represent a period when NDL certainly was faced with ever-increasing competition from HAPAG, Cunard, White Star and the Compagnie Générale Transatlantique. At the same time this was also a period when the quartet of liners in the NDL express fleet worked to perfection and provided a consistent standard of excellence. While it has been customary to regard the Norddeutscher Lloyd greyhounds as maintaining the first class express service until the outbreak of World War 1, it should be noted that the aging *Kaiser Wilhelm der Grosse* was down-graded to carrying only third and steerage after March 1914. Her tonnage was reduced to 13,952 and she operated in a direct Bremen-New York service.

One of the most dismal notices the North German Lloyd ever asked the newspapers to print was the one announcing the cancellation of all sailings in August 1914. No portion of the German economy had more cause to regret the outbreak of hostilities than the Merchant Marine. The prosperity of the lines ceased, many vessels were captured or interned, and others became units of the (Imperial) German Navy. The *Kaiser Wilhelm der Grosse* was at her home port of Bremen and underwent conversion from ocean greyhound to armed merchant cruiser with the intended assignment of commerce raiding. She was armed with six 10.5 cm guns and two 3.7 cm quick-firing cannon. In spite of her 17 years the hull and machinery were sound and she was still faster than all but a handful of ships in the world's merchant marine. She sailed from Germany on August 5 and took a northern route around Scotland where she captured and destroyed the steam trawler *Tubal Cain* on the 7th before passing south of Iceland and disappearing into the vast reaches of the Atlantic Ocean. The raider moved southward to an advantageous position near the Canary Islands by the middle of August. On Sunday, August 16 at 1 pm the big Royal Mail Steam Packet Company steamer *Arlanza* homeward bound from Rio sighted a large four funnel vessel bearing down on her some 200 miles south of Teneriffe.* As the ship drew near her intentions became clear and a swift exchange of six signals occurred:

I. HEAVE TO OR I WILL FIRE INTO YOU.
II. LOWER AWAY AND THROW OVERBOARD ALL YOUR WIRELESS TELEGRAPH INSTALLATION.
III. HAVE YOU ANY WOMEN ON BOARD?
IV. DISMISS ON ACCOUNT OF YOUR HAVING WOMEN AND CHILDREN ON BOARD.
V. 2nd SIGNAL REPEATED.
VI. I HAVE NO FURTHER COMMANDS TO YOUR CAPTAIN.

Chivalry was still thriving in August 1914 and nowhere more so than on the *Kaiser Wilhelm der Grosse*. Not long afterwards the Union Castle intermediate passenger liner *Galician* was captured and treated with the same deference as a passenger vessel carrying women and children. The New Zealand Shipping Company *Kaipara* with mutton and wool, and the Elder Dempster *Nyanga* with West African produce were less fortunate and were sunk as fair game after the removal of their crews. Unfortunately for her, the German speed queen consumed awesome quantities of coal even at reduced speeds and was soon in need of fuel. A rendezvous point was established at the Spanish Colony of Rio de Oro in West Africa where the HAPAG *Bethania,* the NDL *Magdeburg* and two other supply ships, the *Arucas* and the *Duala,* were to bring provisions and above all the indispensible coal.

The *Arlanza,* which had been dismissed after throwing overboard her wireless, soon rigged her spare set while steaming as fast as she could for Las Palmas. She arrived there at 7 am the next day, August 17, and Captain C.E. Down immediately informed the British consul of his narrow escape. Except for acute concern about the safety

of his ship and passengers the news might have been wirelessed ahead since the Radio Officer of the *Arlanza* had the duplicate set rigged within six hours of throwing the original overboard!* The Royal Mail Line and the Admiralty both commended Captain Down for his services.

At Las Palmas HMS *Highflyer* received word of the German colliers' departure from that port on August 23 and learned that they were steaming for the Ouro River. The light cruiser sailed immediately and Captain Buller brought his warship off the River Ouro on the afternoon of August 26 after receiving information that the German raider had been within neutral Spanish waters for more than 48 hours. The *Kaiser Wilhelm der Grosse* was loading coal furiously with colliers on each side and a third standing off. Both Captain Buller and his German counterpart were keenly aware of the dilemma facing them. The German armed merchant cruiser was anchored in neutral waters and had been there for some time. The neutral power had no means of protecting or enforcing its neutrality if it desired to, but the war was young and Britain did not need any unnecessary enemies. Another critical factor was that the armed liner was substantially faster than the light cruiser if she could get to sea, and her armament was fairly heavy. Captain Buller signalled to his opponent to surrender and was informed that 'German warships do not surrender'†. At the same time he was requested to observe Spanish neutral waters. Buller's reply was that he considered the German warship to have violated Spanish neutrality by using the River Ouro as a base and by the duration of her stay. Buller signalled that hostilities were about to commence and that the colliers should be ordered to leave.

At 3.10 pm *Highflyer* opened the engagement with a shot off the bow of the *Kaiser Wilhelm der Grosse* and the German warship replied with a broadside. The battle was joined. The range was about 9,700 yards and the *Highflyer* replied with her starboard battery of 6-in guns. The distance was too great for the British cruiser's batteries. The German's high velocity guns, however, were easily straddling the British warship. The *Highflyer* was forced to close the distance and steamed in toward the raider which continued a telling fire concentrated on the bridge where one sailor was

* Public Record Office, ADM 137/799, p 140, Lt F.V. Lochey, Comdr RN, to Admiralty, August 24 1914. Lochey was a passenger on the *Arlanza* at the time she was captured and freed.

* PRO, ADM 137/799, p 135, Captain C.E. Down to Royal Mail Steam Packet Company, Southampton, August 22 1914, forwarded to the Admiralty for their information.
† PRP, ADM 137/799, p 167, Captain Buller to Admiralty, Secret, August 27 1914. Buller's account of the engagement.

killed. Captain Buller just had withdrawn his men into the comparative protection of the conning tower when a German shell swept the bridge and knocked the searchlight into the ocean.

Any battle between a vessel designed from the keel up to be a warship and a passenger liner serving the necessities of war must be a foregone conclusion even when the crews are well matched. As the range closed the guns of the *Highflyer* simply blew in the sides of the ocean greyhound. The German raider's fire slackened, and she began to list to port with the sea pouring into the holes in her sides. She ceased firing at 4.25 pm and the crew began to abandon their sinking ship which slipped beneath the waves at 5.10 pm. The British cruiser stopped firing when the raider did and Captain Buller offered assistance but the British longboats did not reach the liner before she went down. Furthermore, the surviving crew members took up hostile positions behind sand dunes on the shore and refused to surrender. The British then withdrew and the German captain accompanied by 9 officers and 71 crew reached the Spanish fort that evening where they were given quarters and interned. Some later escaped and returned to Germany.

The *Kronprinz Wilhelm* was the second of the Norddeutscher Lloyd speed queens to be ordered for the express service from Europe to the United States. The success of the *Kaiser Wilhelm der Grosse* assured the contract to the Vulcan Shipbuilding Company of Stettin and it was intended that the new liner would be able to challenge the Hamburg American *Deutschland* built one year before by the same firm. The dimensions of the *Kronprinz Wilhelm* were nearly those of the *Kaiser Wilhelm der Grosse* and she represented both a logical and proper development on the

Outward bound from New York, the Kronprinz Wilhelm *passes a Pennsylvania Railroad tug and a sleek yacht.*

earlier vessel. Her gross tonnage was 14,908 compared with the 14,349 of the *Kaiser Wilhelm der Grosse,* her overall length was 663 ft, beam 66 ft 3 in, depth 39 ft 3 in and draft 29 ft. Because of the monumental nature of her machinery, the net tonnage was a paltry 5,162 and she would really have to move the passengers in order to justify the investment in her construction.

The *Kronprinz Wilhelm* was equipped with two sets of quadruple-expansion engines of 33,000 horsepower with steam provided to each set by twelve double and four single-ended boilers operating at 200 psi. The engines were among the largest constructed at that time and each set consisted of six cylinders with diameters of 34.3 in, 69 in, 98.4 in and 102.4 in. Two of the cylinders were high pressure and two low, with a stroke of 71 in. The boilers were divided among four separate boiler rooms each of which was connected to its own funnel. Coal consumption at full speed exceeded 500 tons a day and the maximum horse power approached 36,000.

In appearance the *Kronprinz Wilhelm* closely resembled the *Kaiser Wilhelm der Grosse.* However, there were differences between the two vessels which could aid in telling them apart. The funnels of the *Kronprinz Wilhelm* were slightly larger and the guy bands were attached fairly close together on the funnels which made her appear both solider and swifter. Furthermore, her forecastle was slightly longer, the boat deck extended a little further aft, and the superstructure, counter stern and knife-like bow made the *Kronprinz Wilhelm* one of the most impressive greyhounds ever commissioned.

The passenger load of the *Kronprinz Wilhelm* was 367 first, 340 second and 1,054 steerage. Accommodation for the first class passengers was placed amidships on the main, upper and promenade decks. The most expensive suites sold for £400 and consisted of a sitting room, bedroom and bathroom. They were referred to as 'cabins de luxe' and there were four, each of which was

The Kronprinz Wilhelm *arrives after a very fast crossing early in her career which stripped the paint from her bow. Passengers crowd the deck to view the docking* (Steamship Historical Society of America).

connected to the Chief Steward's office by telephone. Eight other apartments consisted of bedroom and bathroom for those who valued their privacy in an age when that was rare.

Considerable attention was paid to making the dining rooms on the Norddeutscher Lloyd vessels sumptuous places of meeting and entertainment. The *Kronprinz Wilhelm*'s first class dining room with its 414 seats was no exception. The prevailing tone of the woodwork was a light green which served to highlight some magnificent bronze panels inset into the walls and the oil paintings of the great palaces in which the German Crown Prince had lived, or places where he had spent his student days, such as the cadet school at Plön.

The *Kronprinz Wilhelm* contained a number of innovations which were described as remarkable. An extensive telephone system connected the Captain on the bridge with the heads of various departments of the steamer. The Chief Steward was provided with a formal office of his own similar to those found in land-based hotels. Special attention was paid to the kitchen and food storage facilities. Refrigerated rooms were provided for various kinds of food and the temperature was described as being maintained by 'ice machines'. An interesting and welcome innovation for lookouts was that the ascent to the crow's nest was not by the traditional exposed ladder, but by a ladder running up the inside of the mast. The crow's nest itself was connected to the bridge by a speaking tube. All the clocks of the *Kronprinz Wilhelm* were electric and connected to a master time piece in the chartroom. This eliminated the need to adjust and regulate all the clocks independently. Needless to say the *Kronprinz Wilhelm* was provided with a complete wireless room in order to maintain contact with the shore wherever she might be.

The commissioning of the HAPAG *Deutschland* had seen that liner take the westbound and eastbound records from the *Kaiser Wilhelm der Grosse* in July 1900 with crossings averaging 22.42 and 22.83 knots. Yet the '*Kaiser*' had been able to complete an eastbound crossing of 22.89 in August 1900, before the *Deutschland* had a pair of excellent runs in September of 23.36 knots eastbound and 23.02 knots westbound and reasserted her dominance. The result was that the *Kronprinz Wilhelm* had the honour of the Line to uphold under what became somewhat frustrating circumstances! Her first voyages were marred by heavy seas and strong gales. The maiden crossing on September 17 1901 from Bremen to Southampton and New York with 777 cabin passengers and 608 steerage resulted in the disappointing speed of 19.74 knots under extremely turbulent conditions. The next crossing of the *Kaiser Wilhelm der Grosse* rubbed salt in the wounded pride of the new liner's crew as the older ship romped outward in 5 days, 17 hours, 22 minutes, with an average speed of 22.23 knots. The *Kronprinz Wilhelm* was frustrated a second time with a westbound passage of 5 days, 21 hours, 10 minutes in the face of rough NW winds which held her

The Kronprinz Wilhelm *embarks passengers very close to sailing time with the Boat Train having arrived just minutes before.*

Another of the official photographs of the Kronprinz Wilhelm *is this magnificent starboard shot of the liner with a racing yacht's bone in her teeth, beautifully shown in calm waters.*

average to 21.59 knots. By this time all those on the *Kronprinz Wilhelm* were more than ready to show what their vessel could do under suitable conditions. A vindication was finally achieved when the *New York Herald* noted the arrival of the *Kronprinz Wilhelm* on December 23 1901 after the fastest crossing of her career bringing passengers and mails home for Christmas. She had steamed the 3,050 mile track in 5 days, 15 hours, 20 minutes at 22.57 knots.

In June 1902 an incident occurred which caused some embarrassment to Norddeutscher Lloyd, as the captain of the *Kronprinz Wilhelm* was a little generous in his calculations of the liner's time and distance with the result that NDL claimed a record. Albert Ballin, the Director General of HAPAG, publicly questioned the figures with the result in August 1902 that Norddeutscher Lloyd and HAPAG signed a declaration acknowledging that the *Deutschland* still retained the record. The humiliating sting to the *Kronprinz Wilhelm*'s pride was alleviated partially when she arrived in New York on September 16 1902 after completing a record westbound passage of 5 days, 11 hours and 57 minutes over a 3,045 mile course at an average speed of 23.09 knots. It might be added as a footnote to this competition that the result delivered the *Kronprinz Wilhelm*'s passengers to New York exactly 26 minutes faster than those on the previous record crossing by the *Deutschland* in August 1901. The *Kronprinz Wilhelm* was never able to secure the eastbound record but she had vindicated herself nonetheless.

The matter of who held the 'Record Passage' or the mythical 'Blue Riband' had enormous publicity value even if it was of a transcendental nature.

Atlantic crossings were not always uneventful and the *Kronprinz Wilhelm*'s of October 8 1902 was one her captain cheerfully would have been spared. The big liner crossed the North Sea in deteriorating weather conditions, and found herself in dense fog off Beachy Head. The 660 ton steam collier *Robert Ingham* was bound up the Channel at three knots when Captain Elliott heard a loud foghorn nearby and, in the next instant, the *Kronprinz Wilhelm* rammed the much smaller vessel on the starboard side sending her to the bottom in four minutes flat! The rescue boat of the *Kronprinz Wilhelm* with its crack oarsmen hit the water in record time as the liner slowed and succeeded in rescuing 13 members of the *Robert Ingham*'s crew. The death toll was kept to two, both of whom were asleep below deck in the collier. The *Robert Ingham* had been sliced almost in two by the *Kronprinz Wilhalm* which had not suffered any significant damage in the collision. The German record-breaker proceeded to Southampton where she dropped the victims of the disaster and then left for Cherbourg and New York. Subsequently a British Admiralty Court held the *Kronprinz Wilhelm* solely to blame for the sinking and ordered appropriate damages to be paid. The eventful crossing of October 1902 was not over by any means, however, because the *Kronprinz Wilhelm* also collided with and sliced the bow off a British torpedo boat in the Channel before reaching the open ocean. There certainly were times when one would prefer not to have left harbour, but the demanding schedule of the trans-atlantic mails made punctual departure imperative.

On the whole the *Kronprinz Wilhelm* did not have an excessively adventuresome career before World War 1. One narrow escape captured minor headlines when the big liner was westward bound to New York and rammed a small iceberg while ploughing her way through the darkness of early morning at 16 knots on July 8 1907 off the Grand Banks. This resulted in a badly dented bow and prominent scrape marks down her side. The story was recounted during the horror of the *Titanic* disaster five years later to the German vessel's advantage.

The *Kronprinz Wilhelm* carried many famous passengers during the twelve years of her commercial career. Wilbur Wright, of aeronautical fame, crossed on the German liner in March 1911 and the *New York Tribune* ran the headline 'Wright Crosses Ocean, Takes Water Route to Testify in Airship Patent Cases.'

The summer of 1914 saw a series of events unfold in south-eastern Europe that would embroil the entire Continent in the world's first truly global conflict. The assassination of the Austrian Archduke Franz Ferdinand at Sarajevo on June 28 1914 occurred just as that splendid

World War 1 found the Kronprinz Wilhelm *at New York. She slipped out on August 3 1914, and spent eight months as an armed merchant cruiser. Her officers for the cruise lined up for a formal photograph.*

annual North German maritime and naval celebration, 'Kiel Week', was beginning. The *Kronprinz Wilhelm*'s next North Atlantic run brought her to New York on Wednesday, July 29, and she began to take on coal and supplies in the normal manner. As soon as the serious nature of the European situation was realised an additional 2,000 tons of coal and vast additional quantities of provisions were taken on board. Because of the uncertain political climate, Norddeutscher Lloyd cancelled the sailing of the *Kronprinz Wilhelm* scheduled for Tuesday, August 4 1914, thereby stranding nearly 1,000 passengers, but since the HAPAG cancellation of the giant *Vaterland*'s departure on August 1 had filled New York hotels with 2,700 extra guests everything was relative. The great mid-summer transatlantic migration was about to be disrupted and the dislocation would see the better part of 100,000 travellers trying to get home. Norddeutscher Lloyd had an enormous percentage of its first class tonnage in American ports. The *Kronprinz Wilhelm* shared berths at Hoboken with the *Kaiser Wilhelm II*, *Kronprinzessin Cecilie*, *George Washington*, *Friedrich der Grosse* and *Grosser Kurfurst*.

Captain K. Grahn of the *Kronprinz Wilhelm* received sealed orders from the NDL Agents who, in turn, were under the command of the German Ambassador in Washington. Steam was maintained at a high level by the boiler room gang over the August weekend and then, at 8.10 on Monday evening, August 3, during a raw, gusty summer drizzle, eight tugs assisted the crack greyhound out of her slip and turned her bow towards the open sea. The declaration of war between France and Germany was already history and the British ultimatum a fact. Enemy warships supposedly were stationed off New York and every precaution was taken to make the *Kronprinz Wilhelm* inconspicuous. Tarpaulins, mattresses and any other solid material was placed over windows and portholes. Yet no ship the size of the *Kronprinz Wilhelm* with her distinctive silhouette could expect to disappear unnoticed and the Captain of the Ward liner *Sequranca* coming up from Cuba reported passing the four-funnel liner heading south which was not her normal course.

The secret orders wirelessed to Captain Grahn required him to rendezvous with the cruiser *Karlsruhe* in latitude 25.40N and longitude 72.37W, some 300 miles off the eastern coast of Cuba. On the morning of August 6 contact was made with the German warship which was a four-funnel cruiser of 4,900 tons. The two vessels came alongside each other and made fast with some scraping and denting. The *Kronprinz*

Wilhelm by now had been painted a dull sea-grey with a black top around her funnels. Coal and supplies were frantically transferred to the *Karlsruhe* while two 8.8 cm guns and 300 rounds of ammunition were hoisted on board the liner together with 50 rifles. Lieutenant-Commander Thierfelder of the *Karlsruhe* transferred to the *Kronprinz Wilhelm* with 15 Imperial Navy sailors and assumed command while Captain Grahn served as navigating officer for the duration of the cruise. In the midst of all this activity with the crews divided between the two ships and supplies all over the decks, the British cruiser HMS *Suffolk* was sighted coming fast over the horizon. The German vessels were taken by surprise even though their wireless operators had informed them of the presence of Allied warships in the area. The *Kronprinz Wilhelm*'s band struck up an emotional 'Deutschland uber Alles' and the gladiators of the sea exchanged thunderous cheers as the *Karlsruhe* bravely made a semicircle to star-board in order to give the auxiliary cruiser time to escape. Luckily for them the *Suffolk* took the bait and began to chase the *Karlsruhe* which was a fruitless exercise since the German vessel was faster, while the *Kronprinz Wilhelm* raced off to the south.

The situation for the *Kronprinz Wilhelm* was not good. She only had two small guns with their crews and a pitiful supply of ammunition. Her boilers consumed 500 tons of coal per day at full speed and her bunkers could only hold about 5,000 tons in reserve. The majority of her 500-man crew consisted of stewards who had a limited use on an armed merchant cruiser, yet had to be fed. Commander Thierfelder set to the task with diligence and maintained his huge vessel as an effective naval auxiliary for the better part of the next eight months without once putting into a port!

The *Kronprinz Wilhelm* moved into the South Atlantic and the armament was placed in position. The gun on the port side of the forecastle was nick-named 'White Arrow' by the crew and its counterpart on the starboard side was dubbed 'Bass Drum' because it possessed a deep-throated boom. Mounted on the forecastle, each gun could command nearly 180° of the horizon. The single machine-gun, nicknamed 'Riveter' for obvious reasons, was stationed on the middle bridge where it could be moved from side to side as needed. In order to provide additional coal bunkers, the ship's carpenters dismantled the magnificent grand saloon and turned the space into a giant coal bin. The smoking room was also remodelled for war into the ship's hospital with bunks, benches and cabinets installed as well as

Two of the black gang who worked like Trojans to bunker the armed merchant cruiser Kronprinz Wilhelm *at sea in the South Atlantic, 1914-1915.*

mattresses nailed over the walls in order to prevent the wounded from suffering additional injury if any enemy projectile should splinter the wood-panelled walls.

Lieutenant Brinkman in the wireless room was something of a telegraphy wizard and within a short time could usually tell by virtue of the eccentricities of key handling on the part of the Allied telegraphers which Allied warship was which and where it was in relation to the *Kronprinz Wilhelm*. The oceanic chart Brinkman maintained in the wireless office with flags to indicate enemy vessels was an invaluable aid to Commander Thierfelder.

Commander Thierfelder's goal was to maintain his huge charge at sea as a commerce raider without touching any neutral port since that would make her whereabouts obvious and destroy her most valuable weapon, 'secrecy'. On August 18 Thierfelder rendezvoused with a German supply vessel, *Walhalla,* off the Azores, and the first agonising coaling operation began. Large circular holes were cut through the decks of the liner leading into the depths of the ship's coal bunkers. Through the holes ventilator tubes were run permitting bags or baskets of coal to be dropped directly into the ship. The *Walhalla*'s coal was transferred in containers from her derricks to those of the *Kronprinz Wilhelm* in mid-air at the rate of 800 tons a day so that by the end of the third day the commerce raider's boilers had an additional 2,400 tons of fuel. This was equal to one week of high speed steaming or three weeks of low speed. Approximately 100 of the older staff of the liner were permitted to join the *Walhalla*, thereby reducing the drain on ship's stores without reducing the fighting capability of the vessel.

SMS *Kronprinz Wilhelm* moved into the South Atlantic and positioned herself to harass the South African, River Plate and Australian trades. In the first month at sea her crew had converted a passenger liner into an armed merchant cruiser but captured nothing to show for their efforts. The first ship sighted on August 27 proved to be the Danish three-masted schooner *Elizabetha* of Fanoe which was permitted to continue on her voyage after an inspection of her papers. Immediately thereafter a pitiful prize was a threadbare three-master flying the Russian flag, the *Pittan*. The captain-owner of the *Pittan* was a poverty-stricken soul who knew nothing of the declarations of war and who was grief stricken to learn that his miserable livelihood was about to disappear. The Russian implored the German officers to show mercy and it was agreed that the three-master was of such scant value that she could be spared. The grateful Russian captain gave the German sailors some kegs of brandy and speedily struck the Russian flag as the commerce raider steamed away.

The coal situation was now becoming desperate since the *Kronprinz Wilhelm* had less than three days supply left. Fortuitously, the commerce raider came on the British steamer *Indian Prince* in the dead of night on September 4 and captured her. The next day she was brought alongside the *Kronprinz Wilhelm*, which maintained a speed of two knots in order to retain manoeuvrability. The *Indian Prince* was made fast and captive and captor steamed through the South Atlantic together as the life-giving coal was transferred. By Wednesday, September 9, the *Indian Prince* was stripped of coal and other supplies. Sailors specialising in the delicate art of sea-cock opening performed their surgery on the *Indian Prince* which began to sink, although not fast enough, and she was ultimately helped on her way with dynamite. The *Kronprinz Wilhelm* speedily left the scene for new seas and conquests.

A rendezvous with the German steamer *Ebernburg* brought additional supplies and more coal. Thierfelder, mindful of the back-breaking labour and the tedium of coaling, ordered the ship's band to play martial tunes at the three coaling stations to stimulate those employed in the dirty job. The *Ebernburg*'s reserves were no sooner exhausted than a second supply steamer, the *Prussia*, arrived, and in due course, a third, the *Pontos*, so that there were four German ships nestled in one section of the ocean. The coaling was interrupted by a vain attempt on the part of the *Kronprinz Wilhelm* to aid SMS *Cap Trafalgar* in her ill-fated battle with HMS *Carmania* on September 14 1914. The two converted passenger liners slugged it out near Trinidad and the *Cap Trafalgar* was sunk in the only armed engagement between passenger liners of World War 1. Realising that the German vessel had been sunk when her wireless signals ceased, the *Kronprinz Wilhelm* returned to her coalers and her own duty. The officers and crew of the *Indian Prince* reportedly lightened the gloom of their German counterparts by indicating that the South American trade was paralysed over fear of their whereabouts. Thus the *Kronprinz Wilhelm* performed a valuable service to the German war effort simply by existing. All coaling and transferring of supplies was done on the port side of the liner so that the starboard side could remain relatively pristine. It was thought that it would impress prizes and prisoners on board the commerce raider if she had one good side to present to the world.

The *Kronprinz Wilhelm* struck lucky again on October 7 when she captured the Houlder liner *La Correntina* homeward-bound with an enormous cargo of meat (7,100,000 lb) and full bunkers. Incredibly, *La Correntina* was armed with 120 mm guns superior to the 8.8 cm weapons of the German vessel but had no ammunition for them! Reportedly, the price of beef went up 2d a pound all over Britain when the news of her loss was posted. *La Correntina* was on the return leg of her maiden voyage and constituted a veritable treasure trove of supplies. The 120 mm guns were transferred to the *Kronprinz Wilhelm* and were mounted for show. The crews of captured vessels were given second-class accommodation on the auxiliary cruiser while passengers were given first class cabins until they could be transferred to other vessels. October 8 brought a welcome sight in the NDL *Sierra Cordoba* with provisions from Bremen for the commerce raider and her crew. Once unloaded, the *Sierra Cordoba* carried the crew and passengers of the sunken vessels to safe harbour.

The *Kronprinz Wilhelm*'s next target was the French barque *Union* taken on October 28 with a

welcome cargo of 3,100 tons of Cardiff coal. The *Union* was captured only 40 miles off the Uruguayan coast and, therefore, was towed out to sea for unloading. Violent weather prolonged the ordeal by nearly three weeks during which the sailing ship came close to sinking with her prize crew, so bad were conditions. In this period the French barque *Anne de Brétagne* was also captured with a load of lumber bound from Norway to Australia. As this was of no great value it was decided to sink the vessel immediately, but this proved difficult because of the inherent buoyancy of her cargo. She defied fire, ramming by the *Kronprinz Wilhelm* and dynamite, and was finally left a derelict in the sea lanes.

The 3,814-ton *Bellevue* was captured on December 4 with 5,400 tons of coal, followed on the same day by the French steamer *Mont Agel* which was sunk by ramming. A dry spell then set in during which the German supply ship *Otavi* eluded Allied capture and reached a rendezvous with the commerce raider. On December 28 tedium was relieved by a good catch, the *Hemisphere* of London, with 6,100 tons of coal in her holds. A critical and worrisome development was the discovery of a crack in the propeller shaft which threatened to cripple the *Kronprinz Wilhelm* by radically reducing her speed. Throughout the remainder of the cruise this was an omnipresent problem. The Roland line steamer *Holger* met the auxiliary cruiser on January 6 and brought her needed supplies. Sunday, January 10, saw a smudge on the horizon which soon proved to be a large vessel steaming away from them at full speed. The *Kronprinz Wilhelm* gave chase at full speed while the fleeing ship frantically wirelessed for help. She was the British liner *Potaro* which was soon captured and which Thierfelder elected to employ as a scout for a while.

The Nelson liner *Highland Brae* succumbed on January 14, as did the French three-masted schooner *Wilfred M.* The *Kronprinz Wilhelm* was by now loaded with over 200 foreign passengers and crew from her prizes which it was a pleasure to transfer to the *Holger* on February 12 for transportation to a safe port. At the same time the opportunity was taken to reduce the number of personnel on the commerce raider by all those over the age of 38 who wished to go. Captain Grahn led a group of 73 officers and men to the *Holger* after an emotional farewell. The *Semantha*, a Norwegian sailing vessel with a contraband cargo of wheat, had been taken and sunk on February 3 so her crew were in time to be among the *Holger*'s passengers. After the departure of the passengers, prisoners and excess crew a ten-day

Top *The German supply ship* Sierra Cordoba *was one of the Norddeutscher Lloyd liners which brought welcome provisions to the SMS* Kronprinz Wilhelm. *Here she is shown in a photograph from the commerce raider with the French barque* Union *captured on October 28 1914.*
Above *The* Kronprinz Wilhelm *was short of ammunition from the very beginning of the cruise and resorted to ramming as a means of sinking some tonnage. Here the bow of the liner slices into the side of French freighter* Mont Agel *which had been carrying exactly six sheep, one pig, one ox and a few provisions.*

'dry spell' ensued before the British steamer *Chasehill* with a very welcome cargo of coal was captured on February 22. This was followed by the greatest prize of the cruise when the large French liner *Guadeloupe* of 6,600 tons with 294 passengers was captured. The gallant crew of the *Kronprinz Wilhelm* removed not only the passengers from the French liner but also a good part of their baggage before sinking the ship. Since it was critical to rid the commerce raider of any extra mouths as expeditiously as possible, the survivors of the *Guadeloupe* were transferred to the *Chasehill* and sent into a neutral port at the first opportunity. Two additional prizes fell to the *Kronprinz Wilhelm* when the British steamer *Tamar* was captured on March 24 and the *Coleby* on March 27, but the end was near.

The cruise had been quite extraordinary. Between August 29 1914 and March 27 1915, SMS auxiliary cruiser *Kronprinz Wilhelm* had steamed over 37,000 miles, capturing and sinking 58,201 tons of British, French and Norwegian shipping. All this was accomplished without the loss of a single life among the passengers and crews of the enemy vessels! Throughout the 251-day cruise Commander Thierfelder never ceased to be anything less than a gallant and chivalrous warrior even under the most trying circumstances. In recognition of his accomplishments he was awarded the Iron Cross First Class and 100 members of the crew received the Iron Cross Second Class on March 12 1915. The news came by wireless and was announced to the crew in a formal ceremony. By that time the *Kronprinz Wilhelm* was in poor physical condition. Her bow had been filled with cement to stop it from leaking, the port propeller shaft was fractured, boiler tubes were blowing up periodically, the port side was dented and leaking from the repeated coaling operations while under way, the guns were nearly out of ammunition, and increasing numbers of the crew were down with beri beri because of the absence of fresh fruit and vegetables.

On March 28 the *Kronprinz Wilhelm* steamed toward what many thought would be her last recoaling with a German steamer, the *Macedonia,* near the Bahamas. As the big auxiliary cruiser came over the horizon late in the day steaming due west toward the rendezvous point, the officers on the bridge suddenly noticed a small forest of funnels and masts against the setting sun. The *Macedonia* with the precious coal had been captured! Commander Thierfelder ordered 'Full Speed Astern' and the *Kronprinz Wilhelm* began to back away from the trap as fast as her straining engines would permit. Keeping her bow pointed toward the enemy, the 15,000-ton ship was soon doing an incredible 20 knots in reverse as she kept a narrow profile until the sun set. Then Thierfelder took his charge on a zig-zag north-westerly course

Top left *One of the prizes of the* Kronprinz Wilhelm *was the schooner* Wilfred M. *bound from Barbados to Brazil with cod and potatoes. Again the commerce raider could not afford to waste ammunition and sank the schooner by ramming. The horror of this picture is lessened only by the knowledge that no one was left on board the sailing ship.* **Centre left** *The first ram split the* Wilfred M. *into two pieces, and a second run at the stern was necessary to sink it.* **Left** *A third run at the bow shattered it and pushed it under while a forth run scattered the pieces since the armed merchant cruiser wished to leave no traces of her prize.*

toward the American coast. It was well known that every deep water American port was well guarded by British cruisers but no other alternative appeared viable. By Saturday, April 10, the *Kronprinz Wilhelm* was within 60 miles of the Virginia Capes and the night was dark. Six British cruisers reportedly guarded the entrance to the Chesapeake but Thierfelder still hoped to break through into the safety of neutral waters. Everything was made ready for the final dash in the great engine room where the rattling, prematurely-old, quadruple-expansion engines built up to the maximum speed. Even after eight months of non-stop voyaging the *Kronprinz Wilhelm* could still produce 20 knots as she ploughed the seas towards the Virginia Capes like a demon possessed. Her four great funnels belched towering steams of black smoke, mercifully hidden by the dark night. The liner shook from stem to stern and her officers were said to have had to hold on to the railings in order to remain on their feet as she approached the twinkling lights of an unsuspecting cruiser liner. Six miles out from America the running lights of two enemy cruisers on either side of the narrow channel were detected less than a mile apart. Commander Thierfelder called down to the engine room: 'Lay on, men! Now we're going through'.* Everyone held their breaths waiting to see if a searchlight would detect the big ocean greyhound and then, suddenly, she slammed across the three mile limit into the safety of American waters. The relief was unimaginable.

In Norfolk there was considerable excitement as the *Kronprinz Wilhelm* came racing in, ran up her blue lights, and with a booming rumble on her deep-throated whistle summoned a pilot. Sunday, April 11, was memorable as the *Kronprinz Wilhelm*, with her sailors at attention, slowly steamed past the American Atlantic Squadron whose guns fired a naval salute and whose bands each played the German national anthem in honour of the heroic auxiliary cruiser and her courageous crew. By agreement the *Kronprinz Wilhelm* did not fire a return salute because she was out of ammunition! The liner anchored alongside the *Prinz Eitel Friedrich* which had been a scourge of the North Atlantic sea lanes and had been interned one month before. Commander Thierfelder sought three weeks' grace to repair war damage to his vessel but the American authorities refused under the grounds that the ship was still physically capable of taking to sea.

* Count Alfred von Niezychowski, *The Cruise of the Kronprinz Wilhelm* (New York, 1929), p 296.

Top *The* Kronprinz Wilhelm *had been at sea continuously for 251 days, had steamed more than 37,000 miles and sunk 58,201 tons of enemy shipping when she made a dash for neutral American waters on April 10 1915. Here she is shown at Newport News immediately following her safe arrival having escaped a cordon of British cruisers.*
Above *The* Kronprinz Wilhelm *was interned with the* Prinz Eitel Friedrich *at the Philadelphia Navy Yard* (US Navy).

The *Kronprinz Wilhelm* was drydocked, scraped and painted but it was obvious that she could not function efficiently without much more extensive repairs and refitting. Therefore, Thierfelder agreed that the liner should be interned for the duration so that his crew could receive medical care. Thus ended the cruise of SMS auxiliary cruiser *Kronprinz Wilhelm*, whose commander had performed a miracle in keeping such a huge liner at sea under the most trying conditions without touching a port for 251 days.

The third of the great Norddeutscher Lloyd liners was the Kaiser Wilhelm II *which entered service in 1903. Here she is shown backing out into the North River from her Hoboken pier, circa 1911.*

The select inner social circle of Imperial Germany gathered at Stettin on August 12 1902 to view the launch of the third great four-funnel express liner for the Norddeutscher Lloyd Line. The occasion was made national in scope by the presence of Kaiser Wilhelm II, after whom the new ocean greyhound would be named. His Majesty, wearing his Admiral's uniform, arrived at Stettin on the new torpedo boat *Sleipner,* accompanied by the Imperial State Secretary for the Navy, Admiral von Tirpitz, and was greeted by the Prussian Ministers of War, Commerce, and Railways, as well as the Postmaster General and local civic authorities. All were appropriate for the occasion since the new ship was designed from the keel up to be an armed merchant cruiser in time of war even if her primary reasons for being were to transport passengers brought her by the German railways, and the safe delivery of the Imperial Post. A triumphal arch led to the grandstand erected near the liner's bow. Fraulein Wiegand, daughter of the NDL's General Manager, performed the actual christening ceremony and the *Kaiser Wilhelm II* majestically took to the water as the crowds cheered. The Kaiser spoke briefly during the ceremony and expressed great admiration for the new vessel as representing not only a record achievement for a German yard, but for any shipbuilding enterprise anywhere in the world.

The pride of the Kaiser and of Germany was justified! The new liner was the third express liner in five years for the NDL building programme, but she was much more than just a copy of the *Kaiser Wilhelm der Grosse* or *Kronprinz Wilhelm* since information gathered in the construction and operation of the earlier ships had made many refinements possible. The leading dimensions of the new ship were: length overall 706 ft 6 in; beam 72 ft 3 in; depth from promenade deck to top of keel 52 ft 6 in; load draught 29 ft 6 in; displacement 26,500 tons; gross tonnage 19,361; and with engines producing 44,600 horsepower to drive the twin screws. In terms of her contemporaries, the *Kaiser Wilhelm II* was a foot or so longer than the White Star *Oceanic* which she far surpassed in tonnage, but was some three feet less in the beam than the White Star *Celtic* and *Cedric* which were the only two vessels afloat to exceed her in gross tonnage.

The safety provisions built into the *Kaiser Wilhelm II* were exceeded only by a few warships. She possessed a double bottom extending practically the whole length of the ship. The space between the two skins rose to a maximum of nearly seven feet. The whole was subdivided into 26 compartments which permitted a large quantity of water to be carried in tanks without contamination. The boiler feed tanks were good for 202 tons, the drinking water tanks for 866 tons and the ballast tanks for 2,097 tons. There were 17 transverse bulkheads, and a longitudinal wall separated the engine room into four separate sections.

The *Kaiser Wilhelm II*'s keel had been laid on April 1 1901, so that the launch took place just over 16 months later. Some 11,200 tons of steel were used during construction with the largest single piece being the cast sternpost of 120 tons. The liner's design incorporated four complete decks, orlop, lower, main and upper. In addition there was a spar deck, a second promenade deck and a boat deck.

The basic propulsion system involved 19 boilers, 12 double-ended and 7 single-ended, with a total heating area of 107,643 sq ft, operating at 213-225 psi with the heat coming from 124 furnaces. The bunker capacity was 5,700 tons and between 600-700 tons of coal were consumed each day on the Atlantic run! The boiler rooms and the bunkers together occupied a length of 295 ft. So great a distance existed between bunkers and boilers in the extremes that a railway track nearly 600 ft long ran down the centre of the ship to shift the bulky and heavy fuel from storage to gaping furnace mouth. Even with this mechanical assistance the boiler room staff still numbered 237 people or nearly half the entire crew of the liner. Furthermore, the gigantic, soaring engine rooms occupied another 92 ft of the ship.

Each of the four sets of engines was contained in a separate compartment. The *Kaiser Wilhelm II* and her sister, the *Kronprinzessin Cecilie*, possessed the largest and most powerful quadruple expansion reciprocating engines ever placed in a passenger vessel. The climax of an era stretching back some 40 years was reached in the cathedral-like engine rooms where the cylinders rose nearly 50 ft from the inner bottom with diameters of 37.4 in, 49.1 in, 74.7 in and 112.2 in. The maximum operating speed at 80 rpm was 23 knots although it was considered that the Vulcan vessels were good for 1 to 1½ knots more than their designed maximums. The propellers were four-bladed, each having a diameter of 22 ft 10 in. The *Kaiser Wilhelm II* carried 26 lifeboats and her pumps could deal with 9,360 tons of water per hour. Fire fighting was enhanced by a system of pipes permitting water or steam to be pumped or sprayed into any critical compartment. Electric fire alarms were installed and the captain on the bridge could close all watertight doors by simply touching a button. The ship's equipment included five anchors averaging five tons each. The crew, including wireless staff, exceeded 600.

What the travelling public wanted to know was,

Names and faces to associate with some of the Norddeutscher Lloyd ships are shown in this Hohenzollern family picture. Kaiser Wilhelm II is in the centre of the family grouping with Kronprinz Wilhelm on his left and Kronprinzessin Cecilie seated in the chair to his right. All would have NDL four-funnel liners named for them. The Empress, Kaiserin Auguste Victoria, would have a HAPAG liner named for her.

how did the accommodation compare with that on existing vessels? The *Kaiser Wilhelm II* was designed to convey in splendour 775 first class passengers in 290 cabins and 343 second class in 109 cabins, besides 770 in third class. The main dining room was 108 ft long and 69 ft wide with a seating capacity of 554. All the glory and splendour of Wilhelmine Germany was unleashed in producing a fitting setting for personages of wealth and importance to dine in this truly grand room that soared upwards through three decks. As usual the Vulcan Shipyard made full provision for children and a pleasant junior dining room and playroom overlooked the grand saloon in a kind of balcony.

The smoking room was large and arranged in a horseshoe shape around the funnel casing as before. Two decorative highlights involved a flooring of interlocking coloured tiles and a truly magnificent skylight. A door at the rear of the smoking room led down a hall to one of the most popular rooms on the ship, the Vienna Cafe. There ladies and gentlemen could join together for afternoon coffee and liqueurs in a smoke-free

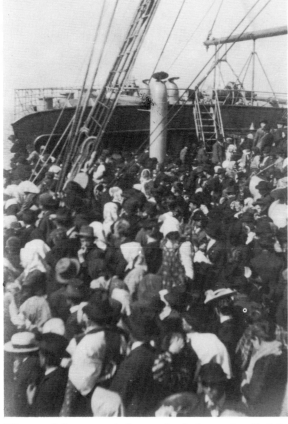

The crowded steerage deck space in the forward well of the Kaiser Wilhelm II (Library of Congress).

environment. Furthermore, it was possible to sit out on the upper deck under a permanent shelter and enjoy both refreshments and fresh air. A ladies' drawing room also was provided for after-dinner relaxation but the Vienna Cafe soon became the meeting place on the ship. The great Imperial Suites provided a drawing room, dining room, bedroom, bathroom and lavatory all *en suite*. One observer commented that it would be quite possible for a millionaire to cross the Atlantic without ever having to mix with non-millionaires. Some restraint in interior decorating was shown in the Imperial Suites where the walls of the cabins were painted in pleasant pastels without heavy gilding, but with little coloured prints to highlight the setting. No detail was too insignificant and a major effort was made to ensure that those worthies travelling in the Imperial Suites would have hot meals in their private dining rooms. To this end special thick dishes were designed which could be super-heated in the galley and which would then keep the food warm for up to an hour prior to serving. At £80 a day in 1903 one certainly had the right to expect hot food even away from the main dining room. In the kitchens of the *Kaiser Wilhelm II* one of the new labour-saving devices was an egg boiler that did hundreds at once in little racks. Sanitation on the ship involved 23 public bathrooms and 53 private facilities which was a remarkably high number for the time.

The *Kaiser Wilhelm II* sailed on her maiden voyage from Bremen on April 14 1903, calling at Southampton later on the same day and sailing from Cherbourg at 1.40 am on April 15. She was under the command of the senior Norddeutscher Lloyd captain, D. Hogemann, with keen expectations of a fast run. The weather squelched all possibilities of the 'Blue Riband' and, even though a commendable run to the west of 5 days, 23 hours over a 3,160 mile course was achieved, the average speed was only 22.10 knots. Rough seas and a high north-easterly swell gave the passengers on the new liner a wild ride. Subsequent voyages proved disappointing as well and NDL was terribly anxious to beat the *Deutschland*'s record in both directions. All through her first season the *Kaiser Wilhelm II*'s machinery performed well but not to record-breaking levels, while the greyhound was plagued with some excessive vibration. In the late spring of 1904 she was taken in hand and fitted with a new pair of propellers. The results were deeply gratifying as she took the record for a single day from the *Deutschland* by steaming 564 miles on Saturday, June 18, at an average speed of 24.35 knots. The complete eastbound crossing of June 14-20 1904 covered a distance of 3,112 miles over 5 days, 11 hours, 58 minutes at an average speed of 23.58 knots, regaining for the Norddeutscher Lloyd Line the eastbound 'Blue Riband'.

In August 1907 the penultimate goal of the Line was achieved with the commissioning of the *Kronprinzessin Cecilie*. Four large 23-knot ships capable of ensuring the regular operation of a weekly express service flew the famed flag of Norddeutscher Lloyd. The *Kronprinzessin Cecilie* was built by the Vulcan Yard at Stettin like her three predecessors and was launched by Her Imperial Highness on December 1 1906. In dimensions the liner was a very close sister to the *Kaiser Wilhelm II* but her gross tonnage was 19,503. Net tonnage in both liners was extremely small, about 6,500 tons, because of the enormity of their machinery.

Accommodation was provided for 742 first class passengers, 327 second and 740 third, while the crew numbered 665. The most expensive accommodation consisted of the two Imperial Suites complete with dining room, drawing room, bedroom, lavatory and bathroom. Each suite went for the genuinely royal sum of £500 a crossing, up £100 from the price for similar facilities on the *Kaiser Wilhelm II* a brief four years before. The eight cabins de luxe with sitting rooms came next, while there were also 12 extra-large staterooms with private baths for the great and near-great.

The Kronprinzessin Cecilie *heading for the open ocean.*

Attention to detail was shown in the grooved contour of the floor of the tubs so that a better grip could be had by the bather in rough weather. The cuisine in the dining room was unsurpassed by any land-based hotel. A fresh fish tank was part of the provision equipment where fish could be kept alive until summoned to grace the dinner of an individual to whom money was of no concern.

The maiden voyage of the *Kronprinzessin Cecilie* began on August 6 1907, from Bremen with a call at Southampton from which she sailed at 2.30 pm on August 7, leaving Cherbourg at 9 pm. She was off Sandy Hook about 3 pm on August 13 with a crossing of 5 days, 23 hours. It was emphasised that there had not been any effort to drive the liner since her machinery was just working-in. However, the advent of the Cunard Line's *Lusitania* and *Mauretania* made the whole issue academic since both vessels were substantially faster even if they were on the Liverpool-New York service and left the Norddeutscher Lloyd quartet dominant on the Channel.

It was fortunate that the *Kronprinzessin Cecilie* came on the line in early August since the *Kaiser Wilhelm II* suffered a disaster at Bremerhaven on July 20. She was being bunkered on Saturday as part of the normal preparations for her Tuesday departure. With the tide out the ship was resting comfortably on the riverbed when the coaling operation began. Since she remained on an even keel the authorities concerned felt no particular need to spread the heavy fuel evenly. But as the tide came flooding up the channel, she wobbled loose from the mud and took a sickening list which plunged the coaling ports below water level, leaving the pride of the German Merchant Marine sunk alongside her pier in her home port! The result was devastating to the NDL schedule since it was necessary to cancel her July 23 sailing in the midst of the high season traffic. Even though she was speedily pumped out, some internal damage had been done and several thousand tons of coal were a sodden mess. The coal was no small part of the loss either since Norddeutscher Lloyd revealed in its annual report for 1907 that the Line had spent £1,630,680 for approximately 1,793,856 tons of coal to fuel the fleet and that this represented a tenfold increase over the previous three decades. The end result on the company books for the 1907 year was a dividend of three per cent which hardly compared favourably with many other industries, although it was a definite improvement over the zero profit of the recession year 1906.

In July of 1908 the *Kronprinzessin Cecilie* steamed westward from Cherbourg in 5 days, 15 hours, 23 minutes over a 3,142 mile track with an average speed of 23.21 knots to beat the *Deutschland*'s record by .06 knots. On the return passage she romped home in 5 days, 11 hours, 12 minutes over a 3,070 mile track with an average speed of 23.71 knots. Weather conditions were just about ideal in August 1908 when the *Kaiser Wilhelm II* went one better than her younger sister by slamming eastbound from New York to Plymouth in 5 days, 9 hours, 55 minutes, over a 3,080 mile course at an average speed of 23.71 knots. A comparison of all four NDL liners shows that there was remarkably little separating their fastest crossing speeds: *Kaiser Wilhelm II* 23.71 knots;

Above *The* Kronprinzessin Cecilie *at Southampton shortly after her maiden voyage* (National Maritime Museum).
Below *Turned and headed down the Water, the* Kronprinzessin Cecilie's *twin propellers begin to kick up a froth. The* Kronprinzessin Cecilie *was almost identical to the* Kaiser Wilhelm II *but 13 in longer and 1 in narrower, with a gross tonnage of 19,503* (National Maritime Museum).

Kronprinz Wilhelm 23.47 knots; *Kronprinzessin Cecilie* 23.35 knots; and *Kaiser Wilhelm der Grosse* 23.00 knots.

Some people have commented that Norddeutscher Lloyd should have selected a turbine propulsion system for the last of the quartet of express liners, thereby bringing her into line with the new British competition. The simple fact of the matter is that the installation of turbines instead of quadruple expansion engines would have made the new liner unique among her running mates with machinery that was by no means conclusively proven. Sane and proper managerial sense dictated that all four ships have similar machinery so that parts would be universally available, crews mutually transferable and a proven, durable propulsion system continued throughout a single class of ship. The inherent conservatism of the Bremen-based management probably means that turbines were never given serious consideration at this time.

During the period 1907-1914 the *Kronprinzessin Cecilie* enjoyed a remarkably un-newsworthy career. Overshadowed by larger and faster vessels almost from the date of her delivery, she rarely captured any headlines although the North German quartet moved thousands of passengers across the Atlantic in fair weather and foul all the year round. In particular the distinguished men who captained the commodore vessel of the Line had an enormous following of wealthy travellers who remained faithful to them and NDL. In fact, when Commodore D. Hogemann retired in March 1913, it was a newsworthy event. Hogeman, with his twinkling eyes, solid build and full beard, was the absolute personification of a 'proper' North Atlantic captain. When he backed the *Kronprinzessin Cecilie* out of her Hoboken slip on March 4 1913, he had made well over a hundred North Atlantic crossings for the company and had been in their service for over thirty years. Many prominent members of the German-American community came to bid him a fond farewell. By any standards Captain-Commodore Hogemann was both wealthy and well-paid even if his responsibility was enormous and the strain of the first magnitude. His personal fortune, built up over the years, exceeded £30,000 and his annual salary from the Line ran between £2,000 and £2,400 a year. In addition he also received a bonus on the basis of how many passengers his ship delivered to New York each year. In the case of an express liner like the *Kronprinzessin Cecilie* this could amount to a very considerable sum indeed.

Captain Hogemann's successor as Commodore of the Norddeutscher Lloyd Line was Captain Charles Polack, recently of the liner *George Washington,* a larger but slower unit of the Line. Polack had risen to the top by being a bit of a martinet who did not tolerate any affront to himself or his command. This was vividly shown when the *Kronprinzessin Cecilie* arrived at New York on July 21 1914, after a tense crossing created by the international scene. The ageing *Grosser Kurfurst* dropped anchor almost simultaneously with the premier ship of the Line, and through a fluke the customs agents boarded the older vessel before Captain Polack's command. Then the *Grosser Kurfurst* proceeded up the harbour first and to compound the indignity her captain endeavoured to dock in the slip reserved for the *Kronprinzessin Cecilie,* which meant that Polack had to cool his heels in mid-stream until the other ship was backed out and berthed properly! The American health officer inspecting the *Kronprinzessin Cecilie* said that if he had just been asked the quarantine flag would have been lowered and the Customs officials could have gone on board immediately since there were no infectious diseases evident. Whatever the case Captain Polack was so livid that he stormed off the bridge to go to the dining room and tell all concerned just what he thought of their incompetence.

In the 1907-1914 period the *Kaiser Wilhelm II* also experienced a relatively uneventful career save for the misfortune of sinking at her pier. However, on the afternoon of June 17 1914, just after passing the Needles in dense fog on a westbound crossing, she was struck amidships by the *Incemore* of Liverpool bound for Antwerp. Two cuts of considerable length were made in her side which extended well below the waterline. One slice was 24 ft long × 5 in wide, while the other was 18 ft long × 9 in wide. A bulkhead was ruptured by the blow, opening to the sea a bunker and a boiler room, but the integrity of the liner was never in doubt. The captain of the *Kaiser Wilhelm II* had closed the watertight doors of his ship as soon as the fog settled in and the flooding was well contained. A collision mat was placed over the holes and the *Kaiser Wilhelm II* returned to port with a distinct list but under her own power. Her passengers were transferred to the HAPAG *Imperator* sailing the next day. This potential disaster again brought very favourable comment about the strength of the NDL greyhounds since it came hard on the heels of the official inquiry into the tragic loss of the *Empress of Ireland* on May 29 1914, in the St Lawrence River with over a thousand dead. The internal subdivisions of the German quartet indeed made them very safe vessels.

Norddeutscher Lloyd in 1912 was second only to HAPAG in the size of its fleet and the variety of its services. Altogether the fleet consisted of 115 ocean-going steamships of which 52 were twin-screw, indicative of their relatively modern construction. The Line also operated 43 river steamers of a combined tonnage of 6,275, two school ships totalling 5,833 tons and 30 steam sloops and lighters equalling 3,371 tons. Under construction was no less than 85,500 tons of steam shipping including a 35,000-ton Atlantic liner with the designated name *Columbus.* During 1913 NDL carried the awe-inspiring total of 175,000 westbound and 64,000 eastbound passengers on the Bremen-Channel ports-New York service. Over 90,000 of the 'westbound total involved steerage class, which serves to put the figures into perspective. Moreover, NDL carried some 25,000 more passengers than the combined Cunard and White Star totals from Southampton and Liverpool to New York. The Line also operated a diversified series of weekly, fortnightly or monthly services to American East Coast ports, the Mediterranean, Gulf of Mexico, Cuba, the Far East and Australia. In 1913 the astronomical total of 662,385 passengers was carried on ships flying the company's blue anchor and chain, while the grand total of passengers carried since 1857 and the founding of the Line was 10,408,113! A surprising comment in the 1913 report was that an agreement had been reached between NDL and HAPAG to pool and share the results of their North Atlantic operations for a period of 15 years. What that might have produced no one can say. To a concern like the Norddeutscher Lloyd with its far-flung, world-wide operations, the greatest possible catastrophe was a war in which the sea lanes were closed and the floating assets of the business became targets for enemy action.

The tension of late July 1914 was evident in the special press coverage given to the sailing of the *Kronprinzessin Cecilie* at 1 am on Tuesday July 28. At the same time the confidence of American banking interests that nothing untoward would occur on the international scene or to the vessel was testified to by the shipping of $10,679,000 (£2,135,800) in gold bars and freshly minted gold coins, and an estimated $3,600,000 (£720;000) in silver in the ship's strongrooms. This treasure was outward bound to British and French banks on a German ship to settle outstanding American accounts. Before World War 1 a substantial proportion of American industry had been financed by European investors who reaped annual profits in bond interest and stock dividends. Furthermore, America bought vast quantities of manufactured goods in Europe, paying for the imports by exporting raw materials such as grain and gold. A shipment of precious metal in excess of ten million dollars was thus not unheard of. The Norddeutscher Lloyd quartet were fitted with strongrooms for carrying the heavy precious metals, while the crews were experts in the speedy and safe transfer of such valuable cargoes from ship to shore, or ship to lighter, even at Plymouth or Cherbourg.

The eastbound crossing was relatively uneventful for the first four days after the July 28 departure. The 1,216 passengers were a cosmopolitan mixture of Americans, Germans and a few British travelling for every conceivable human reason from fear of the international situation to the desire to go grouse shooting in Scotland. The total trip consumed a week under normal circumstances, with a Tuesday departure from New York, a Sunday evening arrival at Plymouth, where the liner lay offshore, a Monday call at Cherbourg and then home to Bremerhaven on Tuesday. Normally the liner would be reprovisioned and coaled on Wednesday, Thursday and Friday, permitting her to take the outward run by Saturday if desired. The *Kronprinzessin Cecilie* sailed from New York on the day that Winston Churchill ordered the British Grand Fleet to sail from Portland for war stations at Scapa Flow. The first day's steaming covered the time frame in which the German Minister at Brussels, Herr von Below-Saleske, received a sealed envelope containing the German ultimatum to Belgium. As the big greyhound steamed eastward at 23 knots the destiny of the world genuinely was being decided. By Friday night, July 31, when the liner was about 900 miles from Plymouth, a wireless message reached Captain Polack ordering him to turn his huge coal-burning charge around and race back across the North Atlantic toward neutral American waters. The capacities of the *Kronprinzessin Cecilie* were to be strained to the maximum. In effect she was ordered to cross the Atlantic twice!

The first class passengers had been enjoying the pleasures of the gala night ball when the *Kronprinzessin Cecilie* began to vibrate somewhat more violently even though the seas remained unchanged. The huge quadruple expansion engines were pounding one of the fastest beats they were ever summoned to perform as glasses began to edge across tables because of the pulsating vibration. While the dance was in progress one of the passengers went out on deck and immediately noticed that the moon had un-accountably shifted to the port side of the liner. Before the full significance of this was universally realised Captain Polack descended from the bridge and summoned all the male passengers in first class to the sanctuary of the *Rauchzimmer*, or smoking room. There, in the centre of the great horseshoe, he gravely announced that a general European war was either imminent or had already begun and that he had been ordered to return to the United States. He reassured all concerned that he had more than enough coal in the bunkers to reach port.

Clear weather soon gave way to dense fog as the big liner sped towards America. Her crew placed canvas over all her portholes and windows, and all external lights were extinguished lest she be betrayed in the dead of the night. The fog was thick but the German ship slackened her speed only slightly to conserve fuel as she silently knifed through the North Atlantic with the devout hope of all on board that no other unsuspecting vessel would cross her deadly bow. Even the foghorn was stifled for the first 24 hours as the liner raced away along a northern track from the potentially dangerous waters of the British Isles. This thoroughly alarmed the passengers and a committee of irate travellers ultimately met with Captain Polack. Mindful of the *Titanic* disaster, they accused him of mercilessly endangering the lives of all on board and that the human beings were of far more importance than the bullion of the modern treasure galleon. Captain Polack assured them that there was little danger since he was running far to the north of the usual steam-ship lanes. This failed to allay their fears but the NDL Commodore did agree to blow the foghorn at irregular intervals. Through the dark nights and the fog-enshrouded days the greyhound steamed on, encountering only a few fishing boats off the Grand Banks. Crew members labouring above and beyond the call of duty retouched the tops of the four smoke, spark and cinder-belching stacks of the *Kronprinzessin Cecilie* with black paint, thereby converting the famous buff of the NDL into the equally distinguished buff and black of the White Star Line. Whether any naval officer would have been taken in by such subter-fuge is questionable, but there was a strong possibility that civilians or casual observers might be. Awards for heroism certainly should have gone to the valiant German crew members working in the fiery hell at the crown of the liner's funnels while she engaged in a wild rolling race for safety with asphyxiating smoke and scorching sparks everywhere.

The smoking room of the Kronprinzessin Cecilie *curved around a funnel casing and was one of the more popular rooms on the ship. Note the music rolls stacked next to the fireplace and the elaborate wood carvings on the walls* (US Navy).

During the eastbound crossing passengers had laid wagers as to the expected arrival time at Plymouth. During the unexpected westbound crossing some of the travellers laid bets as to the ultimate destination of their ship in a world where nothing was certain any more! Among the suggested ports of call were New York, Boston and Newport.

As the dash for American waters neared the critical period the Master of the *Kronprinzessin*

The commercial career of the Kronprinzessin Cecilie *(1907-1914) was brief and she made a hasty return to American waters in August 1914 when war was declared. Carrying a fortune in gold and silver, she slipped into Bar Harbor, Maine, wearing the funnel colours of the White Star Line (black over buff) as part of her disguise* (US Navy).

Above *A superb view of the* Kronprinzessin Cecilie *at Bar Harbor, Maine, in early August 1914 wearing the White Star funnel colours* (Steamship Historical Society of America).

Below *Stern view of the* Kronprinzessin Cecilie *at Bar Harbor* (Steamship Historical Society of America).

Cecilie summoned C. Ledyard Blair, one of his more famous passengers and an avid yachtsman, to a conference. He discussed with the banker which American port to make for and settled on Bar Harbor, Maine, as the best of the smaller northern ports. Blair lived in New York but he loved sailing and his father, D.C. Blair, owned a large summer home at Bar Harbor. The result was that he had sailed the Maine waters often in his 1,000-ton yacht *Diana* and knew every rock from Schoodic Point to Owl's Head in the approach to Bar Harbor. During the early morning of August 4 Blair joined Captain Polack on the bridge of the 20,000-ton liner and between 3-6 am assisted in navigating the ocean-going giant into Bar Harbor. Blair contended he assisted very little but when the *Kronprinzessin Cecilie*'s anchors plunged into the cold waters of the Maine port Captain Polack gave full credit to C. Ledyard Blair for the feat of getting the big liner to a safe anchorage unscathed.

Blair immediately went ashore with a delegation of ship's officers to explain the nature of the situation to the local Customs officer and quarantine doctor. The little village of Bar Harbor awoke to find the largest vessel ever to put into that port dwarfing everything else in the harbour. Initially, because of the black and buff funnels, it was thought that the *Olympic* of the White Star Line had wandered into port, but then the news spread that the liner was indeed the fabulous treasure ship everyone had been reading about.

Mrs A. Howard Hinkle of Cincinnati was a passenger on the ship with her daughter bound for Carlsbad, Germany, for the summer season instead of to their summer home at Bar Harbor. She reported: 'I had commenced to greatly regret that I hadn't gone to Bar Harbor as usual when we turned about in mid-ocean and started back for we knew not where. When I arose Tuesday morning and looked through a port I saw land, and, without having the faintest idea of where we were, I remarked that it looked a little like Bar Harbor.' Her delight was unrestricted when she discovered that the *Kronprinzessin Cecilie* had anchored a stone's throw opposite her home!

The excitement of some passengers on their safe return to the United States soon turned to irritation over the fact that they could not disembark immediately. This Captain Polack could not allow without the permission of the United States Customs authorities which could not authorise anything until Secretary of the Treasury, William McAdoo, issued a special dispensation. The penalty to the Norddeutscher Lloyd Line could have been as high as $1,000 (£200) per passenger for landing them in an unauthorised port and for having transported them between two American ports without first touching a foreign port. The American coastal trade was a sacred preserve of protectionist American shipping. Secretary McAdoo readily waived all regulations and penalties so that the first and second class passengers who so desired could proceed from Bar Harbor to New York by train. Steerage passengers were despatched later, including one additional passenger, a baby boy born to a Slavonic woman on Friday, July 31, while the liner was turning for her race back to America.

The American bankers who had shipped the largely uninsured cargo wanted it back as soon as possible. The United States Coast Guard revenue cutter *Androscoggin* with an armament of four 6 prs was assigned the task of guarding the liner and/or removing the gold and silver. Forty strapping German seamen worked six hours removing the treasure from the liner's vaults. They had to wheel it up a gangplank and through a side port of the German ship on to the deck of the cutter. Its crew became alarmed for the safety of their ship as the weight of the metal increased. Lacking sufficient timbers to shore up the deck, they scattered the 75-pound pigs of silver and 200-pound kegs full of gold coins in order to distribute the load. Once all the treasure was on board the poor little *Androscoggin* she cast off and steamed to the pier where the treasure was checked and re-checked before it was turned over to the American Express Company which sent an armoured train and 300 armed guards to transport it back to New York.

The *Kronprinzessin Cecilie* was guarded at Bar Harbor by the *Androscoggin* for six weeks before two American destroyers relieved her. The NDL

The Kaiser Wilhelm II *was interned in New York when World War 1 occurred. She was then seized by the United States in 1917. Here she barely squeezes into the dry dock at the New York Navy Yard on June 18 1917 (US Navy).*

were anxious for the safety of their vessel and so were the American authorities. The result was a tacit British agreement not to interfere with the shifting of the German liner escorted by American destroyers from Bar Harbor to Boston where she could be berthed safely. This was accomplished during the autumn of 1914 and the *Kronprinzessin Cecilie* lay at Boston for the better part of the next three years until America became directly involved in the war.

Repairs to the *Kaiser Wilhelm II* following her collision with the *Incemore* were completed in good order and she was in mid-Atlantic bound for the United States during the first week in August when war broke out. She arrived at the Ambrose Lightship at 3 am on August 5 with only her running lights showing and without the normal booming signals from her whistles. Only a small number of passengers were on board but the 252 individuals in first and second clearly expressed their delight at being home! The *Kaiser Wilhelm II* tied up at her Hoboken pier where she remained for the better part of the next three years.

Upon the American Declaration of War the interned Norddeutscher Lloyd liners were seized on April 6 1917, and renamed. The *Kronprinz Wilhelm* became the USS *Von Steuben*, the *Kaiser Wilhelm II* was christened USS *Agamemnon* and the *Kronprinzessin Cecilie* was given the patriotic American-sounding title USS *Mount Vernon*. Plans were undertaken immediately to survey the

Outfitted as an American armed merchant cruiser and then designated a troopship, the Kronprinz Wilhelm *was renamed USS* Von Steuben *(Frank O. Braynard Collection-SSHSA).*

liners and to adapt them for trooping duties. The American war effort was pitifully short in high speed vessels with large troop shipping capacities and the three German liners would be of enormous importance to the war effort. Together the three ex-Norddeutscher Lloyd greyhounds made no less than 49 round-trips out of a total of only 481 by all US troop transports.

The *Agamemnon* (ex-*Kaiser Wilhelm II*) underwent extensive reconditioning at the Brooklyn

The Kronprinzessin Cecilie *was seized by the United States on April 6 1917 and converted into a troop transport with sufficient armament to serve as an armed merchant cruiser if desired. Here she is shown at New York in dazzle paint on July 8 1918 (US Navy).*

Navy Yard. The American troops who travelled on her soon christened her the 'Aggie' which became the 'Agony' to many a non-sailor and sailor alike. The German greyhounds were never famous for their stability and the *Agamemnon* with a full load of troops could roll and pitch horrendously. Lieutenant C.K. Cummings, USNR, observed the troopship during a vicious crossing in late January-early February 1918. 'The *Agamemnon* was a sight one could never tire of watching. She would dive down a huge wave and throw her stern high out of the water until her twin propellers could be seen racing furiously, then her bow would rise majestically and shake off tons of water which flew high over the bridge and poured off in torrents.'

The United States Marshal seized the *Kronprinzessin Cecilie* in Boston on February 3 1917 as a result of civil actions against the Norddeutscher Lloyd Line and rumours that her machinery was being sabotaged. The German crew was taken off the ship and it was discovered that numerous engine room plates had been removed or switched. Other damage was minimal. The United States Government formally took control of the ship on April 6 1917, and turned her over to the United States Navy on April 15, whereupon she was shifted from East Boston to Charlestown, New York, for swift conversion into an armed troopship. Plans were made for six 5-in guns to be fitted on the existing German gun emplacements—two aft, two amidships, and two forward—but only the extremes were installed. As the USS *Mount Vernon* the ship was manned by 1,000 crew and undertook her trial trip on September 28, with formal sea-going trials on October 11 prior to departure for New York the next day. Finally she was able to dock at her old Hoboken piers to await the arrival of troops. The *Mount Vernon* on some crossings sailed with nearly 6,000 on board—1,000 crew and 4,800 troops, 1,400 of whom slept during the day so that the bunks were never cold.

The *Kronprinz Wilhelm* lay at Newport News, Virginia, for a while after her internment in April 1915, but then was shifted to Philadelphia, where she was seized on April 6 1917. President Woodrow Wilson issued an Executive Order on May 22 empowering the United States Navy to take over the vessel and repair her. Work proceeded quickly and on June 9 the *Kronprinz Wilhelm* was commissioned into the United States Navy as an auxiliary cruiser and renamed in honour of Baron von Steuben, one of the German-born heroes of the American Revolutionary War (1775-1783).

As the summer of 1917 progressed it became

Dazzle paint scheme for the port side of the USS Agamemnon. *This picture is taken from an old, and unfortunately fractured, glass negative* (US Navy).

evident that there existed a far greater need for transports than for auxiliary cruisers. Accordingly, on September 21 1917, the Commandant of the Philadelphia Navy Yard was ordered to prepare the *Von Steuben* for trooping duties. She sailed from New York at 5.30 pm on October 31 and formed an imposing convoy with the USS *Agamemnon, Mount Vernon, America* (ex-*Amerika*), the armoured cruiser *North Carolina,* and the destroyers *Duncan* and *Terry.* The destination of this American high-speed convoy was the French port of Brest. A normal troop transport convoy took 11-12 days to Europe since war precautions nearly doubled the regular peacetime period. The *Von Steuben,* never short of excitement during her career, added some to the crossing at dawn on November 9 1917. As a huge sweeping turn of the fast convoy was underway the *Von Steuben* arced too broadly. Suddenly, about 6.05 am, the great grey mass of the *Agamemnon* loomed in front of the *Von Steuben* which hit the other troopship a long, hard, glancing blow forward of amidships which buckled the deck for 100 feet, destroyed eight lifeboats and killed one person, while ripping guns from their emplacements. Instantly the Atlantic was ablaze with the floodlights of the great liners and warships, the air was rent with the throaty blasts of foghorns, and chaos temporarily reigned supreme. The bow of the *Von Steuben* was stove-in for the third time in her career but she had no major leaks or other damage. The convoy continued at speed to meet its European escort coming out from Brest, but the *Von Steuben,* reduced to 12 knots, fell far behind as her crew frantically poured cement into the bow section to patch it. The next day, a squadron of American destroyers met the troop transports and the whole fleet of 13 ships turned around and steamed westward to rejoin and protect the crippled *Von Steuben.* Reunited with

their wounded comrade, the entire fleet again reversed course and headed for Brest, entering the French port in an impressive line-ahead at 11.40 on November 12. The first great convoy of American troops in the American Expeditionary Force had arrived . . . with all units accounted for.

The *Von Steuben* disembarked 1,223 troops and passengers and unloaded critical cargo between November 14-19. Minimal repairs also were undertaken to make her a shade more seaworthy and she was given orders to sail again on November 28. The first port of call on this crossing would be Halifax, Nova Scotia, and luck was with her once again. As she was about 40 miles off Halifax shortly after 9 am on December 6 the lookouts reported a towering column of fire and smoke from the direction of the Canadian port. Shortly thereafter a loud bang shook the troopship. The French ammunition ship *Mont Blanc* had blown up in Halifax harbour devastating the surrounding city in one of the greatest civilian disasters of the war. As the *Von Steuben* steamed in about 2.30 that afternoon signs of the catastrophe lay all around. Sections of the city were still burning, ships were sunk and the survivors stunned. Immediately the American officers and crew of the *Von Steuben* rendered every possible assistance to the Canadian authorities. They helped in numerous rescue efforts and then patrolled the streets at night while the troopship remained at Halifax for four days.

The *Von Steuben* resumed her homeward crossing on December 10, arriving at Philadelphia three days later, and continuing to Newport News for coaling. Bunkered, she sailed from Newport News on December 20 with marines for Guantanamo Bay, Cuba, to reinforce the American presence there. Every dry dock on the East Coast of the United States was operating to maximum capacity and none could devote three weeks to repairing the damaged bow of the *Von Steuben.* The nearest available dock was at Balboa on the Pacific side of the Panama Canal. Accordingly the *Von Steuben* left Cuba on December 27 and, having passed through the canal on December 29, immediately went into dry dock, becoming thereby the first of the German greyhounds to touch Pacific waters. Three weeks later she floated out with virtually a new bow in place, sailed back through the canal, coaled at Colon, and steamed north. Between January 28-31 the *Von Steuben* lay at Newport News having two new 5-in guns and a 3-in gun installed to replace those lost in the collision with the *Agamemnon*.

Sailing in convoy she moved down the Delaware from Philadelphia on February 10 and reached Brest without incident on February 24. The return crossing was marred by tragedy on March 5 when a lookout thought he detected a submarine periscope off the port side. Everyone rushed to battle stations and the order was given to open fire. A shell from one of the 5-in guns was defective and exploded immediately after leaving the gun, killing one sailor instantly and mortally wounding two others who died later that night. The 'U-boat' unfortunately turned out to be just a piece of flotsam. During the return crossing the *Von Steuben* coaled at Bermuda on March 12-13 and arrived at Norfolk on March 16. Repairs were made to the damaged area caused by the exploding shell. She left for Philadelphia, from where two more voyages to Brest started. Thereafter her American home port became New York.

Westbound on June 18 the *Von Steuben* sighted

Fresh from the shipyard with a new paint job, the Von Steuben *has a leisurely moment in port. This picture may have been taken after the rebuilding of her bow in January 1918 following a collision with the* Agamemnon *in November of the previous year.*

wreckage floating in the Atlantic. When about five miles distant seven pathetic lifeboats were seen under sail heading in her general direction and she began a zigzag pattern towards them. Twenty minutes later the trap was sprung and the wake of a torpedo was seen slamming towards the bow from abaft the port beam. The gun crews manning their stations began firing at the swiftly approaching torpedo while the wheel was put hard a starboard and all engines full astern in a violent manoeuvre to avoid destruction. Some gunners thought they saw the U-boat's periscope and began firing at it as the twin screws churned the Atlantic to a froth in their frantic effort to slow the greyhound's momentum. Seconds passed almost in suspended animation as the torpedo cut across the bow of the *Von Steuben* within yards of making contact. Relief immediately brought a barrage of depth charges from the heavily armed transport, designed at the very least to shake a certain common commodity out of the U-boat crew. The *U-151* had used the boats from the British steamer *Dwinsk* as decoys for Allied vessels seeking to rescue the survivors. The *Von Steuben* had no choice but to leave the area as quickly as possible. The master of the *Dwinsk* ordered his crew to lay low so that the lifeboats would appear empty and no other Allied vessel would be lured to its doom. Fortunately the gallant master and crew of the *Dwinsk* were ultimately rescued.

The *Von Steuben* reached New York on June 20 and sailed again on June 29 in convoy for Brest. On the third day fire broke out in the forward hold of the troop ship USS *Henderson* and grew in intensity so that there was no alternative but to evacuate the troops in mid-Atlantic. The *Von Steuben* was designated the rescue ship and slowly edged in towards the burning vessel. The flames and smoke admirably silhouetted the towering hull of the four-funnel troopship as she stood by the stricken *Henderson* throughout the night while the men were ferried across. By morning the *Von Steuben* had taken on board more than 2,000 souls to add to her original fully-packed roster! The *Henderson*'s crew declined to abandon their ship, turned her around and steamed back to New York alone. The *Von Steuben* put on all speed for Brest with exceedingly cramped accommodation and reached the French port safely on July 9—a 15,000-ton liner with what may have been as many as 8,000 on board!

Thereafter the routine of the *Von Steuben* was rather normal for wartime. Another half-dozen trips with troops outward bound and sick and wounded homeward. In August 1918 she came

The USS Von Steuben *is shown at Brest. What appears to be a destroyer alongside of the four funnel liner is actually a full-scale painting of a four-stack destroyer as part of the troopship's dazzle paint at this time* (Frank O. Braynard Collection-SSHSA).

home in a violent hurricane that washed three American sailors overboard and injured many others. The single greatest killer, however, turned out to be the influenza epidemic which hit 2,700 troops bound for Brest on the *Von Steuben* in September 1918. The transport arrived with 34 dead and 400 stretcher cases as the epidemic became virulent in the crowded ship. Arriving at New York after her ninth wartime voyage on November 8 she went into dry dock at Brooklyn, New York, on November 10 for drastic repairs and overhauling. While there the Armistice was declared. The *Von Steuben* emerged from her overhaul on March 2 1919, and brought 'Doughboys' home from France until October 13 1919, when she was decommissioned, struck off the Navy Register and returned to the United States Shipping Board. As part of the American war effort during the period 1917-1919 the *Von Steuben* completed 12 'turn-arounds' with an average duration (including time in port) of 40.1 days.

In February 1918 the *Agamemnon* sank for the second time in her career and again while coaling. The coaling ports were open, the load poorly distributed, and down she went when the tide came flooding up the harbour. Pumped out and dried, the troopship was ready to sail in days. This time she served as flagship of the February 27 convoy which disembarked troops at Brest on March 11 and sailed westward the very next day after coaling throughout the night. The convoy had steamed eastbound in horrendous weather conditions and with enormous misfortune went right back into the gale force winds and mountainous seas which began to take their toll on every ship. The severity of the pitching and hogging with little or no let up in speed over the nine days so affected the *Agamemnon* that upon arrival in New York she went to Norfok for repairs and did not return to the North Atlantic until May 6.

Her next outward-bound convoy on May 16 was packed with troops, *Agamemnon* and *Mount Vernon* both having over 4,800 troops in addition to over 1,000 crew. Under similar load conditions

in June the two sister ships narrowly missed each other in the dead of the night to the mutual horror of their officers. Few today can fully appreciate the worries of a fast convoy during World War 1, literally steaming blind through fog or darkness without any resource except the human eye for detecting danger. Early on the morning of July 9 a tragedy occurred within an eastbound convoy. A British freighter, the *Instructor*, suddenly found herself steaming westward, bow on into the path of the on-rushing troopships. The *Instructor* entered the convoy between the *Mount Vernon* and the *America* and frantically tried to manoeuvre out of the way of the 24,000-ton *France* bearing down on her from the second line of ships. In so doing the captain of the *Instructor* over-compensated and placed his ship broadside to the *America*, which ran her down. There was a deafening report, a terrific shower of sparks, and the British freighter disappeared from sight.

Initially painted grey, the dazzle-paint era brought a picturesque change to the *Mount Vernon* in June 1918 when she was repainted in three days by 300 painters working around the clock. The new colour scheme involved dazzle-paint strips and streaks of blue, grey, black and white.

Certainly one of the largest and most impressive convoys of the war sailed from New York harbour on June 30 1918, when the *Mauretania, Von Steuben, Duca degli Abruzzi, President Grant* and *Calamares* moved out with 25,000 troops on board and all their bands playing. As if this was not enough, just to complete the magnificent maritime extravaganza, the convoy was passed in the Narrows by the inward bound *Mount Vernon, Agamemnon* and *Aquitania*. A unique collection of five great four-funnel passenger liners in close proximity and all under steam!

The most dramatic incident of the *Mount Vernon*'s war service occurred on September 5 1918. The big transport was westbound with 1,400 wounded soldiers and a crew of 1,100. She had sailed from Brest the previous day and was

Above *Dazzle paint camouflage for the USS* Mount Vernon, *the service name for the* Kronprinzessin Cecilie. *The design may not have been used* (US Navy).

Left *The USS* Mount Vernon *was torpedoed by the U-82 on September 5 1918, when she was outward bound from Brest. The No 2 5-in gun is shown coming into action during the submarine attack* (US Navy).

Below left *The* Mount Vernon *was carrying nearly 1,400 wounded when torpedoed and her crew immediately swung out the lifeboats so that they would be ready if necessary* (US Navy).

Bottom left *A bucket brigade bailing out the after Troops' Mess Hall following the torpedoing* (US Navy).

making 21 knots at 7.53 am when the lookout cried, 'Submarine! Starboard bow! 45 degrees!' One minute later the *U-82* slammed a torpedo into the aft furnace room 22 ft below the waterline. Thirty-four of the 37 American sailors in the room were killed instantly, either from the torpedo or from the exploding boilers as the ice cold waters of the North Atlantic hit them.

The *Mount Vernon*'s commander was Captain Douglas E. Dismukes of Portsmouth, New Hampshire, and he immediately took every possible step to keep the ship afloat. Immediate defence measures included the release of 500-lb depth charges from the ship's stern. This was quickly stopped because the violent explosions were hindering damage assessment and the liner was slowing appreciably so that there was the very real danger that she would blow her own stern off. The crew worked feverishly to get the wounded and maimed soldiers into the lifeboats although none were actually lowered away.

Once it was clear that the magnificent internal subdivision of the troopship would keep her afloat, it was imperative to get a collision mat over the gaping hole. The bulky mat was dropped over the side of the ship while she slowly glided through the water but it would not pass over the torpedo hole because of the movement of the vessel and the jagged flare of the crumpled steel plates. Charles Lyons, a seaman who later received the Navy Cross for heroism, was secured by a rope tied around his waist and lowered over

Right *The* France *in New York shortly after her Maiden Voyage* (Library of Congress).
Below right *First class de luxe bedroom on the* France (Library of Congress).

Above *The promenade deck on the* France *featured one of the finest sweeps on the Atlantic* (Library of Congress).
Right *The main first class staircase debouched into foyers on the* France *which were designed to impress the traveller from the very beginning with the vessel's magnificence* (Library of Congress).

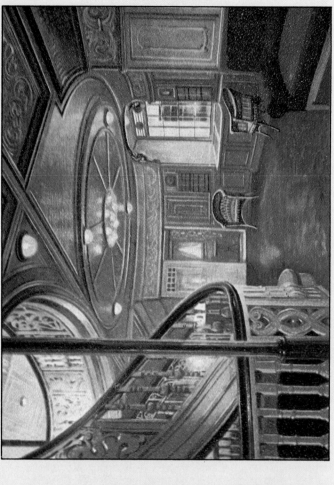

The grandeur of the Deutschland's main staircase gave all the competition reason to think in 1900.

A magnificent skylight graced the Kaiser Wilhelm der Grosse's first class smoking room (Library of Congress).

The classic mediaeval door provided entrance to the first class smoking room on the Deutschland.

The Kaiser Wilhelm der Grosse's ladies' drawing room represents a high point of Victorian interior decorating (Library of Congress).

The Kronprinz Wilhelm's elaborate first class dining room, complete with balcony, skylight and red plush (Library of Congress).

The Kronprinz Wilhelm's combination music room and drawing room featured a white piano and a portrait of her patron (Library of Congress).

The ornate ladies' drawing room on the Kaiser Wilhelm II, where the wives of millionaires could meet in comfort.

The Kaiser Wilhelm II's popular 'Winter Garden' cafe conveyed a delightful 'Gay 90s' atmosphere.

Left *This could very well be 1914; the* Aquitania's *funnels stand resplendent and the ventilators appear almost askew as they point in various directions. Instead it is January 1949 and the liner is near the end of her career* (John Blake Collection).

Below *Her funnels have been repainted, but the* Aquitania *still wears her wartime grey as she moves down Southampton Water soon after World War 2. She was probably employed in repatriation service at the time* (Steam and Sail).

the side of the *Mount Vernon* into the cold North Atlantic. After several minutes of struggling with the contrary mat he managed to get it into position so that the natural suction of water surging in the torpedo hole partially sealed it off. At the same time water was being bailed and the staff of doctors on board were attending to the medical needs of the newly injured.

There was no thought of continuing on to New York some 2,500 miles away when Brest was so much nearer. The *Mount Vernon* slowly swung around and began a race against time back to France. The watertight bulkheads soon proved to be holding so well and the unaffected machinery performing to such a splendid level of efficiency that revolutions could be built up until the troopship with a torpedo hole in her side was ploughing along at a very respectable 15 knots! Fifteen knots with one of four boiler rooms destroyed! An Allied dirigible came out from France in bright clear weather to escort the crippled troopship by keeping an aerial lookout for U-boats. Destroyers also raced to her assistance as soon as her plight became known. The *Mount Vernon* made a majestic arrival at Brest, coming up the channel under her own steam in spite of an 11° list and going straight into dry dock with the help of a group of French tugs for the final manoeuvres. The magnificent character of the vessel's construction had assured her survival even in the face of a torpedo attack and thereby contributing to the safe arrival in port of 1,400 wounded soldiers and 1,100 sailors.

The *Mount Vernon* received temporary repairs at Brest and then crossed to Boston for a complete

A hospital ward set up in the drawing room of the Mount Vernon *during World War 1* (US Navy).

overhaul of the damaged boiler rooms. She rejoined the Cruiser and Transport service on Washington's birthday, February 22 1919, and continued to bring American troops home until September. Since some of her luxury suites were still in good order the *Mount Vernon* had a number of distinguished passengers including Admiral W.S. Benson, Chief of Naval Operations, Newton D. Baker, Secretary of War, and Josephus Daniels, Secretary of the Navy.

The *Mount Vernon* had one more long voyage in her seagoing career when she sailed from New York for Vladivostok. The bitter civil war between the White Russians and the Bolsheviks over control of Russia was grinding to a close late in 1919 and a substantial number of refugees and foreign troops were caught in eastern Russia. Many had fled to Vladivostok on the Trans-Siberian Railway and once having reached there could go no further.

The *Mount Vernon* was transferred from the

The USS Mount Vernon *in dry dock for emergency repairs following the torpedoing of September 5 1918. Later she would cross to Boston for more complete overhaul* (US Navy).

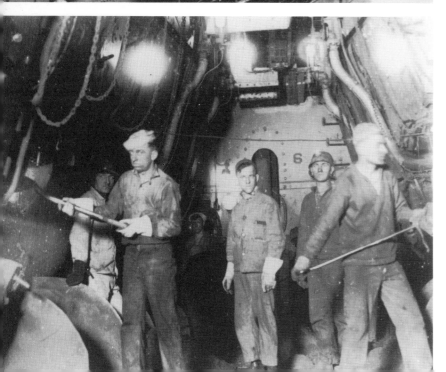

Above *The USS* Agamemnon *survived 18 voyages and carried 78,249 troops and passengers while under the American flag in World War 1. Here she is shown having just arrived at Boston in 1919 bringing units of the 102nd Infantry home from Europe* (US Navy).

Left *USS* Mount Vernon *arriving crammed with troops. The nickname for the transport was the 'Vermin' by the American troops* (Steamship Historical Society of America).

Below left *Stokers at work in the Number Four Fireroom of the* Mount Vernon *circa 1919* (US Navy).

United States Navy to the United States Army Transport Board on September 29 1919 for the voyage. Her funnels were repainted with red, white and blue stripes in the colours of the United States Shipping Board. The outward route lay through the newly opened Panama Canal and the *Mount Vernon* was the largest commercial vessel to use the waterway at that time. The round trip from California to Vladivostok took place without striking incident and the *Mount Vernon* became the only ex-Norddeutscher Lloyd greyhound to cross both the Atlantic and Pacific Oceans. Upon her return to the United States she was docked for a short period at Mare Island, California, where she attracted considerable attention prior to her return to the East Coast.

The *Von Steuben*, *Agamemnon* and *Mount Vernon* were floating assets if they could be employed commercially, and monstrous liabilities if not. The United States Shipping Board was given responsibility for all captured tonnage and

Above *USAT* Mount Vernon *at Mare Island, California, in 1920 after returning from Vladivostok in her one and only trans-Pacific crossing. Note the red, white and blue funnels of the United States Shipping Board* (US Navy).

Below *USAT* Mount Vernon *and the USS* Comfort *(AH-3) docked at the Mare Island Navy Yard, California, in January 1920* (US Navy).

while many grandiose schemes were put forward for the active employment of some of the ships, the final record remains rather dismal. By 1920 there was no further need for the ships as troop-ships and they became colossal grey elephants through no fault of their own. The *Von Steuben* had been so battered by war service under both the German and American flags that there was little question of her fate. She was sold for scrapping at Baltimore by the Boston Metal Company in March 1923.

Twelve different proposals between 1922 and 1932 were made by the distinguished American naval architect William Francis Gibbs to provide useful careers for the *Agamemnon* and the *Mount Vernon*. Nothing ever came to fruition even though the United States Shipping Board agreed to periodic surveys and the War Claims Commission awarded the Norddeutscher Lloyd Line something in the nature of $8,200,000 (£1,650,000) for the two ships. In the end the two greyhounds were laid up as 'reserve transports' off Solomon's Island in the Patuxent River, a tributary of Chesapeake Bay about halfway between Baltimore and Washington, DC. Later they were joined by the *George Washington* and the *America* when those vessels became redundant in the early 1930s. A staff of 47 men served as custodians on the liners and kept their engine rooms in remarkably good condition. One interesting plan of Gibbs' was to convert the propulsion units to diesel and run them in partnership with the *Leviathan*. In this service it was felt that they would have been able to carry enough extra fuel in their sub-divided bottoms not only to drive themselves for a round trip but also to refuel the *Leviathan* in Europe. The United States Congress passed a bill authorising the Gibbs Plan for converting the ships to oil and President Calvin Coolidge signed it into law in May 1928. Unfortunately, 'to authorise' does not necessarily mean 'to fund' and the indispensable money was never approved.

In the 1930s as the Great Depression deepened, periodic attempts were made to sell the deteriora-ting vessels for scrap, but even these fell through.

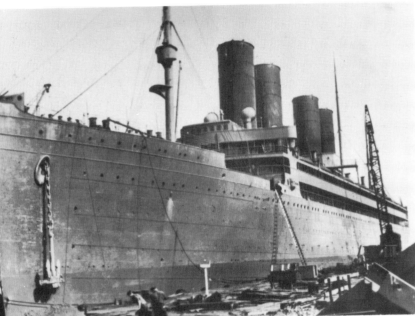

Top left *SS* Mount Vernon *being moved from the James River lay-up fleet in the mid-1920s* (John Blake Collection).

Centre left *SS* Mount Vernon *being scrapped at Baltimore by the Union Shipbuilding Company, 1940.*

Left *The end of the line for the* Kaiser Wilhelm II *at the Boston Iron and Metal Company of Baltimore, Maryland, September 1940.*

An additional name change occurred in 1927 from Agamemnon *to* Monticello *in order to bring her more into line with her consort, the* Mount Vernon. *Mount Vernon was Washington's home and Monticello was Jefferson's, the first and third Presidents of the United States. This photograph shows the two ex-Norddeutscher Lloyd greyhounds laid-up in the Patuxent River, Maryland.* Monticello *is on the near side and the* Mount Vernon *outside of her.*

Finally, with the substantial rise in scrap metal prices as a result of the beginning of World War 2 in Europe another auction was planned. In July 1940 both the *Agamemnon*, renamed the *Monticello* in 1927 in order to bring her name in line with her sister, and the *Mount Vernon* were sold to the Boston Iron & Metal Company of Baltimore for scrapping. The *Monticello* fetched $183,000 because she already was partially stripped during World War 1, and the *Mount Vernon* $178,300 because more panelling would have to be removed. Subsequently the latter was resold to the Union Shipbuilding Company, also of Baltimore, for scrapping.

The wait had been long but the end had finally arrived. The *Monticello* was a grand old lady of 37 yet she had enjoyed an active commerical career of only 11 years, plus a three-year stint as a troop-ship. The *Mount Vernon* had been an Atlantic greyhound for only seven years and a troopship for three more even if she had reached the advanced age of 33 in 1940. A reprieve of even a year might have meant new life as transports in World War 2.

The final critical assessment and judgment on the *Kaiser Wilhelm der Grosse, Kronprinz Wilhelm, Kaiser Wilhelm II* and *Kronprinzessin Cecilie* must be that between 1907 and 1914 they were the premier units of one of the finest transatlantic express services ever offered the travelling public. Built with incredible regard for strength, they endured and triumphed over a number of disasters which would have sunk lesser ships. These four greyhounds stand as a lasting tribute to the men in the management of Norddeutscher Lloyd who had the courage to envisage them, and to the hardy workers of the Vulcan Shipyard at Stettin who produced them.

2 Hamburg America

The Hamburg-Amerikanische Packetfahrt Aktien Gesellschaft ('HAPAG'), or Hamburg America Line, was founded on May 27 1847 by a group of Hamburg ship owners and industrialists who were making fortunes out of the industrialisation of northern Germany and who wanted the capacity to move their goods on German-flag shipping. Initially the line concerned itself with sailing vessels engaged in a Hamburg-New York service. The rivalry for commercial supremacy between Hamburg and the other great north German port of Bremen would remain as constant in the modern era as it had for the better part of a thousand years. In mid-century the primary stimulus for changing the emphasis of HAPAG from sail to steam came from the advances of Antwerp and Bremen. In 1853 Adolf Godeffroy, Chairman of HAPAG, at first opposed the construction of steam vessels during the February annual meeting, and then in December backed the successful proposal when it was evident that concerns in Antwerp as well as Bremen intended to build steamships for the North Atlantic. Almost from its inception the HAPAG steam transatlantic service more than justified its existence when the *Borussia* (1856, 2,131 tons) sailed for New York on June 1 1856, with 402 passengers as well as a strong general cargo. Surviving maritime disasters, competitors and wars, HAPAG steadily grew in prominence on the twin foundations of the German industrial revolution and the great mass migration of European peasants to a better future in America.

A singular development in the history of

HAPAG occurred in 1886 when it acquired the services of 29-year-old Albert Ballin (1857-1918) as manager of the passenger department. Ballin stands out from the maritime history of the North Atlantic as a figure of consummate genius who guided with an increasingly autocratic hand the creation of the largest single publicly owned steamship enterprise in the world. His capacity to envisage grandiose schemes was surpassed only by his capacity for hard work and his attention to detail. The story of HAPAG and of Ballin from 1886-1918 are one. By the early 1890s HAPAG-associated ships sailed from Hamburg for New York via Southampton or direct every Saturday, Monday and Wednesday with extra vessels brought on the line when demand warranted. The universal characteristics of HAPAG vessels were meticulous attention to service without excessive concern for speed.

The commissioning in 1897 of the Norddeutscher Lloyd *Kaiser Wilhelm der Grosse* created a sensation in Germany and incited the envy of the Hapag directors. Ballin travelled to New York on the rival greyhound and, while being impressed by her, clearly felt that the proper course for his passenger operation lay in building a larger if slightly slower response. For once the HAPAG directors refused to follow Ballin's lead and elected to recommend the ordering of a vessel capable of doing NDL one better on their own terms. Hence, the *Deutschland* was born.

The primary qualification for the new liner was quite simply that the Vulcan Shipyard of Stettin should build a ship capable of surpassing the *Kaiser Wilhelm der Grosse*. An average speed of 23 knots was called for and no expense was to be spared in achieving that end. The *Deutschland* was launched on January 10 1900, and finished by the builders in only six months. Considerable publicity

Opposite *A brand-new record-breaker is shown outward bound from New York with a bone in her teeth and her superstructure beautifully highlighted. The photo is by A. Loeffler, one of the pioneering marine photographers in the United States* (Library of Congress).

HAMBURG-AMERICAN LINE, ESTABLISHED ...1847...

Has a fleet of 202 vessels, with a total tonnage of 589,006 tons. Of these 202 ships, 107 are OCEAN STEAMERS, and 19 are large, new, TWIN-Screw passenger steamships.

TWIN-SCREW EXPRESS STEAMERS.

	Reg. Tons		Reg. Tons
Auguste-Victoria	8,479	Fürst Bismarck	8,430
Columbia	7,241	Deutschland	16,502
CRUISING YACHT "Prinzessin Victoria Luise"			5,000

TWIN-SCREW PASSENGER STEAMERS.

	Reg. Tons		Reg. Tons		Reg. Tons		Reg. Tons
Alesia	5,167	Belgravia	10,982	Kiautschou	11,150	Phoenicia	7,412
Ambria	5,148	Bulgaria	11,077	Palatia	7,979	Pretoria	13,190
Aragonia	5,198	Graf Waldersee	13,193	Patricia	13,424		
Batavia	11,046	Hamburg	10,600	Pennsylvania	13,333		

OTHER STEAMERS.

Abessinia	7,717	Canadia	2,404	Rhenania	1,820	Valencia	2,194
Acilia	5,697	Castilia	2,911	Sambia	5,623	Valesia	2,295
Adria	5,472	Cheruskia	3,254	*Segovia	5,872	Westphalia	3,095
*Alexandria	5,700	Christiania	2,811	*Silvia	6,700	Athen	2,199
Allemannia	1,818	Constantia	2,997	*Sithonia	6,700	Dacia	3,470
Andalusia	5,441	Croatia	1,991	Sardinia	3,611	Etruria	4,440
Arcadia	5,454	Flandria	2,041	Sarnia	3,206	Granada	5,125
Armenia	5,471	Francia	2,110	Savoia	2,595	Hellas	2,458
*Artemisia	5,700	Frisia	3,738	Saxonia	5,176	Ithaka	2,268
Ascania	2,046	Galicia	2,860	Scotia	2,558	Karthago	2,821
Assyria	6,581	Georgia	3,143	Serbia	3,694	Lydia	2,731
Asturia	5,290	Helvetia	2,825	Sibiria	3,347	Macedonia	4,344
Athesia	5,751	Hercynia	2,630	Sicilia	2,922	Parthia	2,714
Australia	2,151	Hispania	2,578	Silesia	4,861	Pontos	5,520
Belgia	7,507	Holsatia	3,349	Suevia	4,149	Sevilla	5,172
Bengalia	7,661	Hungaria	1,991	Syria	3,607	Sparta	2,816
Bethania	7,492	Markomannia	3,335	Teutonia	3,066	Troja	2,719
Bolivia	2,646	*Nassovia	3,800	Valdivia	2,176		
Bosnia	7,437	Nubia	3,494	*9 Ocean Steamers, aggregating			69,400
Brisgavia	7,419	Numidia	3,044	River Steamers, Tugboats, Lighters, etc			25,516
*C. Ferd. Laeisz	5,870	Polaria	2,673				
Calabria	3,004	Polynesia	2,171	*Building.		Total Tonnage	589,006

The Hamburg America Line had one of the largest fleets in the world in 1900 which was delineated in the Deutschland *booklet which also discussed other vessels and services.*

was given to her impending maiden voyage and disaster was narrowly averted as many waterways remained treacherous because of inadequate dredging. The Oder was no exception and even though seven tugs escorted the new HAPAG greyhound from Stettin to Swinemunde, she still went hard aground on a mud bank. Nearly two weeks of struggle ensued as the spring runoff had brought so much silt downstream that the very real danger existed of a major island building up around the 700 ft hull. Finally the *Deutschland* wallowed free on a high tide and made it safely to her berth. The hoped-for maiden sailing had to be postponed subject to a survey of the liner and provisioning, but ultimately she was unleashed on the North Atlantic on July 4 1900. She made a call at Southampton and then at Plymouth on July 6, which she left at 10.30 pm to slam westward with all the power at her command. Five days, 15 hours and 46 minutes after passing the Eddystone Light the HAPAG greyhound was off Sandy Hook at 11 pm on July 12. The distance covered was 3,044 nautical miles and the average speed a brilliant 22.42 knots. There was no dispute about the 'Blue Riband' since the westward passage was 0.13 of a knot faster than the previous record of 22.29 knots made by the *Kaiser Wilhelm der Grosse* in March 1898. Homeward bound, the *Deutschland* left her Hoboken pier at 9.30 am on July 18, passed Sandy Hook at 11.35 am, and was off the Eddystone Lighthouse at 7.40 am on July 24, coming to anchor in the sound 50 minutes later. She had covered a track of 3,085 miles and reached Plymouth within 5 days, 15 hours, 9

minutes of leaving New York (Sandy Hook-Eddystone Light).* The eastward run was also a record with an average speed of 22.83 knots, half a knot faster than her Norddeutscher Lloyd rival. At Plymouth the *Deutschland* disembarked around 100 passengers and a large quantity of mail before leaving for Cherbourg and Hamburg.

The requirement that the new HAPAG liner should surpass the Norddeutscher Lloyd *Kaiser Wilhelm der Grosse* virtually assured that the basic dimensions would exceed the earlier Vulcan product. The *Deutschland* had a registered length of 660 ft 9 in, a beam of 67 ft 3 in and a depth of 40 ft 2 in. The overall length was 686 ft 6 in with a displacement of 23,620 tons, a gross registered tonnage of 16,502, but a net tonnage of only 5,196 because of the substantial nature of the machinery and the enormous chambers occupied by the engines, boilers and bunkers. The propulsion unit of the *Deutschland* consisted of two sets of six-cylinder quadruple expansion engines capable of generating 36,000 horsepower. The six cylinders on each set of engines worked in three sets of tandems with three cranks. There were two high-pressure cylinders with diameters of 36.6 in, first and second intermediate cylinders with diameters of 73.6 in and 103.9 in, and two low-pressure with

* N.R.P. Bonsor, *North Atlantic Seaway* (Brookside Publications, Channel Islands, 1980), Vol V, Blue Riband Tables & Footnote 35. Bonsor states that the elapsed time must have been 5d 15h 9m with an average speed of 22.83 knots for the 3,085 miles. The *Times* (of London) July 25 1900, gave an elapsed time of 5d 15h 46m and a speed of 23 knots but agreed on all other details. The *Marine Engineer*, August 8 1900, gave duration as 5d 14h 6m and stated a speed of 23 knots.

diameters of 106.3 in. The stroke was 72.8 in. Each of the propeller shafts was of hollow nickel-steel 24 in in diameter, with twin bronze screws 23 ft in diameter. The engines were driven by 16 boilers, 12 double-ended and four single-ended working at a pressure of 221 psi with 112 furnaces. The boilers were sub-divided into four watertight compartments so that if one should become flooded the others would remain intact. The transverse bulkheads of the ship divided the hull into 17 watertight compartments. A further safeguard lay in a double bottom divided into 24 watertight chambers. Structurally the *Deutschland* was a very solid product but this contributed to excessive vibration which neither the builders nor the line were able to alleviate. Twenty-eight lifeboats were carried.

Accommodation was provided for 467 first, 300 second and 280 third class passengers served by a crew of 553 men and a group of women stewardesses. The principal first class public room was the dining saloon which could seat 425 and to which passengers descended by means of a handsome double-curved staircase. The airy and lofty three-deck-high space of the dining room was splendidly highlighted by a dome of ground glass through which sunlight flooded and was further reflected by gigantic mirrors leaving the impression of a winter garden at sea. The first class combination drawing room and music room on the promenade deck wound around a funnel casing which provided an opportunity for numerous alcoves and secluded corners. In the central portion of this room was a grand piano, well-anchored, and a magnificent full-length portrait of the Kaiser, who was designated 'Our William' by the officers of the *Deutschland* because of the personal interest which Wilhelm II took in the Imperial Merchant Marine.

The men's smoking room also wound around a funnel uptake and again was lighted by a magnificent skylight and plate glass windows. The service in the smoking room was famed for its efficiency while many described the coffee as superlative. An innovation on the *Deutschland* was a grill room where passengers who booked without meals or missed a meal in the dining saloon could order steaks, chops or certain other

Above right *The first class dining room of the* Deutschland *soared three decks and featured a dome of ground glass through which light flooded and was reflected by gigantic plate-glass mirrors. The room could seat 425 passengers at one time.*

Right *The grand entrance hall and companionway of the twin-screw express liner* Deutschland.

The elaborate entrance doorway to the Deutschland's *smoking room featured a mediaeval door under a painting of Hamburg harbour.*

The panelling of the first class smoking room was elaborately carved over the fireplace which sought to enhance the 'club-type' atmosphere of the room.

The first class smoking room of the Deutschland *was reserved for gentlemen and curved around a funnel casing. It contained many small tables and sought to recreate a 'club-type' atmosphere.*

delicacies at an appropriate price. Children travelling in first class had an elaborate playroom. The staterooms on the *Deutschland* contained 'every convenience that experience can suggest or fastidiousness desire.' A large number of the rooms were arranged with a comfortable lower berth and a sofa, and were intended for the sole occupancy of those who preferred a room to themselves. There was an unusual amount of open deck space for exercising, the total length of the promenade deck alone being 520 ft.

The second class accommodation was located aft on the promenade, upper, main and lower decks. Besides the handsome and spacious dining room situated on the main deck, there was a smoking room on the promenade deck, and a finely appointed drawing room for ladies on the upper deck. The third class accommodation can hardly be described as 'steerage' since it was of a superior character with regular cabins, a general public room, pantries and a bar provided for the convenience of the passengers.

In September 1901 a rare juxtaposition of sailings occurred between the *Deutschland* and the *Kaiser Wilhelm der Grosse* which had all the drama of a race. Both liners left New York on September 4. The *Kaiser Wilhelm der Grosse* sailed around noon and passed Sandy Hook at 12.35 pm. The *Deutschland* sailed 55 minutes later and was off Sandy Hook at 1.30 pm. The destination of the NDL greyhound was Cherbourg while that of the HAPAG record-holder was Plymouth. The *Deutschland* overtook and passed her rival around noon on the second day out which must have been a thrilling sight for all the passengers. The *Kaiser Wilhelm der Grosse* arrived at Cherbourg at 10.43 am on September 10 after covering a 3,076 mile track in 5 days, 17 hours, 18 minutes at an average speed of 22.40 knots. The *Deutschland* turned over runs of 507, 535, 540, 549, 545 and 306 to Eddystone Lighthouse, arriving there at 2 am on September 10 after covering a distance of 2,932

Top right *The grill room on the* Deutschland *where passengers who had missed one of the main sittings in the dining room could come and order steaks, chops or a variety of other quick dinners.*

Centre right *The first class children's playroom on the* Deutschland *was intended to keep younger travellers out of sight and sound of their elders, but it was beautifully appointed.*

Right *The first class combination drawing room and music room on the promenade deck curved around a funnel casing but this lent itself to intimacy. The room was dominated by a large oil painting of the German Emperor, Kaiser Wilhelm II, who was referred to by the officers as 'Our William'.*

miles in 5 days, 7 hours, 38 minutes at an average speed of 23.36 knots. The best day's run of the NDL vessel was 520 miles and the HAPAG 549 miles.

In August 1901 the *Deutschland* pushed her best day's runs to 584 miles westward and 552 miles eastward but she was plagued by one nagging problem. Nothing seemed to alleviate an acute degree of vibration towards the stern and, in fact, on some crossings she virtually shook her stern off. Second class passengers were not amused and anyone booked aft of the third funnel might well regret the trip.

The publicity surrounding the record voyages of the *Deutschland* contributed to a spectacular improvement in the passenger figures of the Hamburg America Line for 1900 compared with 1899. The number of North Atlantic crossings soared from 70 to 121 and the passengers carried from 14,000 first and second to 23,000, and from 38,000 to 65,000 in steerage. HAPAG had 19 more sailings than NDL but the Bremen line still surpassed them in first and second class passengers by 70 even if the Hamburg concern transported some 700 more steerage and therefore emerged as the premier line in terms of total passengers carried.

In 1901 the *Deutschland* was challenged by the NDL *Kronprinz Wilhelm* which entered the North Atlantic lists in September and immediately experienced a number of rough voyages during which she could not show her stuff. By June 1902 NDL was very keen on a record passage and the captain of the *Kronprinz Wilhelm* felt sure he had one. The NDL whippet steamed from Sandy Hook to Eddystone Light at an average speed, as first published, of 23.53 knots. This was just .02 of a knot faster than the *Deutschland*, but Albert Ballin exploded when the figures were laid before him. Given the time and distance factors, the average speed did not fit. Recriminations ensued between Hamburg and Bremen and legal actions were threatened. The final result was that NDL had to eat humble pie and acknowledge an error.

Top left *A suite on the* Deutschland *which would capture the fancy of many passengers even if the liner experienced considerable excess vibration.*

Centre left *A detail shot of the second class dining room on the* Deutschland *which experienced quite a bit of vibration. The appointments were far superior to the standards of the day.*

Left *The second class smoking room on the* Deutschland *in some ways was better designed than its first class counterpart. The combination of panelling and brass joined to produce a harmonious decor.*

Minutes signed by experts of the two rival firms on August 7 1902 formally acknowledged the mistake which was cabled around the world. The average speed of the *Kronprinz Wilhelm* had been 23.47 knots, representing a superb performance, but instead of beating the *Deutschland* by .02 knots, it fell short by .04 of her 23.51 knot record established in July 1901. The HAPAG greyhound held the eastbound record until surpassed by the *Kaiser Wilhelm II* in 1904.

In a day and age when rapid transformations were occurring in marine propulsion and design, the *Deutschland*'s achievement was substantial, but at what cost! Few ships ever appear to have been driven as hard as the HAPAG liner. No expense had been spared to make her a winner and no effort would be spared to maintain her image as the fastest ship in the world. No matter what the condition of the seas or nature of the weather, the *Deutschland* was driven like a demon possessed, with a significant toll on crew, structure and machinery. The veteran Captain Albers was in command of the record breaker when she sailed from New York on April 17 1901 and steamed eastward in excess of 20 knots as usual. Within 400 miles of the Scilly Isles in a fierce WSW gale a massive wave hit the liner from behind and sheared off the steering apparatus, sternpost, rudder, and all. Albers elected to bring his charge into port by manoeuvring judiciously with the twin screws, first into Plymouth Sound and then up the Channel and the far more difficult approach to Cuxhaven. The strain of the crossing compounded by the accident of losing the rudder was so great that as the *Deutschland* reached safe harbour Captain Albers suffered a massive heart attack and died. The responsibility of commanding a transatlantic greyhound could be a murderous burden upon even the strongest and most experienced of men. So battered was the *Deutschland* from this crossing that HAPAG laid-up the vessel and had her extensively reconditioned. She re-entered service on November 7 1902 and her sailing from Hamburg and Southampton under the command of Captain Berends was newsworthy.

Top right *The second class ladies' parlor sought to provide a comfortable public room for women when segregation of the sexes was required.*

Centre right and right *A rare piece of memorabilia from the* Deutschland *is this silver napkin ring featuring various ships and scenes from the Hamburg America Line. The anchor and HAPAG initials come first, followed by the* Alte Liebe, Cuxhaven, *the* Deutschland *herself, a two-funnel intermediate steamer, and a single-funnel workhorse of the fleet. The whole sums up the state of HAPAG in 1900.*

Almost immediately she encountered mountainous seas again that created such wild and violent pitching that even the lookout in the crow's nest was drenched. One day out from Cherbourg she was driving along against a severe NW gale when she took a heavy sea over the starboard rail which smashed the iron bulkhead forward on the promenade deck for some 15 ft, broke the post ladder from the promenade deck and carried a port ventilator away. Unfortunately the excitement of the crossing was far from over. As the *Deutschland* passed Nantuckett at 5.20 am on November 13 1902, a bolt from the third crankshaft bearing broke and as a direct result the cover over the low-pressure cylinder was cracked. The engineer on duty reacted immediately to shut off the main steam valve, thereby avoiding further damage, but the liner's propulsion system clearly had suffered. Ship's officers emphasised that only the prompt action of the engineer had saved the ship from grave damage and costly repairs.

The accident produced two loud crashes. Stewards immediately sought to calm the passengers but order was not really restored until the *Deutschland* got under way again at half power. She docked at Hoboken early in the evening of November 13, having lost nearly a day as a result of the accident. Happily the damage could be put right quickly and this was achieved by the engine room crew exerting herculean endeavours so that the ship could take her sailing on Wednesday, November 19.

The *Deutschland* continued to have her problems. In 1903 she stranded for a brief time in New York Bay but got off without significant damage. A gale at Cuxhaven was far more serious late in the same year when the big ship snapped her cables and with the wind shrieking against her towering sides began to drift across the harbour. Some repairs had to be made after she was finally secured by struggling tugs. For a time between July 1904 and August 1906 HAPAG experimented with Dover as the British port-of-call since it was so well situated for any ship using the Channel. A special train from London brought passengers to the 16,502-ton liner docked at the Admiralty Pier in the narrow harbour. With 1,500 passengers and 1,200 bags of mail on board, the *Deutschland* made ready to sail from Dover at 11.35 am on Friday, July 13 1906. The order was given to go astern when chaos suddenly reigned. According to Hamburg America, a hawser snapped triggering a violent chain reaction. According to observers the steamship inexplicably began to go ahead instead of astern. Engines went full astern while anchors were suddenly let loose to stop the

forward momentum. In a matter of seconds the steel bow of the *Deutschland* struck the granite pier a colossal blow, splitting the prow from rail to keel. The metal plates were peeled back like an orange on the starboard side. Water rushed into the void and the forepeak was filled even if the bulkhead held and no other area was flooded. Nevertheless, the crossing had to be cancelled and all the passengers and mails disembarked at enormous cost and with inconvenience to all concerned.

The *Deutschland*'s problems were far from over because a place had to be found to repair her bow at short notice. At first she was scheduled to return to Hamburg but time and money were at stake so Harland and Wolff, Belfast, were brought into consultation. Unfortunately, their dry docking facilities were occupied so Liverpool was surveyed and also found wanting in space. In the end eight days of negotiations brought an agreement for the *Deutschland* to shift to Southampton where the London and South Western docks undertook the repairs. The tug *Hector* assisted the liner from Dover down the Channel to the Solent on July 21 and the repairs took several weeks. The cost of the damage to the dock and ship exceeded £40,000 by a substantial margin and the mid-summer, high-season sailings had to be cancelled. The port of Dover simply was too open and too treacherous for a ship the size of the *Deutschland* to use. HAPAG's decision to return to Plymouth was reinforced when the Swedish steamship *Olans Olssen*, on the morning of October 21 1906, also rammed the Admiralty Pier at Dover, this time toppling Goliath cranes into the water, damaging the pier and buckling her own decks.

By the autumn of 1906, if not long before, Albert Ballin and the HAPAG management were disgusted with the *Deutschland*'s performance. What had succeeded in terms of hull and machinery in the *Kaiser Wilhelm der Grosse*, *Kronprinz Wilhelm* and *Kaiser Wilhelm II* had not combined with any consistent degree of working perfection in the *Deutschland*. It was formally announced in connection with a prospectus to raise £1,000,000 for fleet expansion that HAPAG would devote itself to the slower passenger traffic employing vessels of the largest possible size. A splendid start already had been made with the *Amerika* (1905, 22,225 tons) and *Kaiserin Auguste Victoria* (1906, 24,581 tons) of 18 knots. Profits lay in those ships and in them HAPAG would invest its money. In 1908 Hamburg America vessels totalled 955,742 tons with an average age of only eight years. The ships steamed nearly 7,750,000 miles and completed 1,228 round-trips during the course of the year. This was achieved in the face of acute financial depression in the United States caused by the Crash of 1907 which would not be surpassed until 1929 and which so reduced passenger totals on the North Atlantic that it was deemed prudent to reduce the dividend from eight to six per cent. A time of retrenchment was at hand and the eight-year-old *Deutschland* appeared a prime candidate. A last attempt was made to put new life into the greyhound by reboilering her in 1908, but her performance remained unsatisfactory. In hard times status symbols can be prohibitively expensive and the 23-knot speed queen always had been out of balance with the remainder of the first-class units of the HAPAG fleet. Furthermore, few major liners had ever had as many troubles as that ship with her machinery.

In 1910 the decision was made to rebuild her completely for a new service and a new career. The HAPAG cruising yacht *Oceana* (1891, 7,859 tons), which had served the line as a luxury cruise vessel since 1906, was expendable and it was decided that the *Deutschland* should replace her. Accordingly, the *Deutschland* was taken in hand by her builders Vulcan of Stettin for transformation from ocean greyhound to cruising yacht. The

work took nearly a year beginning in October 1910 and involved drastic changes in the ship. Speed would no longer be imperative so the aft boiler rooms were stripped although the funnels remained for appearance sake. Officially it was stated that the engines were to be 'rebuilt' but the result amounted to their complete replacement. The new machinery involved two sets of four-cylinder, quadruple-expansion units. With only half the previous boilers the new machinery still gave the ship a speed of 18 knots. External reconstruction involved decking over the forward well, installing an additional deck from the mainmast to the taffrail and carrying the boat deck to the stern. Refinement of external appearance brought a white strake from bow to stern and the installation of a magnificent set of polished mahogany lifeboats with a large motor launch carried forward. Internal changes saw the complete removal of second and third class accommodation so that the whole of the 16,500-ton liner was reserved for the exclusive pleasure of her 500 first class cruising passengers. The space allotment per passenger certainly was generous. As a result the gross tonnage rose to 16,703 and the net tonnage jumped to 8,127. During the next three cruising seasons the *Deutschland*, now renamed *Victoria Luise*, was easily the most popular and prestigious

One of the glories of the Deutschland *was the 520-ft sweep of her promenade deck. Here she is shown as the* Victoria Luise *after her conversion into a cruising liner in 1911* (Steamship Historical Society of America).

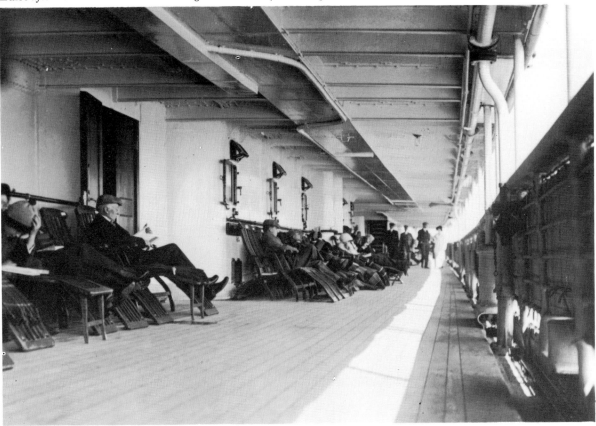

Shuffleboard on the Victoria Luise, *presumably during a cruise to cooler weather if the clothing of the participants is any means of judging* (Steamship Historical Society of America).

The Victoria Luise *on a cruise. Note the missing lifeboats carrying passengers ashore* (Steamship Historical Society of America).

The Captain's Ball on the Gala Evening of a cruise is shown in this picture. The opening ball of 'Kiel Week' 1914 would be held on the Victoria Luise *as host ship with the Kaiser himself present. The next morning the Archduke Franz Ferdinand would be assasinated and World War 1 would begin* (Steamship Historical Society of America).

The Hansa *was demoted from four to two funnels and served HAPAG in this capacity until she was scrapped in 1925.*

cruising vessel in the world. Her trips took her to the Mediterranean, the North Cape and the West Indies while between 1912-1914 she made a number of North Atlantic crossings. In June 1914 the *Victoria Luise* was the principal host liner for the 'Elbe Regatta' and 'Kiel Week', those fabulous Wilhelmine maritime and naval extravaganzas which heralded the beginning of the summer season. In fact the opening ball of 'Kiel Week' had been held in the spacious dining saloon of the *Victoria Luise* on Saturday evening, June 27, with the cream of Imperial society present led by His Majesty Kaiser Wilhelm II in full dress. The very next day, however, the Archduke Franz Ferdinand, heir to the Austro-Hungarian thrones, was assassinated as he rode through the Bosnian city of Sarajevo touching off a sequence of events which led to World War 1 within five weeks. The news was first delivered to the German ambassador to Vienna on the *Victoria Luise* for transmission to his government. As soon as the tragedy was known the destroyers serving as messenger vessels were summoned to steam across the bay at full-speed for the yacht *Meteor* which the Kaiser was visiting in order to inform him of the international incident. The 'Kiel Week' festivities abruptly ended as the harbour reverberated under the death salutes of the assembled warships of the High Seas Fleet.

When war came the *Kaiser Wilhelm der Grosse* was available for duty as an armed merchant cruiser and as soon as she had been made ready for commerce raiding, attention was turned to the *Victoria Luise.* The HAPAG liner was armed for naval warfare and the story goes that her naval commander took her out for trials only to find that she could not produce more than 18 knots at full speed. The story may be more truth than fiction owing to the amazing degree of ignorance shown by naval personnel in all navies before World War 1 of their respective merchant marines. Whatever the case the *Victoria Luise* was no sooner back from her trials than she was laid-up for the duration at Hamburg. Following the

Armistice the liner was in such deplorable condition that of all HAPAG's significant pre-war tonnage, she alone was left to the Line. When you have nothing even a worn out hull looks good.

One aspect of the American dream in 1919 was the creation of a strong United States Merchant Marine capable of maintaining a regular service on a number of the old HAPAG routes, in many cases with ex-German tonnage. Accordingly in 1920 the United American Lines was created with the assistance of the United States Shipping Board to run a North Atlantic service from New York to Hamburg. Learning of these plans Dr Wilhelm Cuno, the successor to Ballin who had died in 1918, went to New York and negotiated a 20-year agreement for a combination of services and tonnage. One of the initial HAPAG contributions was the *Victoria Luise,* renamed *Hansa* and at the age of 20 disfigured beyond recognition by the removal of two of her four funnels. On October 27 1921, the *Hansa* sailed from Hamburg to New York with a revised tonnage of 16,333, accommodation for 36 cabin class and 1,350 third, and a service speed of about 16 knots. Extensive reconditioning followed in 1922 which saw the *Hansa* emerging with accommodation for 220 cabin class, 664 third and another revised gross tonnage of 16,376. Finally in 1924 with the addition of new ships to the Hamburg America fleet the *Hansa* was laid-up and offered for scrapping in May 1925, ending her days at the Hamburg yard of Vulcan-Werft.

Few vessels ever have been conceived with greater hopes, achieved the immediate goal—the 'Blue Riband' of the Atlantic, and had a more chequered career. With the perfect vision of hindsight it can be stated that the *Deutschland* upheld the maritime transportation rule that the principal goal should be to maintain a solid, dependable, well-balanced service and eschew all frills. Within the HAPAG fleet of 1900 there was no place for the *Deutschland* and she remained a liability most of her working life, taking far more than she contributed to the profit and loss of the line.

3 Cunard

Having been awarded an Admiralty mail contract on May 4 1839, the British & North American Royal Mail Steam Packet Company started a regular North Atlantic passenger service on July 4 the following year. The company, which in 1878 became the Cunard Steam Ship Company Ltd, quickly gained an excellent reputation for reliability, and produced many steamers which set an example for the rest of the North Atlantic services. Cunard laid plans in the early 1890s to regain the 'Blue Riband' which they had lost in 1889 to the Inman & International Line, the result being the successful 12,900-ton sister ships *Campania* and *Lucania*. When, however, in 1897 Norddeutscher Lloyd introduced its flyer *Kaiser Wilhelm der Grosse*, Cunard again lost the speed advantage. In rapid succession, HAPAG then commissioned the *Deutschland* and NDL came back with the *Kronprinz Wilhelm* and the *Kaiser Wilhelm II*. The biggest blow of all to Cunard came in 1902 with the formation in America of the International Mercantile Marine Company. This giant combine, masterminded by the American financier J. Pierpont Morgan, quickly bought up most North Atlantic companies, including the White Star Line, until Cunard and the Compagnie Générale Transatlantique (French Line) were among the only major passenger lines remaining independent. Clearly Cunard had to do something.

The 'something' was a 20-year agreement with the British government stipulating that the company remain under British ownership if the Treasury advanced a loan of £2,600,000 to cover the cost of two new express liners, far larger and faster than anything the world had ever seen. As part of the agreement both steamers were to conform to exacting Admiralty requirements that would enable easy conversion to auxiliary cruisers in time of war. The plan called for a pair of 25-knot liners of roughly 30,000 gross tons, with accommodation for more than 2,100 passengers, to cross the Atlantic in less than five days.

The problem of propulsion was one that occupied the designers for nearly two years: whether to install the traditional reciprocating engines or the newer turbines. Since no large liner had ever used turbines, a special committee was designated to study British coastal vessels and others equipped with them. The committee recommended turbines, but Cunard officials were still not ready to commit themselves to the revolutionary form of propulsion. It was decided to experiment with the two new intermediate steamers scheduled to enter service in 1905. The 20,000-ton *Caronia* and *Carmania* were virtually identical with the exception of their power plants. The twin-screw *Caronia* had quadruple-expansion reciprocating machinery while the *Carmania* was fitted with triple screws and turbine engines. Intensive tests were carried out on both ships during their trials and it was ultimately determined that the *Carmania* consistently achieved nearly a full knot more than her sister with the same consumption of coal. In consequence the two superliners would be equipped with turbines.

Because of the many advances in design, exhaustive tests were carried out before the final plans were approved. These included tank tests both in the Admiralty tank and that at John Brown's Clydebank yard. Plans were drawn up by nearly every influential shipyard in the United

Opposite Both the Lusitania *and the* Mauretania *had first class dining rooms that took up space on two decks. They were quite different in decor, the* Lusitania's, *pictured here, done in a handsome Louis XVI style. Although taken at the builders' yard before the protective covering was removed from the carpet, this photograph depicts in stunning detail the spaciousness and elegance of the huge room* (Scottish Record Office).

Kingdom. Finally, contracts were placed in early 1905 with the first of the steamers to be built at John Brown's and the second at the Tyneside yard of Swan Hunter and Wigham Richardson. The keel of the first ship, the *Lusitania*, was laid in February 1905, the *Mauretania*'s keel following several months later.

Work on the *Lusitania* proceeded rapidly and 15 months after the laying of the keel, Cunard's new queen was ready for launching. June 7 1906 was the appointed day and a huge crowd trooped to Brown's yard to see Lady Inverclyde name the vessel her husband had worked so diligently to create. Lord Inverclyde, who had died prematurely at the age of 44 the previous October, was chair-

Above left *The 20,000-ton Cunard Liner* Carmania *was the experiment that finally convinced Cunard officials to install turbines in the* Lusitania *and* Mauretania. *While she was equipped with turbines, her sister ship* Caronia *received reciprocating engines, and the exhaustive tests conducted proved the* Carmania *to be the more economical of the two.*

Left *An interesting aerial view shows the after decks of the* Lusitania *in the final stages of outfitting at John Brown's Clydebank yard.*

Below *A spectacular view of a poised giant. The* Lusitania *sits on the ways at John Brown's Clydebank yard awaiting launch. Notice the giant bronze screws which divers report are still in place on the wreck today and virtually intact (Scottish Record Office).*

Opposite *The* Lusitania, *with an unprecedented launching weight of more than 20,000 tons, slides into the Clyde. A huge crowd, part of which is just visible to the left, came to see Lady Inverclyde name the vessel (Scottish Record Office).*

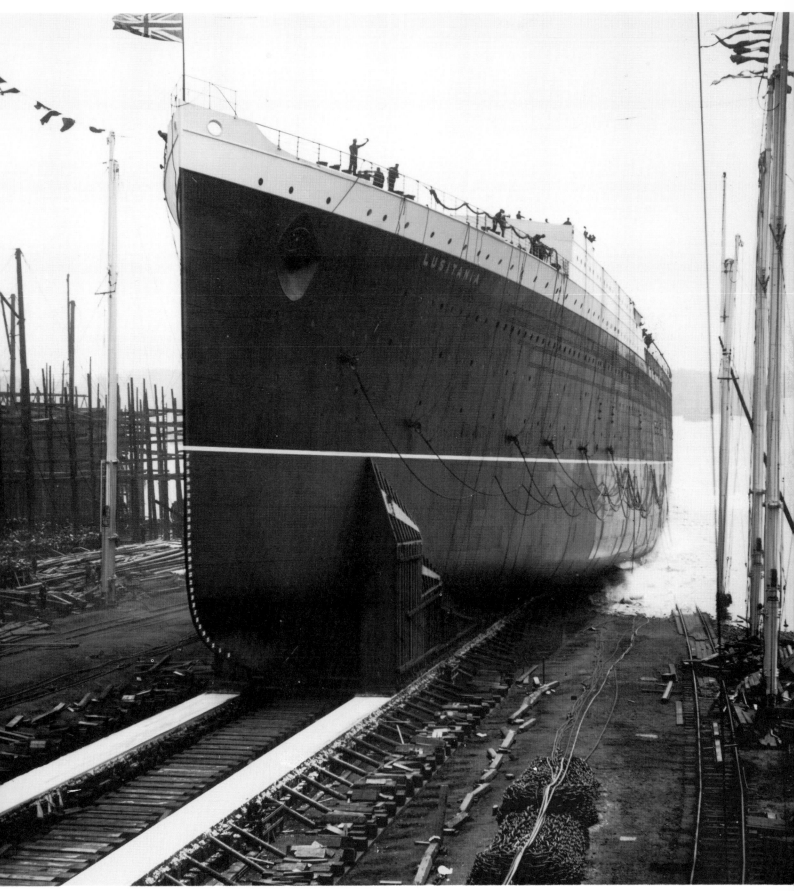

This is the starting platform at the forward end of the engine room aboard the Lusitania, *looking to port. The wheels to the left are part of the power-operated steam valves. The wheels on the right manually control the four main steam lines coming from the boilers. Most of this machinery is for the port engines* (Scottish Record Office).

man of Cunard when the agreement was worked out with the government for construction of the two liners. He, more than anyone else, had been responsible for the daring challenge of the *Lusitania* and *Mauretania*.

Tens of thousands of spectators packed the shipyard and lined both sides of the river to see the world's largest liner, with an unprecedented launching weight of 20,145 tons, take to the water. All went according to plan and at 12.30 pm, beneath a warm and bright sun, the high tide arrived and Lady Inverclyde pushed the electric button that released a bottle of wine and sent it smashing against the vessel's side. Seconds later, to the accompaniment of creaking timbers, the hull began to move and quickly gathered way. As the *Lusitania*'s bow cleared the end of the ways, huge drag chains played out bringing her to a halt within 240 ft. An interesting historical sidelight to

the launching is the fact that the drag chains originally belonged to the fabled *Great Eastern* of 1859. Later a luncheon was held for some 500 guests. Sir Charles McLaren, deputy chairman of John Brown and Company, told the assembled group that the launch placed Great Britain far ahead in the field of maritime achievement.

Fitting-out began immediately with the ship's turbines and boilers being placed aboard. It was a fascinating array of machinery with 25 boilers in all, 23 of which were double-ended. They were arranged in four groups, each group in a separate compartment with the uptakes leading to each of the four funnels. The space below the lower deck was filled with machinery for almost the entire length of the vessel. Admiralty requirements dictated that all the vital machinery be below the waterline. The liner's main engines included two high pressure turbines driving the two outboard shafts and two low pressure turbines for the inboard pair. Two astern turbines were also connected to the inboard shafts. Coal bunkers were arranged on either side of the four boiler rooms with an additional bunker forward of boiler room number one, all the bunkers being made watertight as required by the Admiralty. It was a provision that gave the vessel a measure of safety lacking in many other liners of the period. An added precaution was the subdivision of the engine room into nine separate watertight compartments. The watertight subdivision in the *Lusitania* and *Mauretania* was most complex, there being 175 separate compartments throughout each ship. In addition there was a double bottom which extended around the curve of the bilge. Another feature of the liner, as required by the Admiralty, was the provision for mounts on the upper and promenade decks for ten 4-in guns.

The *Mauretania* was ready for launching on the Tyne on September 20 1906. It was a rainy, blustery day, but that didn't deter virtually all Tyneside from turning out. The honour of naming the vessel went to the Dowager Duchess of Roxburgh. A formal luncheon was held before the actual naming ceremony, high tide not being due until 4.15 pm. Precisely at the prescribed moment, the Duchess turned the little capstan which released the giant launching triggers and sent a bottle of champagne crashing against the ship's hull. Within two minutes, the great ship was afloat. Cunard officials were finally beginning to see the fruits of their labours take form now that both liners were waterborne. The *Mauretania*'s fitting-out began immediately, the intention being that both express liners would enter service the following year.

Above *In this view of part of the* Lusitania's *engine room we see a most unusual piece of machinery. The large screw to the left is the turbine lifting gear, a device utilised because of the low overhead which made block and tackle impractical. It could be fitted either to the turbine casing or the rotor shaft and had to be able to handle a weight of 115 lb* (Scottish Record Office).

Below *A portion of the* Lusitania's *generator room, looking toward the starboard side. To the left is the generator proper for one of the four turbine generators. To the right is the distribution switch board* (Scottish Record Office).

Launch! The Dowager Duchess of Roxburgh has just named the Mauretania *on September 20 1906. The great liner has just touched the Tyne for the first time and is taken into tow by tugs. Virtually every available spot on the river's edge was taken for the occasion* (Swan Hunter Group).

Originally the plan had called for a three-funnel profile with a low superstructure. This was altered to four evenly spaced funnels as opposed to the paired stacks of the HAPAG and NDL liners. There were, in fact, publicity posters circulated by Cunard in the early days of the liners' construction depicting the three-funnel plan. But the four-funnelled profile gave the two ships a distinctive look that denoted speed from whatever angle they were viewed. Although essentially sister ships in the eyes of the travelling public, the two ships were different in a number of ways. Most evident was the large number of cowl ventilators on the upper decks of the *Mauretania* as opposed to the flat-headed type ventilators on the *Lusitania*. There were also differences in the curve of the superstructure front and in the boat and promenade decks which extended out over the ship's side in the *Mauretania*'s case. These variations produced a slight difference in tonnage between the two, so that when the vessels ultimately entered service, the *Mauretania* grossed 31,938 tons as compared to the *Lusitania*'s 31,550. Both ships were 762 ft in length with a beam of 88 ft, and both could carry 2,165 passengers in three classes.

While construction progressed at Clydebank and Tyneside, preparations were being made elsewhere to accommodate the huge vessels. The Mersey Docks and Harbour Board undertook extensive dredging operations in Liverpool that would enable the ships with their draught of 33 ft 6 in to berth at the Prince's Landing Stage. More than 20 square miles of river bed were dredged

while at the same time improvements were being made to the terminal itself to facilitate loading and unloading of passengers, mail and cargo from the big vessels. The existing mooring buoys in the river were deemed inadequate to secure such vast ships and subsequently were replaced with more substantial ones. Alterations were also undertaken at the Canada Graving Dock in Liverpool where the vessels would be dry docked periodically for overhaul. On the other side of the Atlantic, a new channel was being dug into New York harbour and a mammoth new pier, number 54, was under construction there.

In terms of accommodation, the *Mauretania* and *Lusitania* were virtually identical in layout, but differed considerably in decor. The builders were given a relatively free hand in the design of the public rooms and staterooms. Noteworthy differences between the sisters were in the first class dining saloons and first class lounges. The style of Francis I was chosen for the *Mauretania*'s first class dining saloon, the entire two-deck affair being crowned with a cream and gold dome. In the *Lusitania*, the same room was decorated in the style of Louis XVI and finished in white and gold. Nevertheless, both rooms were noted for their splendid mahogany panelling. In the case of the first class lounge, Georgian styling was utilised in the *Lusitania* and the room included a soaring domed ceiling complete with stained or painted glass. The same room on the *Mauretania* was somewhat more restrained and less lofty, being outfitted in the style of an 18th century French Salon. And so it went, with major differences in

Continued on page 76.

The Lusitania's *first class smoke room was a luxurious room decorated in 18th century style. The decor included Italian walnut with carvings in pear wood, an open fireplace and carved mouldings in the ceiling done in deep ivory. Capping off the room was a huge stained glass dome.*

Adams style was utilised in the Lusitania's *writing room and library. The walls were panelled and hung with grey silk. The furniture was Sheraton with a variety of comfortable chairs and settees included along with the various writing tables.*

Second class on the Lusitania *and* Mauretania *was highly regarded for its spaciousness and comfort. Here is the second class lounge on the* Lusitania *with its mahogany panelling done in the Georgian style. This room included luxurious divans with comfortable chairs and coffee tables lighted by an exquisite stained glass dome.*

The Georgian style was popular on the Lusitania and is seen here applied to the second class dining saloon, a rather lofty chamber painted in a soft eggshell white. Individual tables had not yet arrived in second class but the table was beautifully set nevertheless.

Described in promotional material of the period as lofty and expansive, the second class smoke room of the Lusitania was also decorated in Georgian style. It featured mahogany panelling, finely upholstered chairs and sofas and a beautiful domed ceiling.

Louis Seize was chosen for the second class music and drawing room aboard the Lusitania. The panelling was a soft grey, highlighted by tasteful gold ornamentation. Rose carpets and satinwood furniture helped give this room a very warm effect.

The wheelhouse of the Lusitania, showing the efficient simplicity of it all. The brass on the engine room telegraph, binnacle and other gear gleams brightly in this New York harbour photograph. Note that the helmsman's area is enclosed separately at right (Byron Collection, Museum of the City of New York).

The Mauretania's designers chose to decorate the first class lounge in 18th century French style. Highly regarded at the time were the chairs and sofas, all reproductions of Louis XVI. This was considered one of the vessel's most impressive rooms (Everett E. Viez Collection).

Ensuite first class staterooms on the Mauretania were furnished with plush beds instead of berths. The effect was not unlike that of an old country house. The walls were hung with printed silk and a green carpet provided a soft background.

A hallmark of the Maùretania was the large, cheery second class public rooms of the liner. They were handsomely decorated and furnished, a conscious effort being made by Cunard to attract a high class of traveller. This is the library on 'B' Deck, one of two large and comfortable sitting rooms in second class.

This stateroom is typical of the second class staterooms on the Mauretania with space for three or four persons. The panelling was white with red carpet and soft wool hangings. The furniture was mahogany.

Second class accommodation on the Mauretania was considered to be comparable to first class on some earlier liners. The smoke room, located aft of the promenade deck, was Georgian in style and panelled in mahogany.

Above *The Verandah Café was always a popular place among* Mauretania *passengers. Here they could relax after dinner or in the early afternoon and take in the salt air beneath a glazed roof trimmed with evergreens. Here the gardener attends to plants and fresh flowers* (Everett E. Viez Collection).

Below *The* Mauretania's *first class dining saloon. It was divided into an upper and lower room and was panelled in oak which was carved in place. Finished in the style of Francis I, this room was crowned by a cream and gold dome* (Everett E. Viez Collection).

Above *First class entrance foyer aboard the* Mauretania. *French walnut was used in decorating such areas in a 15th century Italian style. The decking is of rubber tiling. To the left is the grillework surrounding a passenger lift* (Everett E. Viez Collection).

Below *The first class smoke room on the* Mauretania, *looking forward. This elegant room was a great favourite of passengers through the years and is outfitted in 15th century Italian style. The woodwork is walnut, sycamore and mahogany* (Everett E. Viez Collection).

Above *Often neglected in discussions of the great liners is the third class, or steerage. But it played an important role in the history of the Atlantic ferry in the early 20th century. The Lusitania's third class dining room, located forward on the upper deck, is anything but elegant but must have been to the immigrant what the Ritz Carlton was to first class (Scottish Record Office).*

Below *A portion of the Lusitania's promenade deck showing the great expanse of deck space which endeared the liner to the travelling public. This is first class territory (Scottish Record Office).*

Continued from page 68.

Above *The* Lusitania's *first class lounge. This photograph shows in great detail the splendid dome and intricate carving work. The highly polished woodwork and the stained glass domes were hallmarks of this famous liner. The carpeting and other furniture has yet to be installed* (Scottish Record Office).

Below *The first class cabins on the* Lusitania *were extremely cosy but nowhere near as gaudy as on other liners of the day. This is a portion of a regal suite bedroom completed in the Louis Seize style with gilt ornamentation and old brocade* (Scottish Record Office).

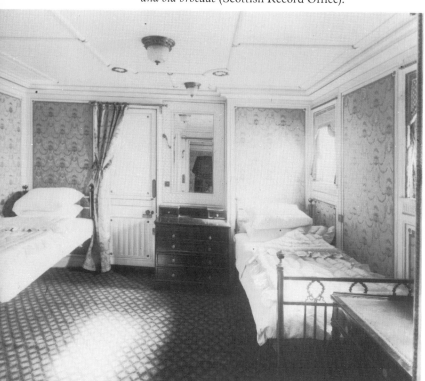

decor in such public rooms as the writing room and library as well as the suites and other passenger accommodation. As was customary at the time, the first class space was generally amidships with second class slightly aft and third class at the far ends of the ships. Grand staircases were, of course, included as well as two separate electric lifts and, in the case of the *Mauretania*, a verandah café, complete with evergreens and a glazed roof at the after end of the boat deck. There were *en suite* and special staterooms and a pair of regal suites on either side of the promenade deck that included a dining room, drawing room, two bedrooms, bathroom and a private corridor. As with most of the first class accommodation, the suites utilised a variety of styles ranging from Adam to Georgian. Not as opulent perhaps as the rooms found on the crack German liners, the accommodation on the *Lusitania* and *Mauretania* was nevertheless extremely comfortable and for years captured the fancy of Atlantic travellers.

Contrary to the myth which has been perpetuated over the years, the *Lusitania,* not the *Mauretania,* held the lion's share of the world's attention. She was the first of the new generation of superliners and as such received front page coverage in every important journal and newspaper on both sides of the Atlantic. Newsmen competed with one another for the privilege of being aboard her for trials and maiden voyage.

The morning of July 27 1907 dawned grey and dreary over Clydebank with the completed *Lusitania* lying alongside the quay at John Brown's. Her four crimson and black funnels presented a brave sight as they towered over the spotless black hull and white superstructure. An attractive strip of white paint continued forward to the bow at the promenade deck level, but was altered to uniform black before her maiden voyage In a few hours the *Lusitania* would be heading to sea for her trials. She exceeded her builder's and owner's expectations by averaging 25.4 knots and on several occasions topping the 26.5 knot mark. One correspondent praised the vessel's 'absolute freedom from vibration', something which could not be said for the *Mauretania* on her trials several months later.

Finally all was in readiness for the *Lusitania*'s maiden voyage. September 7 1907 was a day of unparalleled festivity in Liverpool with much excitement generated over her departure that afternoon. Leaving on the same day for New York was the *Lucania,* the one-time Atlantic record holder. Although everyone knew that the new liner would easily outstrip the older, there was talk among the crews of an unofficial 'race' between the two. At least one waterfront oddsmaker gave the *Lusitania* a 20-hour advantage in reaching New York. The big new Cunarder was scheduled to depart at 7 pm, but was delayed by the *Lucania* which did not clear the Prince's Landing Stage until 5 pm. As soon as she could take her place at the stage, the *Lusitania* began embarking her passengers, a procedure that lasted until well after dark. Those on hand to watch the departure, some 200,000 strong, were treated to the unexpected spectacle of the giant vessel lit from stem to stern as she lay at the berth. Finally, around 9 pm, she cast off to the strains of *Rule Britannia* and a thunderous ovation from the assembled multitude. Heading down the Mersey, the *Lucy* (as she was already known) was accompanied by whistle and horn salutes from nearby ships and tugs. One correspondent reported that 'no vessel in the British mercantile service ever inaugurated her career more splendidly'.

By the time the call at Queenstown had been completed, the *Lusitania*, with 2,165 passengers and 850 crew aboard under Captain J.B. Watt, was beginning to settle into a routine. By mid-day on September 8, despite considerable fog which prevented her from doing her best, she had overtaken the *Lucania* and by 9 pm was out of sight of the older vessel. Spirits aboard the new liner were high and there was great expectation among the passengers of a record crossing. This

Above *Here is the 'E' Deck entrance foyer of the* Lusitania. *The iron gates to the left are the doors to the ship's lift, something of a novelty in those days* (Scottish Record Office).

Below *A splendid starboard view of the* Lusitania *running her trials. Notice the white-painted forecastle which was painted all black by the time the liner entered commercial service in 1907. A comparison of this photograph with one of the* Mauretania *will show easily the differences in profile between the two, the* Lusitania *having far fewer large ventilators* (Scottish Record Office).

All four of those funnels were real! The Lusitania *lays a cloud of smoke as she steams toward Liverpool and the start of her maiden voyage. Notice that the white painted forecastle has been eliminated* (Scottish Record Office).

was not to be, for dense fog banks were encountered on several occasions and combined with rough seas caused the big ship to cut her speed so that she could not even equal, much less break, the German record. The mean speed on the crossing had been about 23 knots with the best day's run 593 miles—about eight miles less than the *Deutschland*'s best effort.

The *Lusitania* arrived off Sandy Hook on the morning of September 13, after a voyage of five days, 54 minutes, and was met by an enormous flotilla of small craft, tugs and steamers which escorted her into the harbour. There was an added touch of novelty in that the *Lusitania* was the first vessel to use the newly completed Ambrose Channel into New York. Pilots and harbour officials admitted relief when the monster

had successfully navigated the new fairway, although the smaller Cunard Liner *Caronia* had used it outward bound earlier in the week. Incidentally, the *Lucania* did not dock until 13 hours later.

Weather on the homeward leg of her maiden voyage also kept the *Lusitania* from cracking the records. During the crossing she averaged 22.6 knots, the best day's run being 530 miles. But upon departure from Queenstown on October 6 on her second voyage to New York, everything went right and the vessel steamed past Sandy Hook 4 days, 19 hours and 52 minutes later, having easily captured the 'Blue Riband' from the Germans. She had averaged 23.993 knots for the crossing with her longest day's run 617 miles. It was the first time the Atlantic had been crossed in

Having completed her triumphal maiden voyage, the Lusitania *rests at her New York pier. For days, crowds of New Yorkers milled about the pier admiring her lean, powerful lines. She was by far the largest vessel yet seen in New York.*

less than five days. The many risks taken in this massive shipbuilding effort, therefore, were more than justified. Britons were ecstatic for they not only had the world's largest liner, but also the fastest.

While the *Lusitania* was capturing the world's fancy, the *Mauretania* was preparing to slip away from her builder's yard for preliminary trials. She left Tyneside on September 17 and put to sea for a series of secret tests, the details of which have generally remained shrouded in secrecy ever since. She steamed back and forth over a 200-mile course between Flamborough Head and St Abbs, during which she was reported to have reached 27 knots. But there was considerable concern over the vibration which was so bad that men on the bridge were nearly shaken off their feet when the ship was only at 20 knots. Dejected, her officers returned her to the builder's yard, worrying that the same serious vibration problems that plagued the *Deutschland* and the *Kaiser Friedrich* (the ill-fated consort of the *Kaiser Wilhelm der Grosse*) would also haunt the *Mauretania*. It soon became apparent that the vibration problem did not stem from the turbines, but rather from the four giant screws. It was not that the propellers were defective, but it must be remembered that the art of propeller design still left much to be desired. Their eventual replacement was the most desirable method of correcting the problem, but it was decided that additional strengthening be undertaken immediately in the after portions of the liner to keep the vibration to a minimum.

Fitting-out was completed within a month and on October 22 the majestic four-stacker departed her builder's yard for Liverpool. The departure was a gala affair, thousands turning out to bid Godspeed to the *Mauretania,* the finest product ever turned out by Tyneside builders. Ships along the river and shorebound factories whistled in salute as the graceful liner headed toward the sea. On the bridge Lady Inverclyde had the honour of giving the command that actually started the voyage once the vessel had cleared the mouth of the Tyne. A host of guests settled down for the trip to Liverpool by way of the north of Scotland and it was a delightful voyage indeed. The weather was excellent and the *Mauretania* performed flawlessly at an average speed of 22 knots. She reached the Mersey around daybreak on October 24 and was immediately placed in the Canada Graving Dock for painting and bottom work. Then followed the official acceptance trials which commenced from Liverpool on the morning of November 3. The vessel ran the 300-mile course between Corsewall Light and Longships

four times at an average speed of 26.03 knots which exceeded the Admiralty's requirements and the *Lusitania*'s speed over the same course. Significantly, the worrisome vibration was substantially minimised. Everyone was delighted. After running the measured mile in the Firth of Clyde, the *Mauretania* returned to Liverpool.

The *Mauretania* left the Mersey on her maiden voyage on November 16 at 7.30 pm to the cheers of 50,000 well-wishers and a fireworks display. If the *Lusitania*'s maiden voyage was less than auspicious because of bad weather, the *Mauretania*'s was even less so. After clearing Queenstown the next day, the new liner ran into some extremely heavy weather that persisted for three days and which caused some anxious moments for those on board. The angry seas tore loose a spare anchor on the forecastle, allowing it to skid dangerously around the decks. Captain John Prichard was forced to turn the ship around stern-on into the storm to permit the crew to secure the wayward anchor. This took three hours to accomplish, during which the *Mauretania* took a terrific beating from the mountainous seas. Several large windows on the upper decks were shattered by giant waves and the iron railing atop the wheelhouse was twisted, mute testimony to the force of the North Atlantic at its worst. The weather continued to keep the speed down and from noon on the 18th to noon on the 19th, the *Mauretania* was held to a passage of only 464 miles. Finally, the weather cleared and she was opened up, covering a record 624 miles in the 24-hour period. But her troubles were not yet over. As she passed Sandy Hook shortly after 11 am on November 22, she was engulfed in a thick fog. Captain Prichard lowered her speed to a crawl and by the time the liner reached quarantine, he decided he had had enough and dropped anchor. The passengers, who had endured the discomforts of the stormy passage, were upset and wanted to be put ashore by tender, but the captain did not permit it. Eventually the fog lifted around sundown and the *Mauretania* finally tied up about 6.15 pm. The voyage had consumed five days, 18 hours and 17 minutes at an average speed of 22.2 knots.

The return voyage was not much better in terms of weather, but the *Mauretania* did manage to average 23.69 knots for a crossing time to Queenstown of four days, 22 hours and 29 minutes. That was 24 minutes better than the *Lusitania*'s best time on the eastward passage. Upon arrival back in Liverpool, the new liner came in for some press criticism. There were those who felt she should have done better in the

The Mauretania *heaves-to in the approaches to New York harbour as she picks up her harbour pilot. This photograph was probably made soon after the loss of the* Titanic *judging by all the lifeboats, but before the promenade deck was glassed-in during the war* (The Mariners Museum, Newport News).

heavy seas and had vibrated too much, one correspondent commenting that she shook so much that it was impossible to read and write on the upper decks. But from the official point of view, vibration was to be expected to *some* degree, this being a problem that has long plagued fast ships and one which would be corrected later in the *Mauretania*'s career. Down through the years the liner would make a solid reputation as a good sea boat. A significant statistic developed during the *Mauretania*'s early voyages. Her builders had estimated a daily coal consumption of 1,000 tons, but on her westbound maiden voyage she burned 856 tons a day and on the eastbound leg 917 tons. Those who contended that the new giants would be impossible to keep bunkered were forever silenced.

Once in regular service together, the *Mauretania* and *Lusitania* engaged in a friendly rivalry as to which was the faster. It was also considered a rivalry between the great shipbuilding centres of Clydebank and Tyneside. Over the next two years, the two liners exchanged the North Atlantic speed record back and forth as they consistently pared minutes off each other's time.

A mishap on her seventh voyage in May 1908 prevented the *Mauretania* from participating in this rivalry for the better part of that year. She was westbound about 250 miles from Daunt's Rock, Queenstown, when she apparently struck a submerged object and lost a propeller blade. This necessitated sailing with only three screws in operation for the rest of the year while new propellers, which had been considered since her

initial trials, were made. Nevertheless, for her next eight voyages she continued to turn in good performances, steaming at about 24.8 knots on the average. During the time her sister was somewhat incapacitated, the *Lusitania* turned in an excellent run in July 1908 by crossing westbound in 4 days, 19 hours, 36 minutes at an average speed of 25.01 knots. The best day's run was 643 miles. Both ships were taken out of service during the winter of 1908-09 for machinery adjustments and the fitting of new propellers which subsequently raised their speed a full knot. The *Lusitania* was first to make her mark westbound, streaking from Queenstown to Ambrose Light in August 1909 at an average speed of 25.65 knots and knocking nearly three hours from the record of July 1908. The *Mauretania* had already made homeward runs at averages of 25.61, 25.70 and 25.88 knots and proved herself to be slightly the faster of the two. Finally, in September she made the westbound crossing at an average speed of 26.06 knots with daily runs of 58, 661, 642, 657, 651 and 115 miles, an aggregate of 2,784 miles, which occupied 4 days, 10 hours, 51 minutes. There was no disputing that the *Mauretania* was the world's fastest liner, a distinction she retained until 1929.

On August 14 1909 the old *Lucania* which, with her sister the *Campania*, had been running on the New York service with the two new liners, was destroyed by fire in the Huskisson Dock in Liverpool. This dramatised the need for that third superliner which had long been under consideration as a running mate to the *Lusitania* and

Mauretania. It was also at this time that the White Star Line had under construction the first two of its three giant liners which would wrest away from Cunard the distinction of operating the world's largest liners. HAPAG also had plans for a trio of even larger vessels and with competition so keen, it was decided that the time was right for Cunard to make another move. The new vessel would be known as the *Aquitania* and in consort with the *Lusitania* and *Mauretania,* would offer a sailing every Saturday from Liverpool. With the fastest ships in the world already under its house flag, Cunard decided with the *Aquitania* to turn to a very large vessel, one with the most luxurious appointments afloat. She was not meant to break speed records, merely to transport passengers in comfort in the finest surroundings possible.

After considerable planning, a contract was placed with John Brown's Clydebank yard for a liner with a speed of 23 knots to make the crossing in about five and a half days. The contract was signed on December 8 1910. Her principal dimensions were 869 feet in length, a beam of 97 feet and a gross tonnage of 45,647. She was designed to carry 597 first class, 614 second class and 2,052 third class passengers along with a crew of 972. There were to be four screws, the propelling machinery consisting of direct-drive triple-expansion turbines, with steam provided by 21 double-ended boilers. Considerable time passed between the awarding of the contract and the laying of the keel, which did not occur until June 5 1911. This was to enable the builders to carry out a series of tests on the hull form. Experience gained through the operation of the *Lusitania* and *Mauretania* entered into the deliberations. Her consorts had been financed largely through government loans, but the *Aquitania* was built completely with funds from the Cunard treasury, indicative of the firm's stability. Nevertheless, she was, like her consorts, designed for possible conversion to a naval auxiliary in the future.

During the period that the *Aquitania* was being designed, the *Lusitania* and *Mauretania* continued to add to their laurels. The *Mauretania* managed a round-trip crossing of the Atlantic and a complete turnaround in New York in just 12 days. That was in December 1910 and was something that had never before been accomplished. The *Lusitania* had her time in the sun a few months later in August 1911 when, because of a seamen's strike in Liverpool, she made two complete round trips to New York and back inside a month, departing Liverpool on the first on August 28 and arriving back the second time on September 25.

By this time the two Cunarders had been eclipsed in size by White Star's new *Olympic* but both continued to be extremely popular.

When new the *Mauretania* and *Lusitania* each carried 16 lifeboats, a number considered adequate under existing Board of Trade regulations, even though they did not provide room for all on board. The sinking of the *Titanic* on April 15 1912 changed all that and when the two liners were withdrawn for their annual refit at the end of 1912, the number of lifeboats was increased to 48.

Meanwhile, preparations were under way for the launch of the *Aquitania,* for never before had anything so large been launched into the Clyde. To ensure that there would be sufficient water and manoeuvring room once the liner was afloat, the shipyard undertook considerable alterations to the Clyde itself. The river had already been widened in 1906 for the launch of the *Lusitania,* but now it was to be widened even more. The channel between Clydebank and Greenock and the open sea was dredged to permit the *Aquitania* to make the passage safely, the river in front of the slip had to be deepened and the fitting-out basin also had to be dredged.

The launch was conducted without difficulty on April 21 1913 before a large and enthusiastic crowd. The honour of naming the vessel went to the Countess of Derby. Upon completion of the ceremonies, the liner was towed to the fitting-out basin where slightly more than a year was spent installing her machinery and luxurious fittings. Historian E. Keble Chatterton remarked at the time, 'If the limit of any art exists it is as nearly as possible attained in the *Aquitania.* If it were possible to have built a better steamship than this it would have been done . . . nothing has been done better in any ship'.*

There was nothing revolutionary in the *Aquitania*'s design. Aside from her outstanding exterior appearance, it was the splendour of her fittings which set her apart from all other liners. It was left to Mewes and Davis of London to decorate the vessel, while the actual design of the public rooms was handled by James Miller. Mewes and Davis are widely known for their work in Ballin's big three HAPAG liners, but their finest work was unquestionably the *Aquitania.* Her rooms were undoubtedly over-ornate by present tastes, but lacked the Teutonic heaviness of the *Imperator* and *Vaterland.*

---

* E. Keble Chatterton, *Souvenir of the Launching of RMS Aquitania, April 1913* (The Cunard Steam-Ship Company Ltd, 1913).

Above *Tugs take the* Aquitania's *hull in tow immediately following her launch on April 21 1913. Another year would elapse before she would be ready to enter service* (Scottish Record Office).

Below *Here is but a portion of the first class promenade area on 'B' Deck aboard the* Aquitania. *This promenade is a full 450 ft in length. Notice the raised terrace at the left. It served a dual purpose: to provide those in deck chairs with an unobstructed view out to sea and to also permit air and light to reach inside staterooms on 'C' Deck. This arrangement appears to have been unique to the* Aquitania (Everett E. Viez Collection).

The *Aquitania*'s design periods ranged from Charles II and Christopher Wren to Louis XVI. The most famous room on the ship was the Palladian or first class lounge. This splendid chamber, located on 'A' deck, was reminiscent of the work of Wren and included a genuine oil painting on the ceiling by an 18th century Dutch master, removed in its entirety from a house of the period. With its large Georgian windows overlooking the garden lounge, the Palladian was long a favourite of travellers. The first class drawing room, with its styles borrowed from various English country homes, exuded a cool graciousness, while the Louis XVI restaurant was resplendent in the opulence of the period. Stretching 140 feet in length and the full width of the ship, this room was tastefully decorated with little paintings taken from the work of Prieur, a well-known decorator of the Louis XVI era. As for the sleeping accommodation, it was on the highest scale possible, and in first class included a variety of large suites, all decorated with copies of well-known English art.

In light of the *Titanic* disaster, life-saving facilities aboard the *Aquitania* were more than adequate. She was equipped with a total of 80 life-boats, 44 of which were double-banked on both sides of the vessel. Altogether the boats could hold 4,584 persons, 1,321 more than the ship was licensed to carry. Her firefighting apparatus was also of the highest standard, as was the watertight subdivision.

Early in 1914 the Cunard Line stopped calling at Queenstown on a regular basis. At about the same time, the *Mauretania* was involved in the only fatal mishap of her long career. An explosion during her annual refit killed four shipyard workers, but it was determined that the blast was caused by the illegal use of a gas cylinder by a worker, and not because of any defect in connection with the ship.

Continued on page 88.

American artist C. Leslie Oursler specialises in paintings of coastal steamers, but he has created this splendid view of the Aquitania *in the English Channel for John Shaum.*

Left *First class accommodation aboard the* Aquitania *was considered quite elegant. Here is an example of a twin-bed stateroom, complete with what appears to be brass bedsteads* (Everett E. Viez Collection).

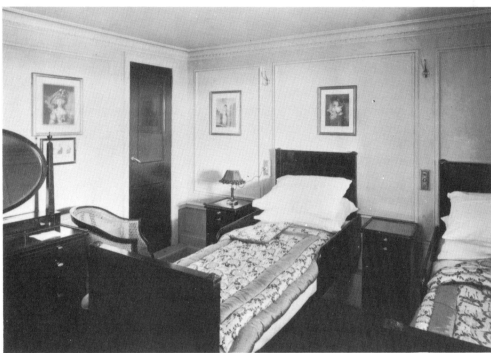

Left *Reminiscent of a fine hotel ashore, this first class stateroom aboard the* Aquitania *features plush beds and heavy wooden furniture finished in 18th century styles. Notice the art reproductions included in all first class staterooms* (Everett E. Viez Collection).

Below left *Early Jacobean is the style selected for the* Aquitania's *grill room, located on 'D' Deck. The grill room was a handsome chamber and provided excellent cuisine in conjunction with the nearby Louis XVI restaurant* (Everett E. Viez Collection).

Opposite *Unquestionably one of the most splendid public rooms on any liner, the* Aquitania's *first class Palladian Lounge is decorated in the style of George I. There are hints of Sir Christopher Wren here. In the centre of the ceiling is a genuine old ceiling painting removed in its entirety from a Dutch house of the period* (Everett E. Viez Collection).

Steam is up in the Aquitania's boilers at Clydebank and she is just about ready to depart on her trials. This beautiful photograph provides many details of this splendid-looking ship (Scottish Record Office).

Continued from page 83.

The *Aquitania*'s maiden voyage from Liverpool was scheduled to begin on May 30 1914. She departed John Brown's yard on May 10 for her trials, making the passage down the Clyde with little difficulty, even though the work of dredging had continued until the last possible moment. Tens of thousands lined the river bank to watch her make her way to the sea. Among those keeping close tabs on the *Aquitania*'s entry into service was a young Cunard officer, then serving aboard the *Carpathia*. Upon seeing the *Aquitania* for the first time, Harry Grattidge made a solemn vow to himself: 'Because we have begun our service in the same year, one day I will be your master.'* Grattidge, who had joined the Cunard Line only two months before, did indeed command the giant liner late in her career, only a few years before being named commodore of the entire Cunard fleet.

For three days the *Aquitania* ran her trials and achieved 24 knots with ease, a speed which easily met contract terms and greatly pleased her owners. From there she proceeded on to Liverpool, where she docked in the Gladstone Graving Dock on May 14 for hull cleaning. The *Aquitania*, incidentally, was the first ship to occupy this dock, which at the time was the largest of its kind in the world. The day before the maiden voyage was due to begin, Cunard opened the liner for inspection. Comparisons were immediately drawn with the giant *Vaterland* which had made her maiden voyage earlier that month. The general consensus seemed to favour the British liner, one contemporary report remarking that she constituted a 'greater symmetry of design'.

Later that day she was taken from the dock and moved to the Prince's Landing Stage to receive her maiden voyage passengers. There had been a good deal of advance publicity surrounding the *Aquitania*'s first crossing, but this was forced to take a back seat on May 30 to the news that the day before, the Canadian Pacific liner *Empress of Ireland* had been sunk in collision in the St Lawrence River with the loss of over 1,000 lives. Liverpool was in mourning since many of the lost liner's crew had their homes there. Cunard reported that no one cancelled their passage on the *Aquitania* because of the disaster, although it was the prime topic of discussion at Euston Station while passengers awaited the Boat Train.

* Commodore Harry Grattidge, *Captain of the Queens* (E.P. Dutton 1956, New York), p.67.

At length, however, the long-awaited maiden voyage got under way with thousands turning out to see her off.

As the maiden voyage progressed, the world was kept informed by wireless. Captain William Thomas Turner reported that the ship worked herself up to speeds better than anticipated. He also remarked that 'the steadiness and absence of vibration are phenomenal'. The maiden crossing was largely uneventful except on June 3 when the vessel was forced to slow to a crawl for several hours because of ice and mist in her vicinity. The *Aquitania* arrived in New York early on the morning of June 5 to be met by a host of small craft which escorted her to her pier. Passengers were unanimous in their praise of the liner, especially the lack of vibration. The average speed during the crossing had been 23.10 knots. She sailed back to the United Kingdom on June 10 and arrived home on the 16th, completing a maiden voyage described as 'highly successful'.

It was now time for the *Aquitania*, *Mauretania* and *Lusitania* to settle down to their three-ship weekly express service, but the new liner was able to complete only three round trips before war broke out in Europe. Two of Cunard's great liners were in port when hostilities started on August 4 1914; the *Lusitania* in New York and the *Aquitania* in Liverpool. The *Mauretania* was en route to New York at the time and received a wireless message ordering her to abandon her regular route, steam far to the north and make for Halifax. The liner immediately cut off all communications, blacked out her lights and ordered an extra watch of stokers. Her speed built to an incredible 28 knots and stayed there for most of the voyage. To make matters worse, a heavy fog settled in and while it obscured the big liner from detection by enemy warships, it increased the chances of collision since many other blacked-out ships were also scurrying for port at the same time. But the *Mauretania* made it to port safely much to the relief of passengers and crew alike.

The *Lusitania* was due to leave New York on the night of August 4, but Cunard decided to hold all its vessels in port, at least for the time being. Across the river at the Norddeutscher Lloyd terminal, the *Kronprinz Wilhelm* got underway and slipped hastily out of New York before a blockading squadron of British warships could take up station off the harbour entrance. At Pier 54, however, Cunard officials pondered the problem: keep the *Lusitania* in port, possibly for the duration of the conflict, or chance a crossing. Finally, after considerable discussion with the British consulate, it was decided to let her sail.

The triumphal maiden arrival of the Aquitania *in New York in June 1914. Note the HAPAG* Imperator *moored across the river* (John Blake Collection).

With the fall of darkness on the night of August 4 the great ship was blacked out and the paltry number of passengers, 200 in all who still wanted to go, were allowed on board. Regular sailing time came and went but still the ship showed no inclination to depart. At 1 am when all was quiet in the harbour, she stealthily slipped away out to sea. Off Sandy Hook she was met by the cruiser *Essex* which had just escorted the *Olympic* in, and a northerly course was set that would take the pair very close to Newfoundland. Nothing was heard of the *Lusitania* for several days and the silence gave rise to countless rumours. Many believed the former record-breaker had been sunk or captured by a German raider. The wireless blackout imposed on the liner contributed to an already mounting state of anxiety on both sides of the Atlantic. But early on the morning of August 14 the *Lusitania*, her four funnels belching clouds of smoke, and with a wide swath of white water spreading behind her, was sighted in the Irish Sea, pounding at top speed towards the Mersey Bar and a safe haven in Liverpool. She dropped anchor in the Mersey at 10.40 that evening, having run unescorted through the foggy weather all the way from the Banks of Newfoundland. Her commander, Captain Daniel Dow, was commended for bringing her home safely.

Now the question arose of what to do with the three big Cunarders. The *Aquitania* had actually been requisitioned as a merchant cruiser several days before the declaration of war and was at Liverpool being stripped of her furnishings and armed for service the day war officially broke out.

In the case of the *Mauretania* and *Lusitania*, it was decided to use them as repatriation ships. The number of neutral Americans caught in Europe at the war's outbreak was staggering and it was clear that a concentrated effort would be required to get them home. Soon the two fast Cunarders were back in service, literally packed to the gunwales on westbound passages with Americans.

Meanwhile, the *Aquitania*'s conversion had been completed in the amazing span of four days and with a Royal Navy crew and a contingent of marines aboard, she sailed from Liverpool on August 8 1914 to begin her career as an armed merchant cruiser. This employment did not last long, for on the evening of August 25 she anchored off the Mersey Bar with heavy damage to her bow. A few days before, she had been in collision near the Old Head of Kinsale with the 9,000-ton Leyland Line steamer *Canadian*. Little is known of this accident, but Lloyd's Casualty Report for August 25 lists the *Canadian* with considerable damage, although not mentioning the vessel with which she had collided. This accident, coupled with the sinking of the German auxiliary cruiser *Kaiser Wilhelm der Grosse* on August 27 by the old cruiser *Highflyer*, proved to the Admiralty that the use of large liners as armed merchant cruisers was impractical. They were limited in cruiser performance by their enormous size, relatively small fuel capacity, lack of armour plating and limited manoeuvrability.

Since there was a need now for only a skeleton transatlantic service it was decided to lay up the *Mauretania* and *Aquitania* until the proper job

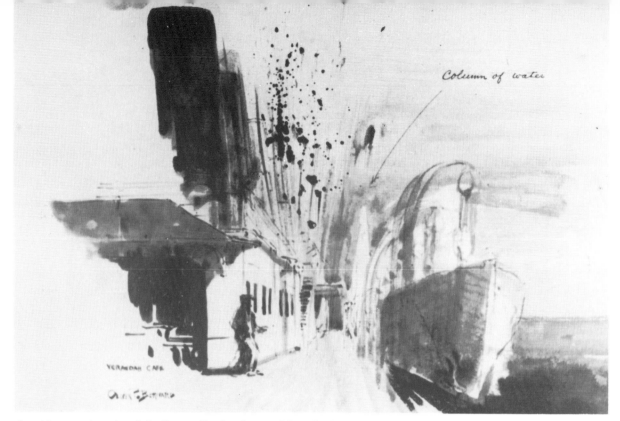

Column of water

A resident scenic artist of the Covent Garden Opera, Oliver P. Bernard was among the passengers aboard the Lusitania *on her final voyage. He was on deck and saw the torpedo strike the liner, and later drew this impression of what he saw* (Illustrated London News).

came along for them. The *Lusitania* stayed with Cunard, sailing virtually by herself on the New York-Liverpool run on a monthly basis. She sailed with watertight doors closed and boats swung out. Her only defence was her great speed and even this was hampered by the decision to shut down six boilers in the name of economy. She could still do 21 knots which was quite sufficient for outrunning submarines, but there was some question whether she could get away from swift German naval vessels or auxiliaries such as the one-time record holder *Kronprinz Wilhelm*.

On May 1 1915 the *Lusitania* departed New York with 1,959 passengers. There had been considerable levity on the pier over rumours that she would be sunk before the voyage was over. The rumours were compounded by a notice ostensibly from the German Embassy appearing in newspapers adjacent to the steamer schedules warning that all Allied shipping encountered in the war zone around the British Isles would be destroyed. It added that passengers travelling on such vessels, regardless of their nationality, would be doing so at their own risk. Only four months earlier, on February 5, the *Lusitania* managed to evade two submarines in the Irish Sea by flying the American flag from her stern. Captain Dow reasoned that this was perfectly legitimate since he had aboard several hundred neutral Americans. As it developed, she steamed full speed in to Liverpool, not even stopping to pick up a pilot, where Dow's tactic met with mixed reaction.

Most of the *Lusitania*'s voyage this trip was uneventful, except for some patchy fog encoun-

tered on the morning of May 7 as the big Cunarder approached the Irish coast. She was travelling at about 19 knots, with extra lookouts posted. She was supposed to have been joined by a Royal Navy escort near Queenstown, but there had been no sign of the escort by early afternoon. One passenger remarked that it had been such a dull trip, she hoped for some excitement during the passage through St George's Channel, the final stretch of water before the sheltered Mersey. The 'excitement' she sought would prevent the *Lusitania* from even reaching St George's Channel.

At 2.10 pm, just as the ship altered course toward land to get a better bearing on the Old Head of Kinsale, a single torpedo smashed into the starboard side without warning. There was a muffled explosion followed almost simultaneously by a much larger one that sent a tower of water and debris high above the bridge. It was this second larger blast which apparently spelled doom for the liner, major damage having been inflicted below the waterline. Even Kapitän-leutnant Walther Schweiger of the German submarine *U-20* was astonished, noting in his log that an 'unusually heavy detonation' had taken place.

Almost immediately the *Lusitania* took a precarious list to starboard and, although still underway, began settling rapidly by the bow. Pandemonium broke out and in the rush to abandon ship, many lifeboats were hastily launched, dumping scores of terrified passengers into the sea. The heavy list prevented most of the

Although some inaccuracies exist, this artist's impression of the torpedoing of the Lusitania *provides a good idea of what it must have been like on May 7 1915. Notice the large hole just beneath the bridge and the explosion farther aft. It must be remembered that there are those who believe the ship was hit by two torpedoes* (Library of Congress).

portside boats from getting away, prompting many people to leap into the water only to be left behind as the sinking liner continued on her course. Captain William Thomas Turner thought he could beach her but commands to the engine room were going unanswered. Even if they had been answered it is doubtful whether anything could have been done: the *Lusitania*'s vitals were torn to pieces. A frantic distress signal flashed out in the hope that the many coastal vessels operating in these waters would come to her aid. Still there was no sign of any naval escort.

As her human cargo spilled from the decks into the water the *Lusitania* leaned farther on to her starboard side, leading many in the water to believe she would roll over on them. Even Kapitänleutnant Schweiger could not bear to watch and ordered the *U-20* out to sea. The great vessel must have been very nearly on her beam ends when, with her bow far below the surface, she lifted her stern clear of the water and poised for the final plunge. Eighteen minutes had passed since the torpedo struck and now the *Lusitania* writhed in her death agonies. Already her bow was on the ocean floor 300 feet below while her stern temporarily was left hanging high in the air. Slowly she began to right herself and then a series of explosions shook her as she settled her stern into the sea until, almost on an even keel, she disappeared from sight in a boiling, hissing cauldron of turbulent water. Debris covered the ocean, through which paddled the pathetically few survivors. Relatively few boats got away unscathed and these, for the most part, were nowhere near full.

It was left to trawlers, tugs and small steamers

(including the *Stormcock* which had once towed the *Great Eastern*) to rescue the *Lusitania*'s survivors. Three large steamers, the Anglo-American Oil Company tanker *Narragansett,* the Leyland Liner *Etonian* and the Ellerman Liner *City of Exeter,* had all been en route to the scene, but were themselves attacked by U-boats. All three managed to escape unharmed but abandoned their efforts to reach the *Lusitania,* convinced that the SOS had been a German decoy to enable submarines to get at them. When the final tally was made, it became clear that of the 1,959 passengers and crew, 1,198 had been lost including 124 Americans.

The world was stunned by the sinking. In England and America it was loudly condemned and many other nations showed extreme displeasure to the Imperial German Government. More outrage followed when the Germans produced a commemorative medal of the event and publicly celebrated the sinking. Many hold the opinion that the loss of the *Lusitania* was a contributing factor to the United States' entry into the war two years later. Although the Germans contended that she had been carrying munitions and may possibly have been armed at the time, the cargo manifest showed 18 empty fuze cases, 125 empty shrapnel cases, 4,200 cases of safety cartridges and 189 cases of miscellaneous non-ordnance military equipment. A court of inquiry in the United States ruled that the liner was indeed an innocent merchant ship that had not violated any international codes. Similar proceedings in England absolved the *Lusitania* of any fault in the sinking and commended Captain Turner for having taken all the necessary precautions. As to why she sank so fast, some theorised that the subsequent explosion following the torpedo blast was caused by boilers exploding or coal dust igniting or a combination of both. Whatever caused the explosion, the damage must have been appalling for a ship so thoroughly subdivided to sink within 20 minutes. The controversy surrounding the sinking of the *Lusitania* is one that has raged unabated for the past 65 years and will probably continue to rage for years to come.

While the *Lusitania* lay on the bottom of the Irish coast, her consorts lay peacefully in port. Finally a use for the giant ships appeared and they were taken into service by the Admiralty and converted to troopships to carry British soldiers to the Mediterranean for the Dardanelles campaign. Both the *Aquitania* and *Mauretania* were commissioned late in May 1915 and dispatched to Lemnos in the Aegean with thousands of troops for that ill-fated invasion. Upwards of 3,000 men were carried on each voyage, the *Mauretania* transporting more than 10,000 troops during her three voyages to the battlefront. The *Aquitania* was at it longer and over a three-month period carried more than 30,000 troops. It was on one of her trooping voyages that the *Mauretania* very nearly met the same fate as her sister. She was bound for the port of embarkation at Mudros with a full load of troops when a torpedo was spotted approaching off the starboard bow. Praying that she would respond as quickly as she had during her trials, Captain Daniel Dow ordered hard-a-port. The giant liner heeled smartly to one side as she turned at full speed, trying to dodge the oncoming missile. The torpedo passed by close alongside; some estimated it at no more than five feet away. Then the *Mauretania* sped from the scene before the submarine could take further action. As far as can be determined this was the only instance in which the vessel was attacked during the war.

Upon completion of their trooping duties the *Mauretania* and *Aquitania* underwent another conversion, this time to hospital ships to be used in bringing home wounded and sick from the Mediterranean campaign. The vast public rooms on the upper decks of both liners became large hospital wards. In the case of the *Mauretania* portions of the promenade deck were glassed-in to provide additional wards. Both ships looked truly magnificent in their hospital ship livery with their white hulls, green stripe and buff funnels. The *Aquitania* began this service in August 1915 and continued on it through most of 1916, transporting more than 25,000 sick and wounded. The *Mauretania* followed in October 1915 and made only three voyages, bringing home 6,298 men. She then went into layup again in the Gareloch before being requisitioned as a troopship for the second time. On this occasion the transformation included the application of the famous 'dazzle' paint scheme in which the liner was camouflaged with large squares and bands of blue and grey paint. She made two voyages to Halifax in October and November 1916 to bring over 6,214 Canadian troops.

Once the Canadian transport service was over the *Mauretania* found herself unemployed again. She was laid up on the Clyde at the end of 1916 and did not see service for most of 1917. The *Aquitania* proceeded to Liverpool at the start of 1917 and likewise was out of work for many months. It was too expensive and too risky to operate the vessels in military service. They probably would have continued in layup for the duration had not the United States entered the war in April 1917. Both ships eventually brought thousands of American troops to Europe.

During this period the *Aquitania* had a harrowing brush with tragedy. On October 9 1918 the liner was approaching the west coast of Ireland, bound for Southampton. She had aboard 8,000 troops; a full gale was blowing and the seas were extremely high. Five US destroyers had met the *Aquitania* to escort her safely to port and were pitched about like corks in the steep seas around the giant transport. The destroyers were steaming in zigzag patterns around the liner, one moment headed toward her, the next moment steaming away from her. It was during these operations that the steering gear of the destroyer USS *Shaw* jammed just as she had turned towards the Cunarder! Commander William A. Glassford saw that a collision was inevitable; he faced the horrible choice of letting his vessel crash amidships into the fully laden troopship or having the *Aquitania* ram his ship. He chose the latter. Rear Admiral Ross A. Dierdorff, then an ensign aboard the *Shaw*, described what happened next:

'Roused from a wardroom transom by the uproar, I ran on deck, froze in my tracks as did many others. To starboard the towering *Aquitania* bore down, the increasing roar of her bow wave quickly drowning out the frantic threshing of our reversed screws. Then with the terrifying screech of steel tearing pitilessly through steel in a sheet of flame, she slashed the *Shaw* in two just forward of the bridge and passed between the pieces.'*

---

* 'The day the Secnav's stars blew off,' *US Naval Institute Proceedings,* July 1956, p.700.

Above left *An Imperial eagle adorns a folder intended to hold colour postcards of the Deutschland.*
Below left *This advertisement appeared in the days when all was still rosy for the White Star Line.*
Above *For many years the Olympic symbolised the White Star Line even though she was eclipsed in size in 1920 by the Majestic. Her picture here adorns the cover of a 1920s passenger list.*
Below *The Olympic appears on a White Star Line brochure in an illustration which captures the atmosphere of the occasion.*

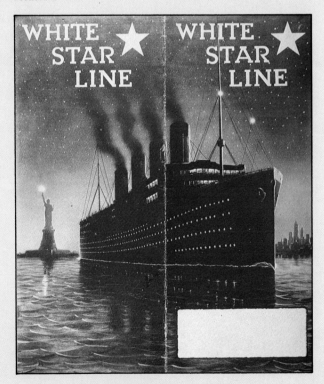

The Kaiser Wilhelm der Grosse at speed with the Imperial German and American flags in one of the beautiful advertising postcards of the period. Note Norddeutscher Lloyd's intertwined 'anchor and key' symbol.

The Kronprinz Wilhelm romps across the North Atlantic in this beautiful artist's depiction of the liner bound for the United States. The ship represents a combination of sleek greyhound and awesome power.

An artist's impression of the majestic Mauretania in New York harbour, probably after World War 1. Artists of the day tried to outdo each other in capturing the true feeling of a giant liner.

A magnificent artist's impression of the Deutschland slamming across on another record-breaking run. The lines of the ship are long, sleek and powerful.

The last of the Norddeutscher Lloyd greyhounds, the Kronprinzessin Cecilie, is shown in this artist's impression at speed with a portrait of her patroness, the Imperial German Kronprinzessin Cecilie.

The White Star Line was floating on a sea of euphoria when it circulated this optimistic advertisement. The first of its trio of giant ships was already in service, with the Titanic expected to join her soon. At the time, illustrations showed the pair as identical, even though the Titanic's promenade deck was glassed-in.

The Kaiser Wilhelm II arrives in New York harbour, escorted by tugs flying NDL's 'anchor and key'.

One of the postcards that circulated during the Olympic's career was this one showing her awaiting the pilot. A little bit of artistic licence has been utilised in depicting the bow.

E.W. Bearman is a retired American railwayman who paints ships and locomotives in his spare time. Here he has captured the Lusitania in her original paint scheme, charging through the sea.

There is no denying that the Britannic was truly beautiful in her hospital ship livery. E.W. Bearman's rendition of her during World War 1 service is exquisitely wrought with fine detail.

Above *The* Aquitania *operated during wartime under several different guises. She is seen here in Canadian waters late in World War 1 as a troopship painted in the distinctive dazzle paint style. She also saw limited service as an auxiliary cruiser and later, as a hospital ship* (Nova Scotia Museum).

Below *An excellent view of the* Mauretania *in her hospital ship livery as she operated between the Dardanelles and the United Kingdom. There is no disputing that she looked superb with her white hull, green stripe and buff funnels. Notice that her promenade deck has been enclosed to make more space for hospital wards* (Imperial War Museum).

Bottom *After beginning her World War 1 career as a cruiser and transport, the* Aquitania *became a hospital ship in 1916. Here she is seen in Southampton Water* (Imperial War Museum).

Above *The destroyer USS* Shaw *is pictured in drydock at Portsmouth after being rammed by the* Aquitania *on October 11 1918 off the Irish coast. Although her bow was shorn off and severe damage done, the vessel did not sink and made port under her own steam (US Navy).*

Below *The* Mauretania *remained in government service for some time after peace was declared in Europe. She is seen here on April 7 1919 entering New York harbour with a load of American troops headed home. A hasty application of Cunard paint restored her to her peacetime appearance, but an extensive renovation still awaited her (US Navy).*

The accident could hardly have been averted. The *Aquitania*, not seriously damaged, was obliged to continue on her way, while the other destroyers moved in to pick up survivors. Shorn in two, the *Shaw*, miraculously, did not sink, although there were some anxious moments as fires started by the collision threatened her magazines. Eventually she was able to make it under her own steam to the Royal Naval Dockyard at Portsmouth where she was repaired and returned to service. Twelve lives had been lost.

After peace was declared, the *Aquitania* and *Mauretania* remained in government service to repatriate American and Canadian troops. Between them the two liners had ferried nearly 130,000 military personnel across the Atlantic during their most recent stint as transports. The *Mauretania* was turned back to the Cunard Line in May 1919, the *Aquitania* having been returned to her owners earlier. Because so many German passenger liners were no longer available to operate in the North Atlantic service and because major British liners like the *Lusitania* and *Britannic* had been lost in the war, it was decided that the *Mauretania* and *Aquitania* should resume commercial service as soon as possible. Following a quick refit, the *Aquitania* returned to the mail run on June 14 1919 from the company's new terminal port of Southampton, the port which had been used for so many years by competing lines. She remained on this service for only four months after which it was deemed advisable to send her to Swan Hunter's for an extensive renovation and modernisation. During this same period, the *Mauretania* was at the same yard having her accommodation restored. But because of the press of work in British shipyards at the time, little was done to her engines which had undergone a massive workout in the war. They would have to wait until later. She left the yard and resumed normal operations on March 6 1920 from Southampton. But a combination of tired, worn-out engines and poor coal resulting from a widespread coal strike, conspired to keep her speed down and her performance was not up to the standard of the pre-war years. Although most of her accommodation was renovated after the war, it had been a rather hurried job and there were many who felt more could be done to bring her in tune with the times. Some observers actually felt the *Mauretania* had become so outmoded that she was just being kept around until new ships could be built.

The *Aquitania*'s rehabilitation at Tyneside, however, was an extensive job indeed. It involved complete renewal of all her luxury appointments

A flotilla of tugs helps ease the Mauretania *around and into her New York pier as she brings home thousands of American troops at the end of World War 1* (Stewart Bale Ltd).

and a complete refurbishing. It was also decided to convert her boilers to oil firing, a decision that would mean not only greater economy but an end to the dirty business of coaling during turnarounds. No longer would there be a need for 350 stokehold hands: 50 would be sufficient with oil fuel. And no longer would the in-port time between voyages be so long. Finally, the liner would be able to improve slightly on her speed. A significant addition to the *Aquitania*'s navigation equipment during the refit was a Gyro compass; she was the first merchant ship so equipped.

On July 17 1920 the *Aquitania* left Liverpool on her first post-refit voyage, subsequent sailings being from Southampton. Her consorts were the *Mauretania* and *Imperator,* the latter being the 51,969-ton former HAPAG liner, the first of the three near-sisters (*Vaterland* and *Bismarck* being the others) which were easily the largest ships in the world. She had been allocated to Britain, placed under Cunard management, purchased from the shipping controller early in 1921 and renamed *Berengaria.* In fact the *Berengaria* and *Majestic* (ex-*Bismarck*) were bought jointly by Cunard and White Star in order to prevent them outbidding each other. This arrangement lasted for about ten years but each Line took over full control of its respective ship.

The 14-year-old *Mauretania* was lying at her Southampton dock on June 25 1921, with most of her crew and officers ashore on leave. Only two of the boilers were being used to keep steam up as the remaining crew went about routine turnaround work. Cleaning men were working on the carpets in some of the first class cabins on 'E' deck and at least one of them was using an inflammable

One need search no farther for a truly beautiful portrait of the 'Ship Beautiful'. The Aquitania *is seen heading out to sea from New York in this stunning view from the Edwin Levick collection* (The Mariners Museum, Newport News).

liquid to work out grease spots. This was strictly against Cunard regulations. Shortly after 1.30 pm a fire broke out in that area, possibly from a match used to light a pipe. The crew sprang to action, rolling out the fire hoses only to find that there was no pressure because of the lack of steam. There was little they could do as thick smoke rolled down the 'E' deck passageways forcing the men to retreat from the heart of the fire. The magnificent wood panelling had ignited in several staterooms and soon flames were licking at the ceilings. Directly above the fire was the elegant first class dining saloon. If the blaze broke through unabated to that area there might not be any chance of controlling it. Shorebound fire-fighters had arrived on the scene and by this time were pumping tons of water on to the flames through side doors and portholes. Then the ship's hoses suddenly came to life as the engineers far below managed to get up steam and start the pumps. Crewmen and Southampton firefighters alike advanced on the fire, trying desperately to contain it in the 'E' deck area. Their efforts soon showed results and it became apparent that given a little time they could control the blaze and eventually extinguish it. But an unexpected development dampened this optimism.

The *Mauretania* was lying with her port side to the pier and all the doors on that side had been opened to accommodate the firefighters. But the starboard doors had remained closed and water was now beginning to accumulate on board. About 5.30 pm one of the port side mooring lines forward gave way under the strain of the extra weight produced by the water aboard. The giant liner suddenly lurched sharply to starboard coming to rest with a list of about 15 degrees, allowing all the water to run to starboard with no way of running out. The officers in charge realised that, with water continually being poured aboard, the *Mauretania* would roll over if other mooring lines parted. The obvious solution was to open the big doors on the starboard side, but this was going to pose major problems since the doors were under more than six feet of water on 'E' deck. Senior First Officer James Bisset organised a small party of volunteers to attempt to get the doors open so the water could drain off. It involved diving beneath the filthy water to loosen the huge nuts on the doors, a process that took the better part of half an hour. Finally the men were able to get the doors open and let all the accumulated water pour out of the ship. Within ten minutes she was nearly back on an even keel. The *Mauretania* had been saved but she was seriously damaged.

Passenger areas on 'E' deck were destroyed and the flooring of the first class dining saloon had been severely buckled by the fire. There was also considerable smoke and water damage to other areas of the ship as well. The problem confronting the company was that she was due to sail for New York within a few days with a full load of passengers. After all, this was the peak travel season. Since her hull and engines had not been damaged it was proposed by some Cunard Line officials that the damaged area be cordoned off, temporary repairs made to the dining saloon and the ship cleansed of the smoke odour so she would not miss her sailing. But at the urging of her master, Captain Arthur H. Rostron, it was decided to cancel the voyage altogether and send the *Mauretania* back to her builders on the Tyne for extensive work. It was also as good a time as any to effect considerable modernisation and convert her to oil burning. In addition, her turbines would receive some much-needed attention. She did not return to service until March 1922, in many respects a new vessel. And once again she became one of the most popular liners on the North Atlantic.

Cunard's express service during much of the 1920s was undoubtedly the best balanced on the North Atlantic, consisting of the large and splendid steamers *Mauretania, Aquitania* and *Berengaria*. This period also saw a different kind of work for the *Mauretania* and *Aquitania,* both ships being sent from time to time during the winter months on extensive luxury cruises from New York and Southampton to the Mediterranean and Caribbean. First to be utilised in this fashion was the *Mauretania* which was chartered by the American Express Company for a Mediterranean cruise departing from New York on January 27 1923, a voyage that lasted six weeks.

In November 1923 Cunard withdrew the *Mauretania* for her annual overhaul, to be undertake at Thornycroft's in Southampton, who were to give the turbines further attention. Unfortunately, the shipyard workers went on strike while the work was in progress, and it was decided to send her over to Cherbourg for the repairs to be completed on schedule. Since the engines were stripped down and uncovered, it was necessary to tow her across the Channel. Six Dutch tugs were engaged for this job and things were well in hand until the tow reached the open Channel where a fresh breeze was springing up. The tugs struggled to control the powerless liner and very nearly lost her during the night when the towing lines parted and she almost drifted ashore in heavy seas and high winds. Fortunately the tugs managed to get their lines back aboard and the *Mauretania* reached safety in Cherbourg where another six weeks were required to complete the engine work. Once back in service, she proceeded to amaze the shipping world with her performance. Here was a liner 17 years old, running faster than she had ever done before. Her best effort was in August 1924 when she covered a distance of 3,198 miles from Ambrose to Cherbourg in 5 days 1 hour 49 minutes at an average speed of 26.25 knots.

While the *Mauretania* made news with her speed, the newer and larger *Aquitania* was impressing everyone with her abilities as an excellent sea boat. On a voyage to New York in January 1924 when the Atlantic was at its angriest, she encountered the worst gale in years. Waves sometimes as high as 60 feet hammered at the ship, but she remained steady enough during the storm for passengers to continue their dancing with little difficulty! During most of the 1920s the *Aquitania* was under the command of Captain Sir James Charles, Commodore of the Cunard Line. Sir James, one of the most famous Atlantic masters, was scheduled for retirement in July 1928 and was completing his final voyage home in command of the great liner when, on July 15, he collapsed in his cabin while the ship was at Cherbourg. After the voyage across the Channel, he was taken ashore, but died in a Southampton nursing home without regaining consciousness. The general consensus was that he had died of a broken heart.

The *Mauretania*'s long reign as speed queen of the Atlantic came to an end in 1929 with the advent of the Norddeutscher Lloyd superliner *Bremen*, a 51,656-ton vessel designed to regain the Blue Riband for Germany. In this she succeeded easily, crossing to New York in June at an average speed of 27.83 knots, and returning at 27.91 knots, thus taking the record in both directions. Her speeds were faster by nearly 1½ knots than the *Mauretania*'s best. But the old liner was not ready to give in. She opened up with all she had upon clearing Cherbourg on August 3 and streaked westward at an average speed of 26.90 knots. Returning home she averaged 27.22 knots, speeds that were appreciably better than she had ever done before.

After more than 21 years the *Mauretania* had relinquished the Atlantic speed record. From that time on she devoted more of her time to cruising and found herself on the express service only during the peak season. The magnificent black hull gave way in 1930 to white which was more in keeping with the cruise image and it must be said that she really looked splendid in that livery. Weekend cruises from New York to the Bahamas and Cuba were scheduled in between Atlantic crossings, voyages that demanded the most of the old liner. Still she continued to amaze and on one such cruise steamed at 31 knots for a period, helped along to a certain extent by the Gulf Stream.

The advent of the new German liners *Bremen* and *Europa* as well as challenges being mounted by the French and Italians made it necessary for the Cunard Line to consider re-equipping its fleet. In 1930 the *Mauretania* was 23 years old, the *Aquitania* 16 and the *Berengaria* 17. The Compagnie Générale Transatlantique had the new *Ile de France* in service and the vessel that would become the *Normandie* was on the way. In Italy, the *Rex* and *Conte di Savoia* were nearly

A variety of vessels can be seen in this pre-World War 2 view in New York harbour, but the Aquitania *easily dwarfs them all. She was never a headline-grabber, but she remains one of the most famous of Atlantic liners* (Steamship Historical Society of America).

ready to make their debut. Accordingly, Cunard placed an order with John Brown and Company in 1930 for the first of a pair of gigantic liners, an 80,774-ton behemoth that would become the *Queen Mary*. A second vessel would follow later for a weekly express service that would be, for the first time, operated by only two ships. But the worsening financial plight called a halt to the construction of 'Number 534' as she was known then. She lay on the stocks in an unfinished state for two full years before the government finally came to the company's aid by agreeing to advance the money for completion of the ship with a guarantee of additional money for a running mate provided Cunard and White Star would agree to an amalgamation. This took place early in 1934 and work on the '534' resumed that April. It was on the *Aquitania* that the double house flag of the newly merged Cunard-White Star Line was first hoisted on July 7 as she headed for New York. The Cunard flag flew at the top of the staff with the White Star burgee immediately beneath it. It was just the opposite on White Star Line ships; both Lines retained their funnel colours.

With work on 'Number 534' proceeding once again, it became apparent that much surplus tonnage would have to be disposed of from the recently merged fleet. Among the ships to be withdrawn was the *Mauretania,* her direct-drive turbines, old-style boilers and accommodation long since outdated. The venerable liner sailed from New York on September 26 1934 on her final voyage, the same day that 'Number 534' was launched at Clydebank and named *Queen Mary.* Her homeward speed was 24.42 knots and by the time she arrived in Southampton, she had been in Cunard service for one month shy of 27 years. More than two million miles had been covered in that long and magnificent career which included 318 Atlantic round voyages and 54 cruises, not to mention her war service. She tied up at Berth 108 in Southampton to await her fate, being joined by the *Olympic* in April 1935.

While the *Mauretania* awaited disposal at Southampton, the *Aquitania* was getting herself into a little bit of trouble, the only accidents she ever suffered in peacetime. On January 26 she grounded at Calshot Spit, but was refloated after only 2½ hours with the help of several tugs. She suffered no damage. Then on April 10, while

returning from a Mediterranean cruise with 300 passengers aboard, she grounded at Throne Knoll in Southampton Water. After seven tugs failed to pull her free, her passengers were ferried ashore. Finally, the ship was lightened by offloading fuel oil and ten tugs, along with her own powerful engines, managed to wrest her from the mudbank after she had been aground for 26 hours. Again damage was minimal and she was able to resume service with little delay.

At Southampton's Berth 108 the *Mauretania* continued to tug gently at her lines through the winter of 1934-35 while rumours spread as to her ultimate fate. There were reports that the famous liner would be sold abroad, reports that met with considerable objection from the public. In the end she was sold to Metal Industries Ltd of Glasgow for demolition. With that news came word that much of the liner's interior fittings would be sold at public auction before she sailed away on her final voyage to Scotland. There were takers aplenty when the sale opened on May 14 at the Southampton docks. Many people, for sentimental or business reasons, crowded the first class lounge to buy items from the ship, including the exquisite panelling, furniture, silverware, china and even the lifeboats. Several rooms were sold largely intact for reconstruction ashore, including the first class dining saloon, lounge and grand staircase. The panelling from these rooms was to have been used in a projected Hotel Mauretania in New York, a project that never got off the ground. But some of the panelling still exists in the dining room of a Bristol pub. No doubt other portions of the woodwork still grace private homes around the world.

On July 1 1935 the *Mauretania* lay at her pier with steam up ready for the final voyage, still majestic but looking rather forlorn. Her masts had been cut down to allow her to pass beneath the Forth Bridge and the white hull was grimy and streaked with rust. Thousands turned out to bid her farewell as she departed Southampton forever. In the crowd on the dock was Captain Arthur H. Rostron, her former commander who felt he had to say goodbye, but he would not go aboard. Likewise, her former chief engineer Andrew Cockburn would not visit her. Both men preferred to remember her as she had been. Her former staff captain A.T. Brown was on the bridge for the final voyage and there was a skeleton crew, a few special passengers and a host of news correspondents. The occasion offered the many reporters the opportunity to wax eloquent, as evidenced in this unidentified dispatch from H. de Winton Wigley aboard the liner: 'The blue peter runs

Opposite *To say that the upper decks of the* Mauretania *were cluttered would be an understatement. But there is no denying that this scene has a certain romance about it that cannot be equalled on today's passenger ships. This view was taken in August 1932* (photo by Walter Lord).

The Mauretania *was so well-loved that when it came time for her demise, it was a national event. The Southern Railway even placed a special train into service to carry people to the auction of her fittings (John Blake Collection).*

SOUTHERN RAILWAY

SALE BY AUCTION ON
THE "MAURETANIA"
of FURNISHINGS, PANELLING and APPOINTMENTS
at SOUTHAMPTON DOCKS.

SECURE A SOUVENIR OF YOUR VOYAGE.

CHILDREN UNDER 14 YEARS OF AGE, HALF-FARE.

PRIVATE VIEW —May 9th.
GENERAL VIEW—May 10th, 11th and 13th.
SALE DAYS   —May 14th to 17th inclusive, and 20th to 23rd
                                                inclusive.
Commencing 11.30 a.m. each day.

CHEAP RETURN TICKETS
from
LONDON
(Waterloo Station)

1st Class.	3rd Class.
s. d.	s. d.
20/-	13/3

Forward :	a.m.	a.m.	*Return :*	p.m.	p.m.
Waterloo .... dep.	8.30	9.30	Southampton West dep.	4.41	6.22
Southampton West arr.	10.29	11.31	Waterloo ... arr.	6.50	8.20

A special service of buses will run between Southampton West Station and the berth in Southampton Docks at which the " Mauretania " is accommodated, at a fare of 6d. each way.

Admission to Private View by Catalogue only, price 5/- each, and to General View and Sale Days, price 2/6d. each.   One Catalogue will admit one person only.

Catalogues obtainable from Hampton & Sons, Auctioneers, 20, St. James's Square, London, S.W.1, at the Offices of Cunard White-Star, Ltd., Southampton, or at the Enquiry Office, Waterloo Station.

REFRESHMENTS will be obtainable on the "MAURETANIA."

TICKETS OBTAINABLE IN ADVANCE AT STATIONS AND AGENCIES.

Waterloo Station, S.E.1.   H. A. WALKER,
                                                                                     General Manager.

C.X. 1068/ 10/30435   April 23433   Printed by M⸰Corquodale & Co. Ltd., London.

Her masts reduced to stumps, the Mauretania *nears Rosyth at the end of her final voyage in July 1935. In only a short time, she will have tied up at the breaker's yard and rung up 'Finished With Engines' for the last time* (Swan Hunter Group).

down from the *Mauretania*'s foremast. Her siren sounds a husky, broken farewell to the people standing on Southampton quay; men slip free the last mooring-rope of all. The final link with the world she has roved so long is broken and the *Mauretania* is sailing away to the port from which there is no return. From across the darkening Southampton water the deep, sudden voices of big ships lament her. The gap between us and the shore widens and this time there are no gay streamers to bridge it until the last moment. It is a final, irrevocable good-bye.' With that, she headed out to sea.

On her way to the breakers, she passed close to Tyneside where thousands lined the shore to see her one last time. Numerous vessels, deep-sea ships and coastal steamers alike, saluted her and exchanged messages with her master. On the night of July 3, just 12 hours before she would shut down her engines for the last time, she performed one last good deed. During heavy weather that evening, she rescued two young men whose motorboat had crashed into the liner's side as they manoeuvred close to get a look at the legendary record-breaker. They were pulled from the sea soaking wet and frightened but nevertheless safe.

Shortly after 6 am on July 4 the *Mauretania* reached her final resting place. 'The half gale whistling down the Firth of Forth caught her under the counter and blew her against the dock wall', reported the *Daily Telegraph*'s correspondent. 'She shuddered. It was a kind of death-throe. Then her engines were stopped. The old heart had beaten its last.' When she moved into her dock, a piper standing on the quay played the lament 'Flowers of the Forest'. Throughout the

scrapping process, officials of Metal Industries continued to be astonished at the excellent condition of her boilers, engines and other machinery. She may have been old-fashioned at the end, but her body and spirit remained robust throughout.

During the late 1930s the new *Queen Mary* was vying with the *Normandie* for the speed record of the North Atlantic. In order to provide valuable performance data for the *Queen Mary*, as well as to improve her own lot, the *Aquitania* in 1936 was fitted with new propellers by J. Stone and Company of Deptford. With them her speed could either be increased by 2½ knots with no additional fuel consumption, or there could be a yearly reduction in running costs of £10,000 if she ran at her previous top speed. The same type of screws were fitted to the *Queen Mary* and she later succeeded in taking the Blue Riband from the *Normandie*.

In 1939 the *Aquitania* reached the age of 25 and it was widely expected that when the new *Queen Elizabeth* appeared a year later, she would be retired. As it happened, war again intervened and when the formal declaration came on September 3 1939, the *Aquitania* was at sea en route for Southampton. She made one more commercial voyage before being requisitioned again as a troopship, the only Cunarder to serve in both wars. In November she began bringing Canadian troops over from Halifax and remained on this run into 1940. In March of that year she was sent south to be based at Sydney in order to transport troops from Australia to the Middle East. On more than one occasion she travelled in convoy with other famous transatlantic liners, including the two 'Queens', the second *Mauretania, Nieuw Amsterdam, Ile de France, Empress of Canada* and

The Aquitania *wore her varied paint schemes well. She is seen here in World War 2 troopship grey. Not bad looking for a 30-year-old liner known affectionately as 'Grannie'* (Stewart Bale Ltd).

Empress of Britain. These convoys were considered the most valuable liner fleets ever to put to sea and they sailed with only one heavy cruiser and two light cruisers as escorts.

Soon after the Pearl Harbor attack, the *Aquitania* stopped in Hawaii for refuelling and was chartered to carry American evacuees to the mainland. Loaded with women and children, the ensuing voyage was nothing if not harrowing. The trip to San Francisco which normally took seven days lasted a month. There were several other large liners in convoy with the *Aquitania,* notably the Matson Line's *Lurline.* There was considerable fog during the voyage and in one instance, the fog lifted long enough for the *Aquitania*'s officers to see the *Lurline* heading right for them. Only through a rapid exchange of whistle signals was a collision narrowly averted.

The *Aquitania* spent the war uneventfully travelling to the far corners of the globe, carrying thousands of troops. She completed her war service by repatriating British troops in 1945 and 1946. She was offered to the United States to assist in the planned assault on the Japanese mainland but was never needed. Throughout the war she had steamed over 526,000 miles without being attacked and carried nearly 400,000 men and women. She continued in government service until March 1948, operating between Southampton and Halifax, carrying Canadian servicemen and their English wives and children back to Canada. She was presented with a bronze plaque by the Canadian government for her wartime service and a service of thanksgiving for her safe return was held in Halifax's All Saints Cathedral. She had, to all intents and purposes, been adopted by Canada. In March 1948 the *Aquitania,* the ship that had been variously known as 'The Ship Beautiful', 'Aristocrat of the Atlantic', 'World's Wonder Ship', 'The Grand Old Lady' and 'Granny', was returned to her owners. Many thought that she was finished, but there was still work to be done. About this time it was proposed that she be used to carry emigrants to Australia, but that service never materialised, the *Aquitania* instead entering into an 'austerity service' between Southampton and Halifax to carry Canadian settlers and a limited number of regular passengers. She underwent a brief refit at Southampton and began the new service on May 25 1948. Two months later the junior officer who had fallen in love with the *Aquitania* in 1914 realised his dream; Harry Grattidge was appointed master of the venerable liner. Grattidge admitted the vessel was by this time a little old-fashioned, but 'it was my sneaking suspicion that her Carolean smoke room . . . was still the finest afloat. I hugged this command to me jealously, for there is nothing so fine as a dream that comes true and does not disappoint'.* Captain Grattidge commanded the *Aquitania* for three months in the waning years of her career.

* Grattidge, *Captain of the Queens,* p.203.

The original agreement with the Canadian government had the liner operating in the austerity service in 1948 only, but it proved so successful that she remained on the run throughout 1949 as well. By this time it seemed as if she would go on forever. However, late in 1949 Cunard announced that the *Aquitania* had finally come to the end of her long and distinguished career. During the final year of her service she carried more than 22,000 settlers to Canada. Plans were made for the liner to go out in style and there were numerous tributes in the press, over Halifax radio and in Liverpool where she had begun her life. It was hoped that she might make one final appearance in the Mersey but for various reasons this did not work out. Her final voyage commenced from Halifax on November 24 1949 and ended in Southampton on December 1. She was laid up and offered for sale the same month.

In February 1950 the old ship was purchased by the British Iron and Steel Corporation for scrapping. She was scheduled to depart for the Clyde on February 19 and the day before, a flag-lowering ceremony was held aboard at Southampton attended by Cunard officials, past crew members and government representatives. The ceremony ended on a touching note, with the famed bugle call 'Sunset'. The next day, with a crew of about 250, many of whom were newsmen and others interested in the ship, she sailed from the same berth from which the old *Mauretania* had left on her last voyage in 1935. The passage was like a funeral procession with ships of all nations saluting the demise of the great liner. From the *Queen Elizabeth* came the message, 'Passengers and crew who had the pleasure of sailing in the great ship *Aquitania* are thinking of her passing'. A Royal Navy oiler signalled 'Good-bye, old faithful' and a frigate summed up all the feelings by saying 'We are proud to have met you!' The final cable came from Cunard chairman F.A. Bates: 'I cannot let today pass without expressing my sadness at this final parting with the *Aquitania*. In peace and war, fair weather and foul, she has done her duty in a manner unsurpassed by any other of her sisters who have helped build up the Company's long history.'

The venerable liner sailed up into the Gareloch, the largest vessel to have done so up to that time, and was tied up at the breaker's yard near Faslane. With the final 'Finished with Engines' the *Aquitania* had logged better than three million miles and a passenger list of more than 1.2 million, and all under one house flag. The job of scrapping her lasted 22 months and it was not until November 1951 that the final section of her double bottom was hauled ashore and cut up. The process produced about 36,000 tons of scrap metal.

Happy memories of the *Mauretania* and *Aquitania* remain even though the ships have long since disappeared. But the *Lusitania* still exists in the form of a shattered wreck on the floor of the Atlantic, and her name is nearly always linked to tragedy despite many achievements in her eight years of service. The various theories surrounding her tragic end have flared anew in recent years with several books on the subject and several attempts to study the hulk on the sea floor. German authorities have continued to maintain that she was a naval auxiliary and as such was subject to attack. There have been suggestions that her manifests were doctored and that she carried nearly 10½ tons of explosives in her holds on that fatal voyage. Still other theories contend that other ammunition stores, not documented, were aboard the liner as well. Furthermore, there has long been speculation that key British officials secretly desired the liner attacked to draw the United States into the war and manipulated circumstances to make possible an attack on May 7 1915. All of this is pure speculation with very little evidence to support it, but it has made good copy in books and magazines over the past several decades and will probably continue to do so for a long while yet.

Despite the sensationalism surrounding the sinking of the *Lusitania,* the three giant Cunard four-stackers hold a significant place in modern maritime history and will be remembered for the records they established, not only in speed, but in faithful service. They will also continue to produce fond memories among those fortunate enough to have sailed in them.

4   White Star

The dawning of the 20th century found keen competition among the major North Atlantic steamship lines, not the least of which was the Oceanic Steam Navigation Company, better known as the White Star Line. This company, under the able direction of Thomas H. Ismay, in the latter part of the 19th century produced some of the most famous steamers ever seen in North Atlantic service. Innovation was an important part of the White Star Line strategy, beginning with the introduction of enclosed promenade decks, running fresh and salt water in passenger cabins and electric lighting. The turn of the century saw White Star operating three splendid steamers, the *Oceanic, Majestic* and *Teutonic*. All three were fine examples of late Victorian marine architecture and their accommodation was highly regarded among travellers. With the 17,274-ton *Oceanic* of 1899, the company opted for a vessel of great size and comfort rather than speed. As has already been stated, Norddeutscher Lloyd's *Kaiser Wilhelm der Grosse* was much faster and more record breakers were in the planning stages. Let the others go for high speed; White Star would woo its passengers by offering them the largest and steadiest ships in the world, combined with extreme comfort.

The first major step in the new White Star policy was the introduction of two 21,000-ton sister ships, the *Celtic* and *Cedric* which appeared in 1901 and 1903 respectively and were the first liners to exceed 20,000 tons gross. But their 16-knot speed and vast amount of cargo space placed them in the intermediate class and left the three

Opposite *The largest ships in the world on the stocks at Harland & Wolff's yard. The* Olympic *is nearing the time of launch, while the* Titanic's *hull takes shape at the left. The two ships occupied space normally given over to three building ways* (Harland & Wolff Ltd).

older steamers to handle the primary service to New York from Liverpool. The success of the new ships prompted two more of the same class, the *Baltic* and *Adriatic,* even bigger ships that rounded out the so-called White Star 'Big Four'. The biggest move, however, was yet to come.

American financier J. Pierpont Morgan, who had been a major force in the merger of many American railroad systems, decided that a similar amalgamation would work on the North Atlantic. In 1902 Morgan formed the International Mercantile Marine Company (IMM) which set out to gain control of just about every major operation on the North Atlantic, including Red Star, Dominion, Atlantic Transport, Leyland and the American Line. The biggest feather in Morgan's cap was to be the acquisition of White Star. His proposal was to pay shareholders ten times the amount of their stock value in 1900. Although the company would be American-owned under the new scheme, the ships would continue to fly the British flag, leaving intact the arrangement with the Admiralty for converting certain of them into auxiliary cruisers in time of war. Despite opposition from some members of the Ismay family and a few stockholders, the sale of White Star to the IMM was completed in December 1902. While a blow to British prestige, it nonetheless meant a steady flow of American dollars to the company, money that would be used to place the firm at the very forefront of North Atlantic shipping lines. By the time the IMM had finished buying up property and aligning itself with other lines, Cunard and the Compagnie Générale Transatlantique (French Line) were among the only major passenger lines to remain independent and even Cunard appeared ready to seek a compromise with the giant combine. As a result, White Star's future appeared extremely bright.

The British government of Arthur Balfour

found the prospect of losing control over both premier British lines too difficult to swallow. An agreement was made with Cunard, therefore, to finance the *Lusitania* and *Mauretania* with government money in return for a pledge to remain under British ownership. These two magnificent ships effectively took the wind out of White Star's sails by being not only the fastest, but by far the largest liners in the world. For all their elegance and Victorian charm, the *Oceanic*, *Teutonic* and *Majestic* just were not in the same class as the new Cunard greyhounds. Even though relegated temporarily to second place among North Atlantic companies, White Star was still easily one of the most prosperous and was already planning the coup that would return it to supremacy. With the *Lusitania* already in operation and the *Mauretania* about to enter service, J. Bruce Ismay, managing director of White Star, went one night in 1907 to the Belgrave Square home of Lord W.J. Pirrie, who was the genius behind the Harland & Wolff ship-yard in Belfast and had long been aligned with both Thomas and Bruce Ismay. When the IMM came along, Pirrie was one of the directors and later joined Bruce Ismay and Harold Sanderson as a partner in White Star. The philosophies of both Ismay and Pirrie were similar when it came to planning ships. Both were firm believers in the big ship concept, and following dinner that night,

The Laurentic *was one of a pair of 14,000-ton steamers built for the White Star Line's Canadian service. She and her sister* Megantic *were utilised in a test for the* Olympic *and* Titanic. *To help determine the wisdom of installing power plants with both turbines and reciprocating engines in the latter pair, that form of propulsion was utilised in the* Laurentic *while reciprocating engines were the sole means of power in the* Megantic. *The* Laurentic, *as hoped, was more economic* (Stewart Bale Ltd).

they sat down to discuss White Star's answer to the new Cunarders. To say that the scheme was grandiose would be an understatement, for the vessels envisioned by the two would easily eclipse the *Mauretania*, *Lusitania* and anything then in operation by the Germans.

From the start, it was planned to build superliners of more than 45,000 tons, the proposal being for a trio of ships nearly 900 feet in length, with the most palatial of accommodation. Initially the plans called for three-stackers with three or four masts, but this was later altered to four funnels and two masts for better balance of design. The fourth funnel was a dummy. Ismay and Pirrie determined they would build not only the largest and most comfortable liners ever, but the safest as well. White Star would operate them from Southampton to New York, utilising the Hampshire port for the primary service and leaving the 'Big Four' on the Liverpool run. Under the new plan, the *Majestic* and *Teutonic* would be withdrawn, with the first of the new liners, the *Olympic* and *Titanic* operating in conjunction with the *Oceanic* until the third vessel of the class could enter service. The plans were completed early in 1908 and White Star set about financing the work by issuing a large number of shares which were quickly bought up. There was, of course, considerable money being invested by the IMM, which supported the ships as the most brilliant jewels in its crown.

As it evolved, the plan was rather traditional but on a grand scale, with the typical three-island type of profile. The vessels were to be 882.5 feet in overall length and 92 feet in beam with space for 2,584 passengers in three classes. Safety was foremost in the minds of the designers and, as a result, the vessels were to be equipped with 15 watertight bulkheads with electrically operated watertight doors that could be closed either at the scene or from the bridge. There was also to be a double bottom extending the full length of the hull and rising above the curve of the bilge. These safety features were designed so that any two main compartments could be flooded without adversely affecting the vessels' buoyancy. In effect, by the standards of the time, the ships were considered unsinkable.

Although speed was not a determining factor in the *Olympic* and *Titanic*, economy was and it was for this reason that a relatively new type of propulsion system was utilised in the giants. Like the machinery that went into the *Lusitania* and *Mauretania*, it was tested in a pair of earlier sister ships. The 14,000-ton *Megantic* and *Laurentic* were being built by Harland & Wolff for White

Star's Canadian service and it was decided to equip the *Megantic* with quadruple expansion engines of conventional style driving twin screws. Her almost-identical sister was completed with triple screws and triple expansion engines as well as a low pressure turbine. It was a plan strongly advocated by the Belfast yard and one that would be utilised in a good many well known steamers built there. Under the scheme, the reciprocating engines would drive the outboard screws with the turbine driving the centre shaft using steam exhausted from the conventional engines. The performance of the Canadian steamers was studied very closely by shipyard engineers and it was determined that not only was it a smooth running system but that the *Laurentic* proved more economical and slightly faster as well. The go-ahead was given to install the new propulsion system in the giant liners, the only ones of the period to be fitted with triple screws. The designed speed of the new White Star behemoths was 21 knots and in order to provide steam to meet this requirement, a vast array of boilers, 29 in all, was arranged in six separate boiler rooms. There were 24 double-ended boilers

Right *It is difficult to conceive of the* Titanic's *huge reciprocating engines, boilers and other machinery tearing loose and crashing through the ship as she stood on end in the Atlantic. Here is one of the reciprocating engines* (Harland & Wolff Ltd).

Below *Shipyard workers put the finishing touches to the second class promenade on the* Olympic's *boat deck. Much paintwork remains to be done, although one funnel is already in buff and black* (Harland & Wolff Ltd).

Above *Shipyard workers fit the propeller shafts of the* Titanic. *This photograph also shows the rudder. These men laboured long and hard on the* Titanic *and her sister ship and they were undoubtedly proud of their work* (Harland & Wolff Ltd).

Below *Two giants of their day inspect the hull of the* Olympic *prior to launch at Belfast. At left is Lord Pirrie, chairman of Harland & Wolff, and J. Bruce Ismay, managing director of the White Star Line. The White Star trio was the brainchild of these two men* (Harland & Wolff Ltd).

and five single-ended ones, five per room except in the case of Number One Boiler Room, which contained four. The engines and boilers took up 520 feet of the ship's length.

Keel-laying ceremonies for the first of the pair, the *Olympic,* took place on December 16 1908, the *Titanic* following on March 31 1909 while the third vessel was scheduled to be laid down as soon as the *Olympic* was clear of the berth. The building of these vessels made it necessary for Harland & Wolff to use two huge building berths side by side in a space normally utilised by three. In addition an elaborate system of overhead gantries and cranes was built to facilitate construction and a specially laid-out boiler shop was also provided. While work proceeded at Belfast, preparations had to be made in other parts of the world. At Southampton it was necessary to rebuild the docks to accommodate the big ships. Channels also had to be deepened. White Star had moved the terminal for its express steamers from Liverpool to Southampton in 1907. The reasoning was plain: travellers heading for Europe desired to be closer to Paris which was rapidly becoming the hub of activity in Western Europe. By using Southampton, the White Star liners could readily touch the French port of Cherbourg, within easy reach of Paris while there was speedy communication between London and the Hampshire port.

Meanwhile, in the United States, a considerable flap developed over providing adequate wharfage at New York. The harbour authorities baulked at the prospect of extending the length of the Hudson River piers an additional 100 feet to handle the giant ships, the idea being to discourage the ever increasing size of transatlantic liners. If New York would do nothing, authorities in Boston would. There was also a proposal to erect a large passenger terminal at Montauk Point on Long Island that would greatly facilitate arrivals and departures. With such pressure on them, the New York authorities finally gave in and agreed to the larger piers. The inevitable simply could not be ignored.

Even though she was the largest ship in the world, the *Olympic* was launched without a formal naming ceremony on October 20 1910. The event was proclaimed by a single rocket announcing the moment of launch. Slowly, the giant white-painted hull, with signal flags spelling 'Success' across the bow, began to move and within little more than a minute, the 27,000-ton hull was waterborne. A host of dignitaries, including the Lord Lieutenant of Ireland and his wife, the Countess of Aberdeen and the Lord

Continued from page 113.

accommodation was described as 'of a very superior character' and far better than any other third class space then available.

The *Olympic* was completed near the end of March 1911 and went into dry dock early in April for cleaning and painting. Trials began on May 2 and lasted until the end of the month, with the liner being opened to public inspection before going to sea on her final trials. Thousands paid a nominal fee to troop aboard and see at first hand the splendours of the world's largest liner, the proceeds going to Belfast hospitals. The *Olympic* did well on her trials, making 21¾ knots, much to the satisfaction of her builders.

May 31 1911 was a momentous day in Belfast. Not only was this the day the *Olympic* was handed over to her new owners, it was also the day the *Titanic* was launched. Thousands packed the yards of Harland & Wolff to witness the occasion. J. Pierpont Morgan himself had travelled to Belfast with J. Bruce Ismay and a large contingent of IMM officials. Shortly after noon, the black-painted hull of the *Titanic* slid effortlessly into the water. With the *Olympic* standing nearby, it must have been indeed thrilling to see the two largest ships in the world side by side. As the *Titanic* was

Left *Honour and Glory Crowning Time look down on the* Olympic's *main staircase. The style was Early English with a touch of Louis XIV evident in the iron scrollwork. The whole affair was lighted by a large overhead dome.*

Below *The* Titanic *slides down the ways at Belfast on May 31 1911. Not too far away, the* Olympic *was getting up steam for a voyage to Southampton and for a short time, the two largest liners in the world lay near each other in Belfast waters* (Harland & Wolff Ltd).

This is a portion of the reception room, located just forward of the Olympic's first class dining saloon. It is an adaptation of Jacobean English, although the wicker furniture is certainly not of that period.

Nestled behind the second funnel on the promenade deck was the Olympic's reading and writing room. It adjoined the first class lounge and was noted for its white panelling and large windows overlooking the sea. The style was late Georgian.

The tables in the Olympic's first class dining saloon are set for dinner. At the time it was the largest room afloat, extending the ship's full width and 114 ft along her length. Jacobean in style, it utilised details of several famous English houses of the period.

The finishing touches have not yet been added to the Olympic's restaurant, located aft on the bridge deck. Small tables have been provided for intimate dinner parties. Light brown French walnut was used for the panelling (Harland & Wolff Ltd).

This photograph provides some interesting details of a first class stateroom aboard the Olympic finished in the Louis XVI style. Extra wide beds and electric heaters were features of these rooms (Harland & Wolff Ltd).

Unquestionably over-ornate by present-day standards, the first class lounge of the Olympic was a favourite of passengers. This fine view provides details of the woodwork, carpeting, furniture and the fireplace (Byron Collection, Museum of the City of New York).

White Star

Right *The* Olympic's *en suite staterooms were described as 'unparalleled' in their luxury. This is a portion of the sitting room of a parlour suite. These rooms were outfitted in various ways, this one in the Adam style.*

Centre right *Contemporary accounts described the first class smoking room on the* Olympic *as the 'finest apartment of its kind on the ocean'. It was certainly one of the most magnificent rooms on the vessel. The painted windows added a colourful touch.*

Bottom right *Here is the famed Turkish Bath of the* Olympic. *This room was said to impart the atmosphere of the Middle East and it is easy to see why. The portholes were concealed by an elaborately carved Cairo curtain and the walls were tiled in large panels of blue and green.*

Mayor of Belfast, were on hand to witness the occasion. The *Olympic* was subsequently moved to the deep water fitting-out dock where the next seven months were spent installing the machinery, accommodation and otherwise completing the ship.

The accommodation on the *Olympic* was in a class by itself. It included the largest room afloat in the first class dining saloon as well as a host of other splendid public rooms. There were also such attractions as the Turkish baths, racquet court, gymnasium and a large swimming pool. As was customary in those days, a variety of styles was utilised in the decoration of the public rooms. The first class dining saloon was Jacobean English and featured details adopted from such great English houses as Hatfield and Haddon Hall. Louis XVI was the period chosen for the restaurant, Louis XV style being utilised in the first class lounge which featured many details copied from the palace of Versailles. Other public rooms were fitted in Georgian style, particularly the reading and writing room and the smoking room. Painted glasswork, resembling stained glass, was featured throughout the *Olympic*'s first class accommodation and added to the almost royal atmosphere aboard this huge liner. As for the first class staterooms, they were rather elaborately laid out to include a large number of *en suite* and so-called special rooms. A variety of styles was also called for here, ranging from Italian Renaissance through Old Dutch to Louis XV. There were a hundred single-berth cabins in first class, which was somewhat unusual for the period. Most of the midships portion of the vessel was devoted to first class, second class being situated slightly aft of amidships and third class at the extreme ends of the ship. Second class fared rather well and it was said at the time that 'such sumptuous apartments' in second class would have been difficult to conceive. Third class

Continued on page 116.

towed off to the fitting-out berth, the assembled guests boarded the *Olympic* for Liverpool, where she was again opened to the public for inspection. It was then on to Southampton for the first time, where the *Olympic* received an enthusiastic welcome.

Wednesday, June 14 was a brilliant day in Southampton. The *Olympic* lay alongside her berth, fully stored and ready to depart. There had been some concern that the maiden voyage might have to be postponed because of a coal-passers' strike, but that fear was allayed when strike-breakers appeared to bunker the liner. Even so, she sailed with five boilers cold because of the shortage of coal. Although designed to carry 2,435 passengers, the *Olympic* was only half full for the voyage which began shortly after noon as a bevy of tugs crowded about her and eased her from the pier. Unaccustomed as they were to handling such a vast ship, more than an hour was required to move the *Olympic* into the stream and point her bow down Southampton Water. Large crowds that had waited throughout the morning for this momentous occasion looked on from the shore as the new leviathan gingerly threaded her way. Lying nearby were Red Star's *Kroonland* and the American Line's *New York* which, according to a contemporary account, were 'dwarfed into bewildering insignificance' alongside the *Olympic*. Although the new liner's maiden voyage was an historic event, it was vastly overshadowed by the news accompanying the impending corona-tion of King George V on June 22. Probably for this reason, little coverage was accorded the maiden voyage until the ship neared New York.

The voyage from Southampton took two hours short of seven days to complete, which was pretty much what White Star had expected. The *Olympic* encountered some rough weather on the way over, but proved herself a good sea boat. Captain Edward J. Smith cabled that all was going smoothly and that the ship had lost a few hours because of fog on Sunday, but was easily able to make up the lost time. There was, however, a bit of a cloud hanging over the anticipated gala arrival in New York. Harbour tug crews were talking about a strike, something that could effectively throw a damper on the maiden arrival since the docking of the *Olympic* would be a challenge under the best of conditions, and almost impossible without tugs. In any event, White Star officials pledged to go ahead with the planned arrival on Wednesday morning, June 21.

Fortunately for all involved, the strike failed to materialise and the *Olympic* dropped anchor at Quarantine shortly before 7 am. Already a sizeable fleet of tugs and pleasure craft had gathered to escort her on her triumphal entry into New York harbour. 'She looked to be a genuine sea monster' as she lay off Staten Island, wrote a reporter who witnessed the scene. The trip up the Hudson River to Pier 59 was uneventful and, when the ship arrived off the newly extended pier, 12 tugs were in attendance. The docking was described as a delicate task that took the better part of an hour to complete. One of the biggest problems was in trying to line up the vessel's side ports with the pier gangways. It was a tight fit to say the least.

A brand-new Olympic *swings at anchor preparatory to her maiden voyage on June 14 1911. It was not a particularly smooth crossing but it did serve to prove that she was a good sea boat* (Stewart Bale Ltd).

Passengers on the maiden voyage had nothing but praise for the new *Olympic* and were especially enthusiastic about the tremendous amount of space on board. One commented that it took the better part of the voyage to find one's way around. There was very little vibration, according to the passengers, but some did complain about the thud from the wing propellers which could be felt in the after end of the first class dining saloon. Among the happy first class passengers was J. Bruce Ismay. He was ecstatic about his new ship and wrote to the Liverpool office of the White Star Line at length about the trip. 'Everything on board the ship worked most satisfactorily,' he wrote, 'and the passengers were loud in their praises of the accommodation and table. The machinery worked excellently and there was no hitch of any kind in connection with same.'* Ismay had spent most of the voyage studying details of the liner and there were many notes accompanying his letter home, notes intended to improve the *Olympic* and make the *Titanic* an even better vessel.

Once the festivities of the maiden voyage were over, the *Olympic* settled into the mail service with the *Oceanic* and *Majestic*. Only three months later the new liner ran into trouble. September 20 1911 found her outward bound from Southampton with 1,313 passengers aboard. The weather was good and everything was going according to plan as she steamed down Southampton Water towards the Spithead Channel. At the same time the

* Wilton J. Oldham, *The Ismay Line* (*The Journal of Commerce*: Liverpool, 1961), p.172.

cruiser *Hawke* was proceeding down the Solent headed for the same location. The two saw each other with plenty of time to spare and, although arriving near the Bramble Bank at about the same time, they should have passed without difficulty. Yet for no apparent reason, the 7,350-ton *Hawke* crashed into the starboard side of the liner about 80 feet from the stern, tearing a hole 40 feet long in the hull. The bow of the *Hawke* was badly damaged and there was some fear that she might sink, but the *Olympic* was not nearly as severely damaged. Both ships stopped and closed their watertight doors but abandonment was unnecessary. Within a short time the *Olympic* moved on to Osborne Bay where she dropped anchor while the damage was surveyed. Later she went to Cowes, where most of her passengers were ferried ashore. The next day the liner returned to Southampton. The *Hawke* meanwhile had proceeded safely into Portsmouth. The potential for real disaster existed since the *Hawke*'s bow had torn into several second class staterooms. Fortunately all the occupants were in the dining saloon having lunch at the time and no one was injured.

Background photograph *The mood in New York harbour was festive as the* Olympic *arrived on her maiden voyage on June 21 1911. A variety of ships stood by to escort the world's largest liner to her berth. The ship is seen here at quarantine* (Library of Congress).

Inset photograph *A bevy of tugs manoeuvres the* Olympic *into position off Pier 59 at the end of her maiden voyage. It was not the easiest of tasks, primarily because the pilot and tugs were not used to handling a ship of such vast proportions* (Library of Congress).

Above *A controversial collision involving the* Olympic *and HMS* Hawke *occured on September 20 1911 near Spithead. The cruiser rammed the liner on the starboard side near the stern. This is an interior view of part of the damage after a temporary wooden patch had been affixed* (Harland & Wolff Ltd).

Below *Very few pictures exist of both the* Titanic *and* Olympic *together. This one was taken in 1911 when the* Olympic *returned to Belfast for repairs after colliding with the* Hawke. *Before her promenade deck forward was enclosed, it was quite difficult to distinguish the* Titanic *(left) from her sister ship. Note, however, that the second class promenade aft on 'B' Deck was unenclosed on the* Olympic. *On the* Titanic *the area was mostly enclosed to accommodate the restaurant on the port side and the Café Parisien on the starboard* (Harland & Wolff Ltd).

The *Olympic* was sent back to the Harland & Wolff yard at Belfast for repairs that lasted about six weeks. While this was going on, so was some heated haggling over just how the collision occurred and who was at fault. Suits and countersuits were filed in the Admiralty Court. The testimony was conflicting and for quite some time it appeared most of it would go in the *Olympic's* favour. But in the end the court fixed the blame for the collision solely on the liner, based primarily on evidence which suggested that the *Hawke* was drawn towards the *Olympic* because of the suction generated by her tremendous hull. The verdict subsequently went to the Court of Appeal and House of Lords but to no avail. The White Star Line stood behind Captain Smith and the liner's pilot George W. Bowyer through the whole affair and some months later expressed its continued confidence in its commodore by awarding Smith command of the new *Titanic*.

Even after the *Olympic* had returned to service from her repairs, there was plenty of White Star Line activity in the Belfast yard. Work on the *Titanic* was proceeding at a rapid pace and there was every reason to believe she would sail on her maiden voyage in April 1912. At the same time, the third ship in this mammoth trio was about to begin taking shape. The keel of this vessel, Yard Number 433, was laid on November 30 1911, but there has long been some controversy over what name she was to carry, and it was widely reported after the loss of the *Titanic* that she would be named *Gigantic*. It seems clear, however, that White Star had no thought whatsoever of using this name, and that no name had been seriously considered when her keel was laid. She was to be built to the same plans as the other two and was scheduled to enter service in 1914.

As a result of those meticulous notes made by Bruce Ismay on the *Olympic's* maiden voyage and because of the many comments made by passen-

gers on that liner, several changes were made in the appearance and accommodation of the *Titanic*. The most obvious was the enclosing of the forward end of the promenade deck with sliding glass windows to protect passengers from ocean spray. Additional first class cabins were added on the promenade deck and 'B' deck, the deckhouses on the latter level being extended out to the side of the ship. Here were also added two private promenades adjacent to the parlour suites. A noteworthy feature of the *Titanic* was the Café Parisien, a verandah-type room off the restaurant decorated in French style with climbing ivy, wicker furniture and tables and chairs arranged in a Continental style. Use of the reception room adjoining the first class dining saloon had far exceeded expectations on the *Olympic*, so White Star decided to incorporate this feature into the *Titanic*'s restaurant as well. It was a large and spacious room and was finished in Georgian style. More space was provided for diners in the first class dining saloon, the capacity being increased to more than 500 passengers at a single sitting. The number of staterooms was also increased to other decks throughout the ship, so that in the end, her passenger capacity was slightly increased to 2,566. The *Titanic*'s gross tonnage, by virtue of the alterations, was 46,329, compared to her sister's 45,324, giving her the title of world's largest liner.

Work on the *Titanic* was finally completed in March 1912 and she was opened for an inspection by the press on March 30. As expected by the White Star Line, everyone was suitably impressed and all was made ready for the liner's sea trials. Monday April 1 was the date fixed for these but high winds outside Belfast harbour made it necessary to postpone them for 24 hours. Shortly after 6 am on April 2, the *Titanic* sailed away from her berth for the first time and headed into Belfast Lough. After her compasses were adjusted, she

Top right *The* Titanic's *gymnasium was located on the boat deck and it was here that John Jacob Astor sliced open a lifebelt to show his wife what was inside. Astor was lost in the sinking of the* Titanic (Harland & Wolff Ltd).

Centre right *Here is a typical first class stateroom on the* Titanic's *'B' Deck. Many passengers had already climbed beneath the warm blankets of big beds such as these when stewards came knocking to tell them to go on deck with their lifebelts* (Harland & Wolff Ltd).

Right *Several alterations were made to the* Titanic *from lessons learned from her sister. One of these alterations was the Café Parisien on 'B' Deck, adjacent to the restaurant. Utilising wicker furniture and climbing plants, it gave the impression of an open-air verandah* (Harland & Wolff Ltd).

Escorted by a small fleet of tugs, the Titanic *steams out of Belfast for her trials on April 2 1912. The liner moved swiftly and easily through the trials and headed on to Southampton for the start of her maiden voyage* (Steamship Historical Society of America).

set her course for the Isle of Man and headed out on her speed trials. As with the *Olympic,* everything worked to perfection and by 6 o'clock that evening, the liner was back in Belfast only to put to sea again later that night bound for Southampton. It was midnight on April 3 when she steamed into the Ocean Dock and tied up practically unnoticed among the bustle of the busy port. A week remained until the start of the maiden voyage but there was still plenty to do. The Board of Trade inspectors boarded the *Titanic* to look over the safety equipment. As if by premonition, they were unusually thorough, causing Second Officer Charles H. Lightoller to comment that the chief inspector would accept no one's word on even the slightest detail: he must see for himself.

Although the largest liner in the world, news of the *Titanic's* maiden voyage was buried under news of the coal strike then going on in England. There was some concern that this would prevent the ship's bunkers from being filled and perhaps result in a delay in the maiden voyage. To compensate, White Star scrounged up an adequate supply of coal from a variety of sources. The *Olympic* brought over a large amount of American coal, even carrying some of it in her public rooms. The White Star *Oceanic* and the American Line *New York,* both in Southampton as the *Titanic* prepared to sail, provided coal from their bunkers. In an effort to conserve as much as possible, some of the coal was not properly watered down in the *Titanic's* bunkers and a fire broke out that occupied the crew for the duration of that ill-fated maiden voyage.

Finally, all was in readiness. Wednesday April 10 dawned clear but cool. A total of 1,316 passengers was booked for the trip, only about half the ship's capacity, and it was a glittering passenger list, comprising the cream of American and British society. The first class roster included such luminaries as John Jacob Astor, Benjamin Guggenheim, John B. Thayer of the Pennsylvania Railroad, J. Bruce Ismay and a host of others. Some equally famous names were to have been aboard but had to cancel out, among them J. Pierpont Morgan himself and Lord Pirrie. Even the cargo was glamorous and included a priceless jewelled copy of *The Rubaiyat of Omar Khayyam* and the new French Renault car of William E. Carter.

A few minutes before noon, the *Titanic's* whistle roared its heart-stopping farewell, the gangways were withdrawn, the hawsers dropped and the giant vessel slowly began to move away from her dock. A small armada of tugs pulled her into the stream and slowly her huge engines began to turn. As the *Titanic* headed away from the Ocean Dock, she had a near brush with disaster. Her bulk was so enormous and she dragged so much water along with her that as she passed the *New York* and *Oceanic* docked side by side at Berth No 38 she literally sucked the American liner away from her moorings. A collision seemed inevitable as the *New York's* stern swung menacingly toward the port side of the *Titanic.* It looked as if the 10,499-ton liner would hit the new ship abreast of the fourth funnel. She would have, had not Captain Smith cut his engines and allowed the tug *Vulcan,* which had just let go from

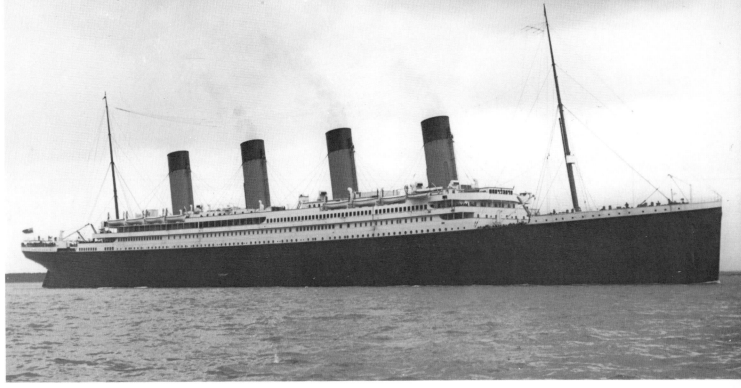

If any photograph can be singled out as the photograph of the Titanic, *this is it. The big liner has departed Southampton and is headed for her first stop at Cherbourg* (Beken & Sons, Cowes).

the *Titanic*, to get a line on the *New York*. As the American Line vessel was towed back to her mooring, the *Titanic* slowly got under way again and for a moment it looked as if there would be a repeat performance as the *Oceanic* strained at her lines. Fortunately her hawsers held as the new liner passed safely down Southampton Water bound for the Solent.

The trip across the Channel was uneventful except for the revelation by members of the lookout crew that the ship carried no binoculars. First Officer William M. Murdoch made a note to pick some up when they reached New York. One wonders whether the events five nights later in mid-Atlantic would have turned out any differently had the lookouts been provided with glasses. At dusk, the *Titanic* dropped anchor in Cherbourg harbour to take on additional passengers and mail before departing about 8 pm for Queenstown. She stopped off the Irish port shortly before noon the next day to take on her final passengers, most of whom were emigrants headed for a new life in America. After two hours, the liner weighed anchor for the last time and pointed her bow towards the open sea. After passing Fastnet Light, the *Titanic* gradually worked up to top speed and quickly left land astern. Her passengers settled down into the routine of shipboard life, revelling in the privilege of making the maiden voyage on the largest ship in the world.

Sunday April 14 was a beautiful day, although a bit on the cool side, and the *Titanic* was cutting easily through the North Atlantic, her maiden voyage more than half over. It had been an uneventful trip so far and the new ship was performing beautifully. Thomas Andrews, managing

director of Harland & Wolff, who was making the crossing to help iron out any kinks that might arise, was delighted. The ship was solid as a rock and apparently did not suffer from the vibration problems inherent in other large ships of the day. In fact, the only problems confronting Andrews had to do with coat hooks in cabins, the galley hot press and the decoration in the Café Parisien. Captain Smith and Bruce Ismay were equally pleased. The only possible cause for concern was the reports being received from other ships of ice lying ahead of the *Titanic*. But if the captain was overly worried he did not show it: the weather was clear and the lookouts were keeping a sharp eye out for ice. Even as darkness closed in, he had no plans to reduce the giant ship's speed. The *Titanic* continued to charge across the calm Atlantic at 22½ knots.

All evening long, the two wireless operators were inundated with passengers' private messages and it was no doubt for this reason that they neglected to pass on to the bridge a message from the Atlantic Transport Liner *Mesaba* giving explicit details of the icefield ahead of the White Star liner and telling of heavy pack ice and several large icebergs. It also told exactly where to expect it. But because of the novelty of wireless and because the ship was within range of the station at Cape Race, the *Mesaba*'s message was consigned to the spike until the flood of private messages could be finished. Outside the temperature was dropping rapidly and was down to freezing by 10 pm. But inside the ship, all was cosy and pleasant and there was not the slightest hint of concern among either passengers or crew. Another message telling of ice came in around 11 pm from

The final stop of her maiden voyage. The Titanic *lies at anchor off Queenstown on April 11 1912. Within a few hours the liner would turn her bow toward the open sea and leave Ireland behind forever* (National Maritime Museum).

the Leyland Liner *Californian*, stopped not far away at the edge of the huge icefield. Chief wireless operator John G. Philips ignored the message, asking the *Californian* to keep out so he could continue with his messages for Cape Race.

Up on the bridge, First Officer Murdoch quietly paced back and forth, peering into the blackness ahead. The sky was brilliant with stars but there was no moon. Up in the crow's nest on the foremast, lookouts Frederick Fleet and Reginald Lee surveyed the great expanse of black sea spread out before them. Both men bundled up, trying to keep warm against the blast of cold air hitting them as the *Titanic* forged ahead.

Then Fleet saw something. He strained his eyes against the darkness and then banged the crow's nest bell, at the same time picking up the telephone to the bridge.

'Iceberg right ahead!' he reported.

On the bridge Murdoch ordered the wheel hard to starboard (which meant that the ship's bow would swing to port), rang Full Speed Astern on the engine room telegraph and closed the water-tight doors. Then he waited. The berg now filled the wheelhouse windows and was almost on top of the ship. Then, ever so slowly, the bow began swinging to port as the *Titanic*, her two outboard screws thrashing full speed astern,* tried to dodge the berg. It looked as if she might make it, but the mountain of ice was too close. It slid by along the starboard side, dumping tons of ice on the forward decks, while at the same time catching the liner's hull well below the waterline. The razor-sharp ice ripped open the *Titanic*'s plates all the way from the forepeak to Boiler Room Number 5. It was just about 11.40 pm on Sunday April 14 1912.

Slowly the big liner drew to a stop. All over the ship people were murmuring, wondering why.

* The turbine did not operate in reverse, meaning the centre shaft sat useless during this manoeuvre.

On the bridge the answer was readily evident as Thomas Andrews listened to damage reports and studied the ship's plans. Water was pouring in below decks and there was nothing anyone could do about it. There was no way, Andrews explained, that the *Titanic* could stay afloat with that kind of damage. Considering the rapid rate at which the sea was surging in, he estimated the ship could only stay afloat about an hour and a half. Immediately, Captain Smith mustered his officers and ordered them to fill the lifeboats and lower away, knowing full well there was room for only about 1,178 persons in the boats. More than 2,200 persons were aboard.

A few minutes after midnight, wireless operator Phillips tapped out the first distress signals and at first the replies were encouraging. Steamers like the *Frankfort, Mount Temple, Virginian, Birma* and *Olympic* all were within range of the sinking liner's wireless. But it was the Cunard Liner *Carpathia* that offered the most hope: she was only 58 miles away and making fast for the *Titanic*. But her captain estimated it would take four hours to get there. The big question was, would the *Titanic* last that long?

Soon after, the first of the boats began to leave the ship, but they were lowered away more empty than full for the simple reason that the women and children refused to go. After all, the *Titanic* was still steady and the comfort of her warm interior was certainly preferable to a tiny boat on the cold sea. Then there were those who could see the lights of a steamer in the distance, no more than eight or ten miles away, some estimated. Considering the endless stream of signals emanating from the Marconi office, it seemed a foregone conclusion among everyone that she would soon respond to the *Titanic*'s plight. To dramatise further the need for aid, the stricken White Star liner began firing rockets and morsing the nearby ship, but to no avail. She sat out there, apparently oblivious to the tragedy in the making.

The controversy that erupted over this incident continues to generate heated debate even to this day.

Those who did choose to take to the boats were greeted by a disconcerting sight as the boats pulled away from the *Titanic*. She was still on an even keel, but her bow was low in the water and her screws were visible above the surface at the stern. Many of the passengers still on board were beginning to wish they had gone with the small armada of lifeboats that was beginning to collect several hundred yards away from the still brightly lit liner.

Lower and lower sank the great ship until, at 1.28 am, Phillips radioed to the *Carpathia* to hurry, that the engine room was flooded. By this time, there was a great crush for the remaining boats and the ship's officers were forced to form human rings around each boat to let only the women and children through. The tilt of the deck had increased markedly and those left behind found it difficult to stand. Finally, at 2.05 am, the last lifeboat, a collapsible, pulled away from the liner, leaving more than 1,500 people behind.

The *Titanic*'s bow was far below the surface and her stern was rapidly rising high out of the water. Amazingly, all the lights still burned brightly, casting an eerie glow on the sea. In the boats, they gazed in horror as the giant ship's stern swung higher and higher. Then, seemingly all at once, everything moveable on board broke loose and slid toward the bow. The enormous engines and boilers tore free from their mountings, the lights went out, the forward funnel ripped free and toppled into the sea. The *Titanic*, half her bulk beneath the water, stood straight on end, remained there for a brief time and then slid quietly and cleanly from sight. It was 2.20 am, Monday, April 15. When the *Carpathia* arrived on the scene a little more than an hour later, she picked up 705 half-frozen persons, survivors of one of the most appalling and mystifying marine disasters in history.

Many questions remained to be answered. First was the question of lifeboat capacity which was dictated by antiquated Board of Trade regulations which based the boat capacity on the vessel's tonnage, not on how many passengers she carried. This was a matter which would be quickly rectified as would the question of steamer tracks during the ice season. From henceforth, transatlantic liners used a route more to the south, and in 1913 the International Ice Patrol was formed to keep track of iceberg movements. Then there was the question of manoeuvrability. Had the *Titanic* continued on her course and just reversed her

Above *This may very well be the iceberg that sank the* Titanic. *It was photographed not too far from the scene of the sinking because hints of paint along its base indicated a recent collision with a ship.*

Below *The Cunard Liner* Carpathia *was plodding along en route from New York to the Mediterranean when she picked up the* Titanic's *distress signal. All 705 survivors were rescued by the little Cunarder.*

Her four funnels marching in stately procession along the boat deck, the Olympic *gives the impression of being at least a mile long! Here, at New York, we see the many lifeboats and collapsibles added in 1913.*

mystery steamer was the *Californian.* Her wireless shack utilised only one operator and was shut down for the night and she failed to hear any distress signals. But her officers contended, while admitting they *did* see rockets that night, that she was 20 miles away in heavy ice, too far away to be of any help. Some students of the disaster believe there was a ship, or ships, between the *Titanic* and the *Californian.* One that may have been in the vicinity was the Norwegian sealer *Samson* which reportedly saw lights and rockets that night. This is a story which has been 'making the rounds' for many years, but it just does not seem to hold up for there is other information to suggest that the *Samson* was, at noon on that very day, off the North Carolina coast—more than 1,000 miles away! But regardless of how many ships there may have been in the vicinity at the time, the fact remains that the *Californian* did indeed observe rockets and did not investigate. The reason will never be known, but the incident did prompt the staffing of wireless posts on a 24-hour basis to ensure that never again would two ships lie so close together with one not knowing that a disaster was occurring on the other.

Repercussions from the *Titanic* disaster were widespread. Ships carried extra lookouts, rows and rows of lifeboats suddenly materialised on decks and floats and rafts were everywhere. Especially hard hit was the White Star Line. On April 24 1912 the *Olympic* was preparing to depart Southampton on her first voyage since the loss of the *Titanic.* Already the company was planning drastic alterations to the *Olympic* to prevent a recurrence of the accident and had installed 24 additional collapsible lifeboats as a temporary measure until the liner could be despatched to a shipyard. But shortly before she was due to sail, the ship's entire complement of firemen, greasers and trimmers walked ashore, refusing to sail. They complained that the collapsibles were old and unseaworthy and they would not return aboard until wooden boats were substituted for the canvas collapsibles. But the company maintained the boats were adequate and sailed the *Olympic* to an anchorage off Spithead where the boats were tested and where some *did* prove unseaworthy. Squabbles involving union and non-union seamen ensued and the *Olympic*'s voyage was first postponed until April 25 and then until April 26. Finally the voyage was cancelled altogether and the *Olympic* was kept in port until May 15 by which time better boats were placed aboard.

At the end of the 1912 summer season, the *Olympic* returned to Harland & Wolff's Belfast

engines, she probably would have crashed head-on into the berg and probably would have survived. Or had she continued full speed ahead and turned to port at the same time, she may very well have missed it completely. But the combination of the turn and reversing of the engines (with the loss of power and manoeuvrability from the centre shaft) conspired to place the ship exactly in the wrong place at the wrong time.

But the biggest question, and one which will probably remain forever unanswered, is why did the ship lying only a few miles away fail to respond to the *Titanic*'s calls for help? The inquiries into the disaster concluded that the yards for major reconstruction as a direct result of the *Titanic* disaster. She was there for six months, being gutted in many respects and rebuilt so that she would be about the safest vessel anywhere. The double bottom was carried farther up the ship's side, allowing the installation of side bunkers amidships as a precaution and to increase buoyancy. Several key bulkheads were also extended upwards. This was a massive undertaking, for it required the removal of the ship's funnels, boilers and other gear as well as the re-routing of much electrical and plumbing work. At the same time, double-banked lifeboats were installed all along the boat deck, increasing the number of lifeboats from 20 to 48. Because of the alterations, the *Olympic*'s tonnage was increased to 46,350.

While the *Olympic* was undergoing reconstruction, her unfinished sister ship lay nearby. Framed to the height of the double bottom, construction had been suspended pending the outcome of the *Titanic* inquiries, but was underway again. Similar changes had been made to her as well, increasing her beam an additional two feet. A much more complex series of watertight compartments was included and it was planned to install a system of gantry boat

davits to facilitate the launching of lifeboats. The new liner was named *Britannic* for the simple enough reason that this name was considered lucky, having been successfully borne by a vessel operated by the company from 1874 to 1903.

Finally, after all these alterations had been carried out, the big ship was ready for launching on February 26 1914. Again a huge crowd of invited guests gathered at Harland & Wolff's to see the new leviathan take to the water. In keeping with White Star tradition there was no formal naming ceremony. Following the launch, Henry Concannon, on behalf of the owners, told a reception at Belfast's Grand Central Hotel, that 'neither thought nor money has been spared, and when you see the finished article we feel sure that we shall have your approval, as we have had your good wishes today'. Once again, despite its awful setback, the White Star Line seemed at the pinnacle of success.

Outwardly, the *Britannic*'s appearance was very similar to that of the *Titanic* and *Olympic*. The forward end of the 'A' deck promenade, like that of the *Titanic* (but unlike the *Olympic*) was glassed-in and an enclosed well deck aft on 'D' deck was included which was absent in the earlier vessels. The *Britannic*'s poop deck also was

Below left *As the* Olympic *steams past the lower New York skyline, steerage passengers get their first close look at the New World. Within minutes, she would be at her pier.*

Below right *This is what the* Olympic's *forward deck looked like from the bridge. Although taken in New York, this photograph, with a little imagination, gives an idea what the view must have been like on the* Titanic *as the iceberg loomed ahead* (Photo by Everett E. Viez).

Above *The hull of the* Britannic *takes shape on the Harland & Wolff slipway. This view is looking down on the liner from the huge gantry superstructure* (Harland & Wolff Ltd).

Below *Launching day draws near for the* Britannic *as the finishing touches are put on her hull. For some reason, the* Britannic *was launched with a grey hull; the* Olympic's *was white and the* Titanic's *black* (Harland & Wolff Ltd).

Top *It is February 26 1914. The* Britannic's *mammoth hull takes to the water for the first time. Notice the difference in the shelter deck aft which is enclosed on the* Britannic, *unlike her two sister ships. Also notice the structure on the poop deck which enclosed the third class smoking room* (Steamship Historical Society of America).

Above *The* Britannic *is moved to her fitting-out basin where the finishing touches will be provided. In profile she was more similar to the* Titanic *than the* Olympic. *Note that she was built with the forward end of the promenade deck enclosed* (Harland & Wolff Ltd).

somewhat higher than that of her sisters, contributing, some feel, to a disproportionately lofty stern. Unquestionably the most significant differences were the huge gantry-like lifeboat davits adjacent to the first and fourth funnels. These somewhat ungainly looking innovations were added to make it possible to launch all the lifeboats from either side regardless of how badly she might list. The boats were to be arranged in several large groups: the foward davits would handle a motor launch, two emergency boats and three lifeboats per side. Two groups of 12 boats were by the forward funnel and 14 were located amidships. There was also a large group of boats clustered about the fourth funnel. Together these were designed to accommodate 790 first class, 830 second class, 1,000 third class and 950 crew and provided more than enough space for the number of people the *Britannic* could carry. As originally designed, the *Britannic* grossed 47,500 tons, but alterations increased this to over 48,158 tons. She was the largest liner built in the United Kingdom prior to the *Queen Mary*. Delivery of the new ship was scheduled for spring 1915 and she must have been nearly completed when World War 1 broke out in August 1914. She was dry-docked a short time later to receive her three propellers and, although war was now raging, work proceeded on

Above *Shipyard workers install the* Britannic's *huge reciprocating engines. Like her sisters she utilised both reciprocating engines and turbine propulsion. The outboard screws were driven by the old-style engines while the centre shaft was powered by a low-pressure turbine utilising steam from the conventional engines* (Harland & Wolff Ltd).

Below *One of the* Britannic's *29 boilers is hoisted aboard at the fitting-out dock. There were 24 double-ended boilers and five single-ended ones, arranged in six separate watertight compartments* (Harland & Wolff Ltd).

preparing her for the Southampton-New York service.

As for the *Olympic,* she was en route to New York on August 4 when word was received that war had been declared. She arrived with no problems, having been escorted on the last leg of her voyage by the cruiser *Essex* which then turned around and escorted the *Lusitania* out to sea. All British shipmasters were fearful of German warships or converted merchantmen that might be prowling off the American coast. The passengers who had been scheduled to return to England on the *Olympic* were transferred to the *Adriatic* which steamed home by way of the northern route and avoided any enemy ships. Four days after the outbreak of war, the *Olympic* put out to sea from New York with only her crew aboard. They busied themselves painting over the large windows and covering parts of the ship with grey paint. They paused long enough to taunt and wave at the German crewmen aboard the giant *Vaterland,* tied up at Hoboken, New Jersey, across the Hudson River. She was in the midst of her fourth voyage and would never again sail under the German flag. The *Olympic* made it back to the United Kingdom safely but put in at the Clyde instead of Southampton which had been abandoned for the duration as the terminal port. While several other White Star liners were taken over for war duty, the *Olympic* remained in commercial service, if it can be called that. She sailed blacked-out at night, with her watertight doors closed and her boats swung out. Her main chore was to bring home as many Americans as possible who had been stranded in Europe by the war, and this she did admirably, always managing to avoid German warships. It was on one of these voyages that she performed one of the most courageous naval feats of the war.

The morning of October 27 1914 found the *Olympic* steaming off the coast of Northern Ireland, headed home. Ahead of her lay the Second Battle Squadron en route to gunnery practice off Lough Swilly. Among the squadron was the 23,000-ton battleship *Audacious,* built only the year before by Cammell Laird & Company. Just after 8.30 am the *Audacious* was rocked by an explosion in the port engine room which tore a large hole in her side. With water pouring in and listing to port, the battleship dropped out of formation and headed for land. But the sea soon reached the other engine spaces, and by 11 am the *Audacious* had lost all power. The signal went out for tugs as the battleship wallowed in the long swells, her stern very low in the water. At about the same time, the *Olympic*

Very little has been done to alter the Olympic's *appearance in this photograph in Halifax harbour during her early years as a troopship. Her buff funnels, however, have disappeared under a coat of black paint. Armament is minimal* (Nova Scotia Museum).

arrived on the scene, much to the surprise of the smaller naval vessels nearby. It was assumed that the *Audacious* had been torpedoed and it struck the Royal Navy people as rather strange that the huge liner would heave-to with a large contingent of passengers when an enemy submarine was believed to be in the area.

Captain H.J. Haddock, the *Olympic*'s master, asked if he could be of any help, so the *Audacious* requested that the liner take her in tow. First they removed all but 50 of the battleship's crew by small boat and then succeeded in getting a line between the two ships. This was short-lived for, as she cruised nearby to assist, the cruiser *Liverpool* ran over and cut the line. The tedious task of rigging a new line and passing it to the *Olympic* was undertaken and this time all went well. But as the tow got underway, a new problem presented itself. The *Audacious*, by now full of water, rolled heavily and became almost impossible to control. The result was that after only a relatively short tow, the line parted. At the same time, the sea began to kick up and the senior naval officer at the scene concluded that the *Olympic* was too large to handle such a tow and that the *Liverpool* should have a go at it. Having received the thanks of the *Audacious'* commander, the liner continued on her way. Later that night, word was received that the battleship had blown up and sunk making it necessary for the Admiralty to detain the *Olympic* in Lough Swilly until the problem of security could be worked out. The liner remained there for nearly a week while officials pondered how to keep the loss a secret from the enemy since many of the ship's passengers had not only witnessed the incident but

photographed it as well. During this period, it was determined that the *Audacious* had been sunk by a mine and that there were more than 200 mines in the area at the time. That revelation sparked considerable debate over whether Captain Haddock had been justified in risking the big White Star liner in such a situation. In the end, it was considered a courageous feat that called for the utmost in seamanship, and Captain Haddock's judgement on the matter was never again questioned.

Once the *Olympic* had completed the task of repatriating American citizens, she was taken over by the Admiralty as a troopship. Fresh troops were required for the Dardanelles campaign and it was up to the *Olympic* and several other large liners to see that they got there safely. She made four voyages to the Mediterranean, on one of which she encountered an enemy submarine off Cape Matapan, but managed to outrun it with little difficulty.

While the *Olympic* was busy making a name for herself, her sister ship *Britannic* was fitting-out at Belfast. Although the White Star Line had baulked at the suggestion that she be requisitioned for war duty, it was inevitable that she be taken over. On November 13 1915, the *Britannic* was taken up as a hospital ship. By now the Dardanelles campaign was faltering and it became necessary to effect a large-scale evacuation of wounded. Shipyard workers ripped out much of the luxury accommodation they had just finished installing and in the haste of readying her for service were forced to erect canvas partitions in the place of more substantial ones. The first class dining room became the main hospital with the

adjoining reception room serving as the emergency operating room. Most of the other public rooms were converted into large wards while many of the larger staterooms were prepared as private rooms for officers and senior enlisted men. Most of the doctors and nurses lived on the upper decks so they could be near their patients. As a hospital ship, the *Britannic* was equipped with 2,074 berths and 1,035 cots for casualties, a medical staff of 52 officers, 101 nurses, 336 orderlies and a 675-man crew.

Her four funnels were painted buff and her hull and superstructure white. It was broken only by a green stripe running the entire length of the hull just below the 'E' deck level. Two red crosses were painted on her hull sides, one abaft the forward funnel, the other between the cluster of lifeboats by the fourth funnel. In addition an illuminated red cross was strung between the first two funnels. Only five of the planned eight gantry-type davits were installed: there were none on the poop deck nor on the portside forward. Open spaces on the boat deck were taken up by 14 boats mounted beneath conventional Welin-type davits. This gave her a total of 58 lifeboats, motor-boats and collapsibles. Upon completion the *Britannic* was turned over to Captain Charles A. Bartlett, RNR, marine superintendent of the White Star Line who had supervised her construction.

She left Belfast on December 11 1915 for brief trials and went the next day to Liverpool where she was officially commissioned as a hospital ship. There were no crowds or bands to greet her; only a handful of onlookers watched in silence as the towering vessel was warped into her dock. Twelve days later on December 23 she departed

Right *Prepared for use in advance publicity flyers, this artist's impression depicts the* Britannic's *main staircase and dome. The White Star Line was known for its high standards of luxury and there is little doubt the* Britannic *would have carried these to new heights* (Harland & Wolff Ltd).

Top left *No photographs appear to exist of the* Britannic's *public rooms as they would have been outfitted for passenger service. But there are several excellent artist's impressions. Here is what the first class smoking room would have looked like* (Harland & Wolff).

Centre left *The* Britannic's *first class lounge was very similar to that on her sister ships, but may have been intended slightly more ornate as suggested by this drawing* (Harland & Wolff Ltd).

Left *This is the* Britannic's *first class restaurant, which would have been just about identical to that on her sister ships. A total of 518 passengers could have been served in a single sitting* (Harland & Wolff Ltd).

Liverpool for her port of embarkation at Mudros on the island of Lemnos, to take aboard her first load of wounded. She stopped at Naples on December 28 for bunkering and then moved on to Mudros where she embarked 3,300 sick and wounded over a four-day period. Her first round trip was uneventful and she arrived back at Southampton on January 9 1916. Following a quick turnaround she steamed back to the Mediterranean and anchored at Naples in company with the *Aquitania* and *Mauretania*. These three ships were much too big to enter the smaller harbours near the battlefront so many casualties were transferred to them in Naples by shallower draft hospital ships. The *Britannic* was

HM Hospital Ship Britannic *loads wounded from the* Galeka, *another hospital ship, as the two lie at Mudros. Notice how she towers over the smaller vessel* (Imperial War Museum).

back in Southampton on February 9 and remained tied up for seven weeks before starting on another mercy mission. During this period the *Olympic,* still serving as a troopship, was attacked twice by submarines but managed to avoid torpedoes. On yet another occasion, a torpedo did actually hit the *Olympic,* but fortunately it was a dud and caused no damage. The *Olympic* seemed to be as lucky as the *Titanic* was unlucky.

The spring of 1916 found the *Britannic* back in Belfast where she was laid up after serving briefly as a naval hospital at the Isle of Wight. Her hospital ship days appeared over, for the Admiralty released her from naval service on June 6 and it is believed that some of her hospital fittings were removed soon after to prepare her for reconditioning as a passenger liner. If work did begin anew on outfitting her for the mail run it all came to naught for on August 28 she was once again taken over by the government and ordered back to Southampton, whence she sailed for Mudros on September 23.

On her fifth Mediterranean voyage, the *Britannic* became the subject of a minor international dispute. On the return leg of her voyage she made an unscheduled stop at Naples at which time she took aboard, among others, an Austrian invalid named Adalbert Franz Messany for repatriation. His charge that the ship was carrying some 2,500 troops below decks brought a swift protest from Germany. The claim was strongly denied and the Admiralty declared that no troops had ever been carried on board. Messany later said he obtained the information from an unin-

jured British officer named Harold Hickman who was aboard the *Britannic* for treatment of malaria. Eventually the incident was forgotten and no additional diplomatic action was taken.

Her sixth voyage outbound began at Southampton on November 12 1916, a year less one day since she had been requisitioned for hospital service. She had aboard 22 surgeons, 77 nurses, 290 orderlies, three chaplains and a crew of 673, for a total of 1,065. At Mudros she was scheduled to pick up about 3,000 injured personnel. There was calm weather for most of the trip and the morning of November 21 dawned without incident and found the big liner steaming about four miles west of Port St Nikolo in the Kea Channel between the Greek mainland and the Cyclades Islands. It was a clear, sunny day and the Aegean was exceptionally calm. At twelve minutes past eight o'clock while breakfast was still being served, the *Britannic* was rocked by an explosion on the starboard side forward. It occurred near the bulkhead separating holds two and three and shattered the bulkhead causing both holds to flood. It was later ascertained that the bulkhead between holds one and two was also damaged, opening those compartments to the sea. Boiler rooms five and six were also making water soon after the blast leading to the assumption that the bulkheads separating them from the holds were damaged. This meant that, despite the elaborate structural alterations made on the stocks, the ship sustained nearly the *same damage that proved fatal to her sister Titanic four years earlier!*

Some survivors later said they heard another explosion almost immediately after the first but this has never been substantiated. There are those who served in British hospital ships during World War 1 who claim that these vessels carried munitions deep in their holds that could conceivably have accounted for a second blast. Others have long held that she was torpedoed not once, but twice, even though the overwhelming evidence points to her having struck a mine.

But at 8.12 am on November 21 1916 there was no time for such speculation. Captain Bartlett knew immediately that his ship was seriously damaged because of the starboard list taken by the *Britannic* as the explosion died away. With the shore looming large the captain felt there was a chance to save her and decided to try and beach the crippled vessel on Kea Island. Emergency quarters were sounded and the boats made ready for launching in the event the liner could not safely reach shallow water. At the same time an SOS was sent out.

When emergency quarters were sounded, the nurses were all herded up on deck and loaded into the lifeboats as a precaution. The Reverend John A. Fleming, one of the liner's chaplains, felt they might be in the boats for a long time if the ship had to be abandoned, so he dashed below to the pantry and brought up several loaves of bread and distributed them among the lifeboats. By now the *Britannic* was listing rather heavily to starboard and her bow was deep in the water. She rapidly was becoming unmanageable and it soon became clear that she would not make it to shore. Reluctantly, Captain Bartlett ordered the engines stopped just as the steering gear failed. But before this order could be carried out, two half-full lifeboats launched hastily without approval from the bridge, were drawn into the revolving port wing propeller, now above the water, and smashed to bits. As the listing *Britannic* drifted to a halt in the calm sea crewmen tossed deck chairs into the water in an attempt to assist swimmers. Fortunately the sea was warm and most swimmers had no difficulty managing with the deck chairs until picked up by the rest of the lifeboats which were now being lowered.

Within a short time most of the vessel's company had abandoned the ship. Among those still aboard were Captain Bartlett and several officers as well as a small band of engineers who had valiantly remained at their posts providing power to the ship. At the last moment they made their escape through the dummy fourth funnel. When he was certain everyone else was off the sinking ship, Captain Bartlett walked off the bridge into the rising waters and was picked up a short while later by a motor boat. Arriving on the scene about that time in answer to the distress signal were HMSs *Heroic, Scourge, Foxhound* and a French tug. The tug captain suggested a towing attempt, but the deteriorating seaworthiness of the big hospital ship ruled that out.

At 9 am, less than an hour after the blast, the *Britannic* rolled over on her starboard side and began her final plunge. As she did so huge clouds of smoke billowed forth from the ventilators and other openings as the fires below were drowned by the inrushing waters. From within the hull came the muffled sound of exploding boilers and as the ship began to slip from sight, each of the four funnels broke off and sank into the sea. Finally, her stern pointed skyward, she hesitated for a moment and then disappeared from sight. The *Britannic* settled to the bottom 620 feet below the surface with the dubious distinction of being the largest individual war loss to the British merchant marine. Of her large company, only 28 persons were lost, many of the casualties occuring when the two lifeboats were destroyed by the spinning propeller. Given the rapidity with which she sank there is little doubt that the toll would have been much higher had she carried a full load of wounded.

The controversy over exactly what caused the explosion that sank the *Britannic* raged for years afterwards, and it was not until 1928 that Lieutenant Commander Gustav Siess, former captain of the German submarine *U-73*, stated that his ship was indirectly responsible for the liner's loss. It developed that from April to November 1916, his submarine was busy laying mines from Lisbon to Malta, mines which sank the battleship *Russell* and later the *Britannic*. Commander Siess lamented the fact that the clearly marked hospital ship fell victim to one of his mines, but added that mines do not have the capability of picking their targets and that submariners such as himself often had to bear the responsibility for work done by mines.

About the same time that the *Britannic* was lost, the *Olympic* was being overhauled, painted in dazzle patterns and fitted with six 6-in guns. In April 1916 she made a round trip to Canada to carry a diplomatic mission to Halifax and afterwards returned to trooping duty, bringing Canadian and, later, American troops to Europe. When the United States entered the war, the *Olympic* was used almost exclusively to ferry the 'doughboys' across the Atlantic. It was during this period that she acquired the nickname of 'The Old Reliable'. Her port of entry was Brest,

One has to look very carefully to pick out the fine lines of the Olympic *amidst the dazzle paint scheme which was used extensively on troopships in World War 1* (Imperial War Museum).

where she arrived after a rather harrowing experience on March 6 1918. Plans called for the liner to pick up her escort off the French coast but heavy fog made this impossible at first, so for eight anxious hours the *Olympic* steamed in figure-eights at 17 knots trying to find her escort. Throughout all this, her officers felt certain she would accidentally happen upon an enemy ship. But luck was with her once again and she came through unscathed. Two months later, things were a little more exciting.

The *Olympic* was in the English Channel early on the morning of May 12 loaded to the gunwales' with American troops when she sighted a surfaced submarine about half a mile off the starboard bow. Captain Sir Bertram Hayes, in command of the liner, decided his only recourse was to ram the submarine before it sighted the blacked-out liner. As the *Olympic*'s bow swung to starboard, her forward gun opened fire at the U-boat but missed. The submarine tried to get away, but the huge troopship was too close. A few minutes before 4 am the *Olympic*'s bow struck the submarine a glancing blow and tore a gigantic hole in her side.

'The shock of the impact was much greater than I expected,' recalled Captain Hayes, 'I had always thought of submarines as being frail things, but it jumped us off our feet on the bridge.'*

* Sir Bertram Hayes, *Hull Down* (Macmillan Company: New York, 1925), p.231. A splendid account of the *Olympic*'s war years.

As a transport, the *Olympic* was prohibited from stopping to pick up survivors and since she appeared undamaged, she continued on her way to Southampton. Thirty-one survivors of the *U-103* were rescued by the American destroyer *Davis*. When the *Olympic* reached port it was found that her bow had been twisted about eight feet to port and dented in several places. It appears to be the only documented instance of a liner serving as a transport sinking an enemy vessel in World War 1.

The rest of the *Olympic*'s war career was rather an anti-climax and by the time hostilities were over, she had carried more than 188,000 troops and civilian passengers, covering more than 184,000 miles without a casualty. Her war record had certainly been exemplary, prompting the 59th Regiment, United States Infantry, to present a special commemorative tablet that was placed on the main staircase when the ship was reconditioned after the war. Before returning to Belfast for reconditioning, however, the liner was used for repatriating many of the Canadian troops she had brought over during the war. While so employed many tributes, largely in the form of silver services, were presented by the grateful people of Canada, not only to the ship but to her skipper Captain Hayes as well.

On August 12 1919 the *Olympic* arrived back at Harland & Wolff's for her postwar refit, a mammoth undertaking that took more than six

Above *The* Olympic *steams down Belfast Lough on June 17 1920, fresh from her post-war refit at Harland & Wolff's. It was said that she was even more magnificent after this refit than when first built* (Harland & Wolff Ltd).

Right *When converted to oil after World War 1, the* Olympic *was the largest oil-burning steamer in the world. She would hold the distinction only a short time however. This is a view of one of her boiler rooms in the oil era.*

months to complete. In addition to modernising her passenger accommodation and replacing the many mechanical parts that had been worn out by strenuous war service, it was decided to convert her from coal to oil fuel, cutting the number of engine room staff from 350 to 60 men. During this period, the Southampton-New York service was maintained by the *Adriatic* and the Red Star *Lapland,* neither of which was really suited to that express run. White Star, dealt a major setback when the *Titanic* sank in 1912, had suffered another severe blow with the loss of the *Britannic,* and now had only one large express steamer, the *Olympic,* for the mail run. It became clear that additional first-class tonnage would be required.

When the *Olympic*'s restoration was complete early in the summer of 1920 she was opened to the public for inspection at Belfast. Between three and four thousand people visited her during the two-day open house, the proceeds of the admission fee going to area hospitals. Everyone was unanimous in their praise of the liner, declaring her 'like a new ship'. She sailed on her first post-war voyage on July 21 from Southampton, her

passenger capacity reduced to 2,150 through extensive renovations. But the *Olympic*'s return to service convinced White Star officials they must have at least one consort immediately in order to provide an adequate service. They turned to the Shipping Controller who was in charge of all former German tonnage taken over as war reparations. White Star decided in favour of Norddeutscher Lloyd's 34,351-ton *Columbus,* then lying uncompleted at the Schichau yard in Danzig. The world's largest twin-screw vessel and the largest ever to be driven by twin screws and reciprocating engines, she was re-named *Homeric* and placed in service with the *Olympic,* the 33,600-ton vessel ordered at Belfast in 1914, and on which little or no work had been done, being cancelled in her favour. The new White Star express service was rounded out in May 1922 with the acquisition of the former Hamburg America liner *Bismarck,* re-named *Majestic.* At

Left *This photograph tells the whole story. Framed by a sign on the Southampton waterfront, the* Olympic *lies in the floating drydock undergoing hull work in the 1920s.*
Below *This is a particularly fine photograph of the* Olympic *as she steams down Southampton Water headed for the open sea. This may have been near the area where she collided with the* Hawke *in 1911. The date is the mid-1920s.*

56,551 tons she was the largest liner in the world, but in the eyes of many Britons she was not in the same class as the *Olympic*. Consquently the older, more graceful four-stacker continued to attract a large following that preferred her to the ex-German ships.

The years immediately following the war were kind to the *Olympic* which continued to prove herself an excellent sea boat and as reliable as an express train. Her performance was never better, on several occasions averaging the crossing at about 23 knots. Owing to a drastic decline in third class travel following the introduction of the United States Immigration Restriction Acts of 1921 and 1924, the *Homeric* and *Majestic* began in 1926 to cater for a new class of passenger, tourist third cabin, in addition to first, second and third. The *Olympic* followed suit in January 1928 and so popular did this arrangement become that by October 1931 the second class of all three ships was taken over by what had been re-named tourist class.

Ever since the war ended, the International Mercantile Marine Company had been involved in quiet negotiations with a number of parties over the sale of all its British-flag holdings since the Morgan combine never was the success envisioned. As a result, the Royal Mail Steam Packet Company, then in the process of building up a gigantic shipping combine of its own, acquired the White Star Line in 1927 and returned ownership to Britain. Although a great source of pride for the nation, it was an ill-conceived move since Royal Mail was in the midst of financial problems. But at the time the important thing was that, after nearly 25 years under American aegis, the White Star Line was again a British concern. The Royal Mail chairman, Lord Kylsant, had a special affinity for White Star and planned to use it as his group's showpiece. With that in mind, he planned the most daring move of all and on June 18 1928 the line announced that it had placed an order with Harland & Wolff for a 60,000-ton, 1,000-foot liner to succeed the *Homeric* on the mail run since she was too slow. The new liner was to be named *Oceanic* and was to be the largest diesel-powered ship in the world.

This proved to be the beginning of a new batch of troubles. First there was considerable difference of opinion as to whether she should be turbine or diesel propelled. Second, there was the question of a loan to help finance her construction. Third was the delicate financial situation of the Royal Mail group which by now was getting too big for its own good. Finally the worldwide depression ended the entire grandiose scheme. White Star

dropped the *Oceanic* project in favour of the 27,000-ton motorships *Britannic* and *Georgic* which, as it turned out, were the last liners built for the famous old company. Conditions around the globe were changing drastically, causing the company to re-evaluate the tourist third class and to alter the passenger capacity in the *Olympic* and other liners. Eventually the carrying capacity of the famous four-stacker would be cut to 1,447 spread over three classes as compared to 2,584 passengers when new. As the Depression took hold in the early 1930s the *Olympic* and other White Star liners were forced to turn to cruising to help make ends meet. Both the *Olympic* and *Majestic* operated three and a half day trips from New York to Halifax during their layovers between Atlantic crossings. For a time the *Olympic* was even based in Boston for a series of cruises to Quebec, the North Cape, Halifax and Bermuda.

Traffic on the North Atlantic reached a low ebb early in the 1930s, prompting the disposal of many ships. Even the construction of the giant Cunard liner which was to become the *Queen Mary* was affected. Laid down at Clydebank in 1930, work was suspended on her for over two years because of the Depression. There just was not a market for so many big ships. With both White Star and Cunard in trouble, the British government decided that there was no alternative but to come to the rescue. If the Cunard and White Star interests were to merge, the government proposed, money would be advanced for the completion of the *Queen Mary*. It was the only way out and on December 30 1933 the directors of both companies agreed to the merger. On May 10 1934 a new concern, Cunard-White Star Ltd, came into being and for many of the older ships, especially those flying the White Star burgee, it signalled the end of the line. With the completion of the *Queen Mary* in sight, it became clear that the combined lines would no longer require the services of many of the 25 liners they owned. One by one the older ships departed for the scrapyards.

Only five days after the new company came into existence in 1934 the *Olympic* made headlines. With Captain J.W. Binks on the bridge, the huge liner was picking her way through extremely heavy fog bound for New York early on the morning of May 15. Somewhere not too far ahead lay the Nantucket Lightship which guarded the shoal waters off the US coast. A few minutes after 10 am the *Olympic*'s lookout suddenly reported seeing something dead ahead. Captain Binks called for full speed astern as his liner forged

A pathetic relic of the glory that had once been. The hulk of the Olympic *is towed by a fleet of tugs from Jarrow to Inverkeithing. Much of the ship has already been dismantled and it was left to Thomas W. Ward's yard to reduce her to scrap.*

ahead at 16 knots. He ordered the watertight doors closed. To the horror of all concerned, directly in the path of the oncoming liner was the tiny Nantucket Lightship, moored to the ocean floor and helpless to avoid the impending disaster.

'The *Olympic* is on top of us!' screamed a crewman to Lightship Captain George Braithwaite but there was nothing anyone could do. The 46,359-ton *Olympic* crashed into the side of the 133-foot Lightship dead amidships, cutting her cleanly in two and sinking her almost immediately. Within three minutes the liner's boats were in the water searching for survivors. A passenger aboard the *Olympic* described the debris-littered seas as 'heavy with oil and bodies floating by'. Some of the surviving lightship crewmen could be seen clinging to hatches in the water. Seven men were plucked from the seas but three died aboard the *Olympic* leaving only four of the eleven-man crew to survive the collision. As for the liner, she suffered very little damage in the accident. A passenger, Sir Arthur Steel-Maitland, MP, recalled feeling only a 'slight jar' at the time. Others knew nothing of the incident until the vessel stopped to pick up survivors.

Blame for the collision was laid directly on the *Olympic*, although lengthy litigation followed the accident. One positive result of the collision was that no longer would ships follow the lightship's radio beacon, swerving at the last possible minute to avoid hitting her. The 12 hours preceding the collision had been harrowing ones for the lightship crew, having been nearly rammed by two ships including the French Liner *Paris*. In fact earlier that same year, the lightship had actually been brushed by the liner *Washington* but with only minor damage. As in the case of the *Titanic*

many lessons were learned from the collision that would help avoid a recurrence in the future.

The *Olympic* continued on the mail run for another ten months and on March 27 1935 left Southampton on what was to prove her final transatlantic round voyage. She arrived home on April 12 and was taken out of service. As she lay at Southampton's Berth 108 rumours abounded, the most persistent being that she would be converted into a troopship. But nothing materialised and the great liner, now nearly 25 years old, remained tied up in company with Cunard's *Mauretania*. In July the famous old Cunarder sailed away to her doom and the *Olympic* was not to be far behind. In August she was opened to prospective buyers for inspection. A buyer materialised the following month when the *Olympic* was sold for £100,000 to Sir John Jervis, an industrialist who also happened to be a Member of Parliament. He promptly resold the ship to Thomas W. Ward Ltd of Sheffield for demolition, a proviso of the deal being that she would be broken up in the Tyneside town of Jarrow to provide work for the many labourers made idle by the Depression.

October 11 1935 was the day appointed for the *Olympic*'s final departure from Southampton. She sailed under her own steam manned by a skeleton crew obtained from other White Star ships. It would have been cruel to ask any of the *Olympic* veterans to take her to the scrappers. The Southampton docks were crowded with thousands of people that day, many who had fond memories of trips on the 'Old Reliable', others who came down because they knew that while they could build them bigger and faster, there would never be another *Olympic*.

At the Marquis of Granby Hotel near Sheffield, there is an 'Olympic Room' utilising original panelling and a doorway from the liner's first class smoking room. The clock and carpet, both in excellent condition, are also from the ship (Thomas W. Ward Ltd).

She arrived on the Tyne during the afternoon of October 13 and had to wait outside the port of Jarrow in deep water until the tide was just right. Because of her great draught only an hour was available for her to come up the river to her berth. Within half an hour of ringing up 'Finished With Engines' for the final time, the great liner's keel was firmly in the river mud. Less than a month later, on November 6, an auction of her fittings got under way in the first class lounge. Furniture and panelling quickly found buyers. So did smaller items such as dinner gongs, framed state-room notices, silver and china. As with furnishings from several other large liners, some of the *Olympic*'s woodwork and furniture was re-installed in area hotels where it continued in use for many more years.

Demolition of the vessel continued for the better part of two years, during which the workers dismantled all her superstructure and part of the hull. But the yard at Jarrow was rather limited in space so it was decided to move the hulk to Ward's Inverkeithing yard for final scrapping. On September 20 1937 she left Jarrow at the end of a tow line for her final berth. The *Olympic*'s hull was in excellent condition when she was scrapped and had it not been for the Depression and the merger she may very well have remained in service long enough to be used as a World War 2 troopship. Considering how valuable the *Aquitania* was in this service she would have been very useful to the Allies. Ironically, the pride of the White Star Line and the man who master-minded her ended their careers within a month of each other. Having been in retirement since 1913, J. Bruce Ismay, who had watched not only his three-ship dream dissipate but his great steamship line as well, died at his London home on October 17 1937.

The intervening years have not dimmed interest in the White Star giants. If anything, interest in them has grown to the point where one, the *Britannic,* has already been visited at the bottom of the sea with the promise that the other, the *Titanic,* will soon be the subject of a series of deep-sea dives.

The great White Star Line trio was born amid much promise and although marred by great tragedy remains to this day one of the most famous class of liners ever built.

A magnificent shot of the France *in New York fresh from the 1923-1924 overhaul which converted her boilers to oil-fired from coal* (Frank O. Braynard Collection).

5 Compagnie Générale Transatlantique

The industrial revolution seized hold in France during the 1840s, the supporting figures usually being that in 1840 there were 600 steam engines of all types in the country but by 1847 the number had risen to 4,853. The earliest attempts at a French North Atlantic steamship service in 1847 and 1856 did not succeed but the advantages and possibilities of steam over sail were evident to many who watched the Cunard efforts across the English Channel. Two enlightened and gifted maritime entrepreneurs, Émile and Isaac Péreire, founded the Compagnie Générale Maritime (CGM) in 1855 with the goals of maintaining a European coastal service, a world-wide sailing ship trade, and establishing the French flag on a fleet of North Atlantic steamships. A combination of fortuitous economic and political developments occurred in 1860. The Compagnie Générale Maritime succeeded in acquiring the concession of L'Union Maritime (1858, Le Havre) to establish a mail service to North America and the West Indies as well as the very substantial backing of the French government in the form of an annual subsidy and advances on that sum interest-free over twenty years. A decree of His Imperial Majesty Napoleon III dated August 25 1861, authorised a name change from Compagnie Générale Maritime to Compagnie Générale Transatlantique (CGT).

Initial tonnage was built by John Scott & Co of Greenock but the Péreire brothers were so incensed by the quotations received from French builders that they bought a strip of land at St Nazaire, near the mouth of the Loire, and with contract assistance from the Scottish firm elected to develop their own shipyard and to construct their own ships. The result was the birth of that great maritime enterprise which eventually became Chantiers & Ateliers de St Nazaire and which maintained a century-long partnership either directly or indirectly with the Compagnie Générale Transatlantique.

Advances in French Line vessels were often tied directly to the signing of new mail contracts between the line and the French government. The agreement between CGT and the French Postmaster-Générale in the late 1890s called for ships capable of maintaining an average speed of not less than 20 knots for an Atlantic crossing in the Le Havre-New York service. The French Line honoured the contract by ordering *La Lorraine* (1900, 11,146 tons) and *La Savoie* (1901, 11,168 tons), both of 20 knots, and the fondly remembered *La Provence* (1906, 13,753 tons) of 22 knots. While quite popular, the only shortcomings of these vessels were that they were smaller and slower than contemporary British and German mail steamers. This was particularly critical on the Channel service where the big Norddeutscher Lloyd and HAPAG greyhounds left the French competition far behind between 1897-1912. The situation was unacceptable competitively, particularly after the commissioning of the *Lusitania* and *Mauretania,* the transfer of White Star ships from Liverpool to Southampton, and the vast size of new German tonnage.

Something dramatic had to be done and Charles Roux was more than willing to accept the challenge when he became President of CGT in 1904. It was announced with great pride in 1907 that the company was entering into negotiations to build the largest ship the line had ever ordered, tentatively named *La Picardie*. At least in part the size of the new unit was dictated by the progress made in expanding the port of Le Havre at the mouth of the Seine. Negotiations with St Nazaire were somewhat protracted and the keel of *La Picardie* was not laid until early 1909. Between the keel laying and the launching, the *France* (I) (1865, 3,200 tons) was scrapped after a 45-year

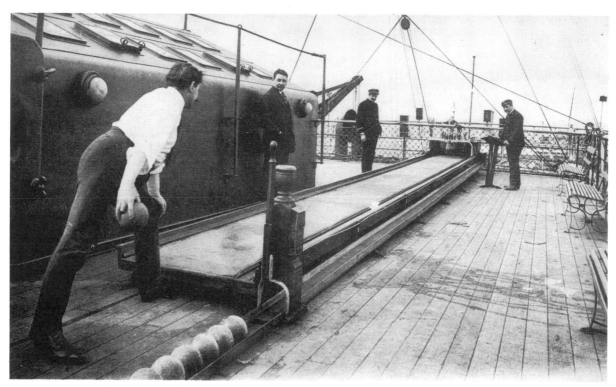

Deck games on the France *included bowling with stewards to keep score.*

career and the decision made that a vessel nearly twice the size of any previous unit in the fleet should bear the name of the entire country, not just a province. This would create some confusion in the public eye since all the French Line mail steamers were named after provinces and carried the prefix 'La' as part of their names. Accordingly, many sources during the first decade of her existence, including the United States Navy during World War 1, referred to the ship as *La France* rather than the shorter and correct *France*.

The *France* (II) was launched on September 20 1910, immediately gaining the distinction of being the largest ship built so far in a French yard, the only four-funnel liner ever built in France, and the first large turbine-driven vessel to fly the French flag. In every way she warranted and received an avalanche of superlatives. Her 23,666 gross tons exceeded by over 4,000 tons that of the *Kronprinzessin Cecilie,* her nearest rival as a Channel-based greyhound. The overall length of the new flagship was 732 ft, length between bulkheads was 690 ft 1 in, breadth was 75 ft 6 in. The displacement of the huge liner was 29,654 tons so that many newspaper accounts described her as a 30,000-ton ship, but the net tonnage was only 8,432 tons owing to the enormous space occupied by the propulsion unit.

The CGT management was every bit as daring as Cunard when they elected to fit their new liner with turbines. Chantiers & Ateliers de St Nazaire obtained a licence to produce the Parsons steam turbines but substantially modified the design

after experimenting with a number of small vessels, notably the *Charles Roux* (1908, 4,104 tons) of the Mediterranean service. After observing the performance of the *Charles Roux,* St Nazaire ended up by producing the first triple-expansion marine turbine for the *France.* The four turbines were coupled directly to the quadruple shafts and could produce 42,000 shp. Technically, this was intended to give the liner a service speed of 23.5 knots. However, the performance was substantially better than that since the *France* achieved over 25 knots at her trials in March 1912. Steam was provided by eight single-ended and 11 double-ended, cylindrical, coal-fired boilers. The bunkers could take 5,045 tons of coal and she needed most of it on a normal crossing since she consumed between 650-720 tons per day. Fifty years later the *France* (III) (1962, 66,348 tons) maintained an average speed of 31 knots on approximately 720 tons of oil, the same amount of fuel by weight even if a direct comparison is not warranted.

Fitting out was delayed by a bunker fire but the *France* was given a tumultuous welcome on her maiden arrival at Le Havre on April 13 1912. The sides of the piers and quays were hidden beneath flags and bunting and so great a crowd gathered to greet the liner that units of the French Army were called out to insure against disorders and accidents. In view of the fact that Le Havre in 1912 was a hotbed of unionisation and labour management strife, the role of the army was almost certainly as much to protect the invest-

Above *The promenade deck of the* France *was a favourite place of rest and relaxation where passengers were served by a cadre of stewards who never forgot a face, name, or deck chair preference!* (Everett E. Viez Collection).

Below *The first class Café Terrace was situated aft of the smoking room and was one of the most popular areas on the ship in fair weather* (Everett E. Viez Collection).

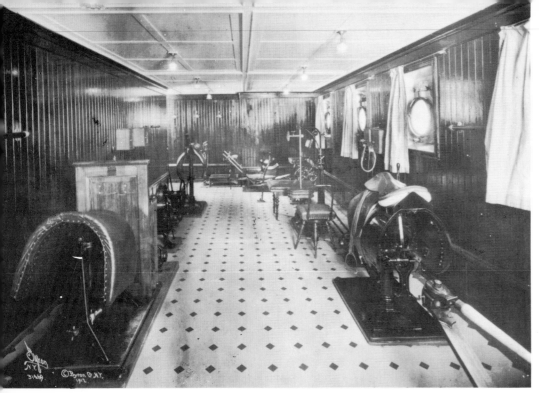

Gymnasium on the France (Library of Congress).

Louis XIV returns from the hunt in one of the oil paintings gracing the Grand Salon *with two of his favourites on either side of the king wearing more than he would have liked.*

The Grand Salon de Conversation *of the France was one of the reasons why she was nicknamed the 'Chateau of the Atlantic'. The vast first class public room was decorated in all the grandeur of Louis Quatorze complete with a portrait of* Le Soleil Roi *after Rigaud.*

ment of the CGT as it was public safety. It was deemed an affair of state that nothing interfere with the maiden sailing of the pride of the French Merchant Marine.

The external contours of the *France* gave an impression very similar to the 1890 drawings of what a five-day boat should look like—very long and sleek, lean and racy. The four oval funnels of the liner were smaller than those of her rivals and situated in the middle two-fifths of the ship. The bow jutted out before them, but 40 per cent of the vessel's length lay aft of the fourth funnel. The appearance of great speed was emphasised by a broad white strake running from bow to second mast.

The internal fittings of the *France* may well have been the most expensive per public room ever used in the decor of an Atlantic liner. The basic theme was the full-blown opulence of Louis XIV, and a substantial effort was put forth to recreate the grandeur of Versailles afloat. The large embarkation hall on 'F' deck was calculated to stun the arriving passenger not only by its considerable size, but also because it was graced by two sweeping staircases patterned after the Bibliotheque Nationale in Paris. Immediately forward of the embarkation hall was the first level of the three-deck-high first class dining saloon, which was lighted and ventilated by double ports enclosed by stained glass windows with black and gold frames. The electric lighting was hidden in clusters of snowdrops which gave a picturesque effect when in use. The cuisine on the *France* may well have been the finest ever served on any passenger liner crossing the North Atlantic. Other lines endeavoured to excel in their national specialities and often succeeded very well indeed since one of the great pleasures of any crossing was the sumptuous food. However, the chefs of the *France* worked miracles no matter what seas the great ship was steaming through and the matchless splendour of the dining saloon provided an appropriate and complimentary setting for each gourmet feast.

The boat deck was almost completely devoted to first class passengers. Ascending to the deck by the grand curving staircase which rose through five decks, a comfortable 'galerie', or enclosed promenade, with floor to ceiling windows lay before the passenger. Strolling aft one entered the *Salon Mixte* where ladies and gentlemen could gather in a typical ornate Victorian parlour complete with heavy furniture, skylight and palm trees. Immediately aft of the *Salon Mixte* was another enclosed gallery running along the fourth funnel casing which led to one of the most bizarre public rooms on any transatlantic liner, *Le Salon Mauresque,* or Moroccan Room. The repeated clashes of France and Germany over Morocco and control of the Straits of Gibraltar had stimulated a new European interest in all things Moroccan. Quite simply between 1908-1914 there was a Moroccan fad in full swing with an emphasis on Moorish art and architecture. The CGT capitalised on this by making one of the smaller public rooms on the *France* into an elaborate Moorish living room and coffee salon. Everywhere was a riot of geometric patterns from the fine oriental carpets on the floor to the magnificent tiles on the walls and the intricate carvings on the ceiling. A marble fountain supplied a constant flow of water *à la Alhambra* but kept ice cool for American palates. At appointed times French Line personnel each wearing baggy pantaloons and a fez served strong coffee in little cups.

Walking still further aft on the boat deck the male traveller could enter the sanctuary of the smoking room. No funnel uptake divided the room as in the German greyhounds, instead the room stretched the width of the deck house and was described as a 'câfé' by the CGT complete with a terrace shielded from North Atlantic gusts by wall-like extensions of the deck housing aft. On the terrace a dozen tables made a beautiful setting for outdoor coffee whenever weather conditions permitted, heightened by the playing of the ship's orchestra in the afternoon.

If the traveller reached the boat deck by the staircase and elected to stroll forward, the magnificent and awe-inspiring *Grand Salon de Conversation* would overwhelm the senses. The *Grand Salon* was unmistakably Louis XIV in style even to massive oil paintings of the king, one after Rigaud's likeness in the Louvre showing the king in majesty, and the other representing him returning from the hunt. These faced each other across the room and were accompanied by smaller paintings of the king's favourites with substantially more clothing about their persons than the king would have approved—if other examples in French chateaux are any indication! Victorian propriety sometimes weighed heavily on feminine charms. Everywhere lavish decoration abounded. The ceiling, covered with gold fleurs-de-lis, curved upward to an elaborate domed skylight of the finest polished glass. Pale, fluted Corinthian columns supported the ceiling as they marched down the room, their eucalyptus leaf capitals splendid with gold leaf. The solid armchairs were fit for a king and upholstered with either high plush or the crewel fabric the French Line was always so fond of for public room furniture. The

A first class suite on the France was designed to surpass even the accommodation of a grand hotel. The style of this particular suite was described as being after 'The Directory'.

The first class Salon Mixte for ladies and gentlemen after dinner was designed to make the wealthy passenger feel at home with the heavy furniture, palm trees and glass of a Victorian or late 19th century parlour.

A Moroccan fad gripped the European public stimulated by the competition between Germany and France for control of that kingdom. A Moroccan Room was one of the first class public rooms and was famous for its after-dinner coffee.

final touch was provided by a full-length, specially created Aubusson carpet of the most magnificent character. The visual result gained for the *France* the nickname, 'Chateau of the Atlantic', for the sheer overwhelming opulence of her interior decor.

Forward of the *Grand Salon* on the port side lay the telegraph room and, separated by a passageway, the gymnasium. On the starboard side, the well-appointed library with a pair of first class cabins beyond completed the deck. Passengers travelling on the *France* found little to fault with her appointments or conveniences which included for the first time on a French ship two lifts tucked into the space forward of the grand staircase.

The *France* sailed from Le Havre on Saturday, April 20 1912, under the command of Captain Poncelet for her maiden voyage to New York. The ship's orchestra played one jaunty French marching song after another as the giant liner slowly left her pier, a tradition maintained to the end, even if over the loudspeakers of the *France* (III) in 1974. The glorious occasion was dimmed by the universal horror of the world over the catastrophic loss of the White Star liner *Titanic* just five days before! The CGT did everything conceivable to reassure their clientele about the safety of their ships and the navigational precautions taken by their masters. It was widely publicised that the new *France* was equipped with sufficient life-saving apparatus for all and that this included 22 lifeboats on her boat deck with accommodation for 52 each, totalling 1,144 places, in addition to two boats capable of carrying 25 each, and life rafts forward and aft on the boat deck capable of caring for 32 people each. It was not mentioned, however, that out of a maximum capacity of 2,476 passengers and crew, over half (1,282) would have to rely on the life rafts and that since the crew numbered 613, and some of them unquestionably would be needed to man the lifeboats, all 916 steerage could expect the invigorating alternatives of a life raft or having to swim for it! At least they *did* have an alternative, unlike the tragic figures on the *Titanic*, and the two liners would have arrived in New York within a week of each other on their maiden voyages.

Above right *A view across the first class dining salon of the* France *with fresh flowers on every table shortly after a sailing.* (Everett E. Viez Collection).

Right *The grand staircase provided a matchless entrance for the first class traveller into the dining salon. Few Continental hotels could match, let alone surpass, this extravagance* (Everett E. Viez Collection).

Left *The first class dining salon on the* France *was designed to provide an appropriate setting for the gourmet feasts emerging from the kitchens. Towering three decks high, the room was splendidly appointed with numerous mirrors to enhance its expansiveness.*

Right *The* Grand Salon *could be converted into a chapel for Sunday morning services. The large American flag was a gift of the United States Government to the ship and it with the* Tricolore *served to mask the portrait of Louis XIV for divine services.*

Captain Poncelet took the new long southern route also publicised by the French Line in the New York papers which was intended to avoid any possibility of icebergs. During the crossing on the fifth day out fog was encountered off the Grand Banks and Poncelet took his charge even further south to get clear of it since the giant ice field that had spelled disaster to the *Titanic* was still in existence. The *France* made the passage of 3,276 miles from Le Havre to the Ambrose Channel Lightship in 6 days, 4 hours, 31 minutes. Her best day's run was 561 miles on the last full day and she averaged 22.45 knots for the crossing. In all she brought 163 first, 162 second and 949 steerage passengers to New York.

The passengers on the maiden crossing praised the *France* for her stability but others noted on later crossings that she could roll very substantially and that there existed considerable vibration towards the stern. Both problems were tackled in the first off season and the tendency to roll was alleviated by extending and enlarging the bilge keels. Vibration was reduced by installing newly designed propellers on the inboard shafts. Captain Poncelet was asked to evaluate his new command and he described her simply as a 'good ship', but

he clearly had a warm regard for his last command, *La Provence*, which had a high reputation for steadiness. Diplomatically he refused to compare the two vessels. Delays at Quarantine and the difficulty inherent in handling a new vessel at her New York pier delayed the actual docking by nearly four hours. This gave reporters time to interview the distinguished passengers including Louis Bleriot, the famous French aviator who had won the London *Daily Mail*'s £10,000 prize for the first Cross-channel flight, and who was on a vacation to America.

The *France* remained several days at New York for the traditional publicity and hoopla surrounding the maiden crossing of a great liner. On the eastbound run she crossed in 5 days, 20 hours, 46 minutes at slightly over 23 knots which was a speed record for the French Line. Among her first class passengers was Osmont Theyner, the cotton broker, who had survived the sinking of the *Titanic* and who received an emotional welcome at Le Havre from friends and family. The *France* had performed solidly and the CGT was well satisfied with their new flagship.

The new liner had one more round trip to New York before the French maritime industry was hit by a major strike. The CGT was among the most obstinate of steamship lines in refusing to negotiate with its men. At the same time the line persuaded the French government that the mails must go through. When the strike hit with the arrival of the *France* on June 8 the management appealed to Paris for aid and received it in the form of 163 bluejackets recruited from naval vessels in the western ports so that *La Provence* could sail with a strike-busting crew on June 16. The strike leaders were incensed because the French Line refused even the government entreaties to negotiate while the Messageries Maritimes of Marseilles were willing to do so, and made the fact known publicly.

Troops were called out at Le Havre to guard the *France* and to guarantee the safe departure of *La Provence*. Wisely, the strike leaders responded by keeping their men home in the knowledge that there were not enough sailors to man every mail boat and that Paris would soon tire of the disruption and cost to the navy. The Central Committee of the Seamen's Union called for a 24-48 hour strike in order to demonstrate solidarity with Le Havre workers. *La Provence,* with her bluejacket sailors, reached New York late owing to bad weather and the unfamiliarity of the stokers with the liner's boilers. An effort to submit grievances to binding arbitration failed and the summer of 1912 proved to be a long hot one in terms of labour relations. Some ameliorating factors for the French Line were that the stewards did not join the strike because the sailors had not supported them in the previous year. Interestingly, the wages paid to French naval sailors at this time were some five to six times lower than those paid to their striking counterparts on the *France.*

The nationwide seamen's strike was a financial disaster to French shipowners but the CGT remained adamant in refusing to grant higher wages to its men. Rioting occurred at Le Havre on July 5 with some property damage. Among the leaders were some women wearing red sashes calculated to inflame public opinion with visions of barricades and the Paris Commune. However, if the French public was aroused by the threat of anarchy, the justice of the seamen's claims was emphasised when the officers of the French Line working the Mediterranean fleet decided to join them and paralysed the Corsican and Algerian services. In the end negotiations did occur and some upward adjustments in wages were achieved by the autumn.

When World War 1 broke out in August 1914 the *France* was at Le Havre having just brought a portion of the summer rush of tourists to Europe.

Immediately many Americans vacationing in France tried to flee the war zone amid wild scenes at the French Line offices. Fears were engendered that the German armies might cut the railways to Le Havre and plans were described in the press to take passengers bound for the *France* down the Seine in pleasure steamers so that they would not miss the sailing. The *France* was scheduled to depart on August 4 and she was completely sold out with some 2,000 travellers holding tickets and permitted only to take hand luggage. So pressing was the demand that the officers agreed to give up their cabins so that additional Americans could be accommodated. The scare was heightened by the fact that any large city like Paris is highly dependent on the regular arrival of foodstuffs from the countryside which had been disrupted, thereby creating a scarcity. Furthermore, in an effort to stabilise and maintain the currency in the immediate panic, French banks were either closed or significantly limiting withdrawals—so much so that the American Consul-General in Paris, Henry W. Diederich, even wired Washington to appeal for a relief ship. In New York the scene was equally frantic as the French Navy took over the CGT offices in order to provide accommodation for Frenchmen returning to the colours. *La Lorraine* sailed on August 5 from New York with 2,000 French reservists on board dramatically singing *La Marseillaise* at the top of their voices as the liner backed out into the North River and bid adieu to 8,000 well-wishers on the shore. Sentiments changed to intense hostility as *La Lorraine* passed the liners of Hamburg America and Norddeutscher Lloyd tied up at their Hoboken piers on her way down stream.

The *France* reached New York without incident and delivered her grateful passengers. Never more profitable, she saw many more Americans safely home before being taken over and commissioned as a unit of the French Navy. Initially she was renamed *France IV* and fitted as an armed merchant cruiser but it was soon realised that she was too big and valuable for that service. Therefore she was re-employed as an armed transport and specifically delegated to carrying troops to the Eastern Mediterranean for the Dardanelles Campaign, which tried to split the Ottoman Empire away from her Axis Allies. Next she served as a hospital ship and the most common World War 1 photographs date from this period with the liner painted white and large red crosses adorning her sides. The war took a heavy toll on the ship, which could carry over 4,000 soldiers at a time, and it was found necessary to overhaul her at Toulon early in 1917. The opportunity was

Top *The* France *as a hospital ship in World War 1 with the name* France IV. *This followed her initial designation as an armed merchant cruiser. As a hospital ship she served in the Mediterranean bringing wounded home from the Dardanelles.*

Above *After the American Declaration of War (April 1917) the* France *served as a transport carrying units of the American Expeditionary Force to Europe. This rare photo shows her in dazzle paint late in 1917* (US Navy).

Below *The* France *sails from New York in the late 1920s carrying some of the annual migration of vacationing Americans to Europe. The liner was never more popular to thirsty Americans than during Prohibition* (Everett E. Viez Collection).

The France *slams by the* Paris *in mid-Atlantic around 1925 in a dramatic meeting with her larger consort* (Everett E. Viez Collection).

taken to extend the boat deck aft to the stern and fit a docking bridge since manoeuvring was frequently difficult in little known harbours or anchorages. The *France* emerged just in time to transport American troops to Europe as soon as the American Expeditionary Force could be made ready in the fall of 1917 following the American Declaration of War.

In July 1918 the *France* was part of a huge fast-troopship convoy which sailed from New York for Brest. Included in the convoy were the *Orizaba,* the *America* (ex-*Amerika*), *Mount Vernon* (ex-*Kronprinzessin Cecilie*) and *Agamemnon* (ex-*Kaiser Wilhelm II*). During this crossing the British freighter *Instructor* suddenly found itself bow on to the fast transports and in a frantic effort to avoid the on-rushing *France* ran foul of the *America* which hit her amidships and sank her instantly. The *France*'s World War 1 service was marred by only one other incident when an explosion occurred in her boiler room in 1918 which killed nine men and injured many more. Following the accident she was returned to the French Line and employed during late 1918 and early 1919 in carrying American troops home from Brest. Her most joyous arrival in New York was on Christmas Eve 1918 when she steamed in with 3,865 troops on board. In 1919 the *France* began to carry a few commercial passengers as well as troops and some of the totals were spectacular. On February 2 she sailed from Bordeaux with 516 first, 56 second and 4,167 troops! A total of 4,739 passengers and 613 crew!

The *France* rejoined the Le Havre service on August 6 1919. Over a year later, on January 16 1921, she steamed into New York with the largest number of commercial passengers ever carried by a French Line vessel—170 first, 462 second and 1,959 third class, a grand total of 2,591 fares.

A joyous event indeed was the maiden voyage of the new *Paris* (1921, 34,569 tons) which began on June 15 1921. The *Paris* had been under construction when war was declared, launched on September 12 1916 and laid-up in Quiberon Bay until hostilities ceased and she could be completed as planned. The French Line took advantage of the fact that the *France* desperately needed a major reconditioning to convert her from coal to oil-fired boilers during 1923-1924. At the same time passenger accommodation was revised from 535 first, 440 second and 950 third (1912) to 517 first, 444 second and 660 third (1924) in recognition of the drastic changes in American immigration policy after the war. On May 10 1924 the *France* returned to the Havre-Plymouth-New York service, the Plymouth call being reintroduced in 1922. She was just in time for the high season and together with the *Paris* and the *De Grasse* (1924, 17,707 tons) maintained the premier French Line schedule until the maiden voyage of the great *Ile de France* (43,153 tons) on June 22 1927. The shipping slump of the 1920s saw the scrapping of *La Lorraine* in 1922 and *La Savoie* in 1928 after the *Ile de France* entered service. The intermediate units of the French Line subsequently included the *De Grasse, Lafayette* (1930, 25,178 tons) and *Champlain* (1932, 28,124 tons).

The slack winter months of 1928-1929 saw the *France* taking occasional cruises, particularly to the Mediterranean, but her uneconomical propulsion system made the cost prohibitive. When the American Stock Market crash of 1929 drastically reduced the number of passengers and the amount

The France *backs out of Pier 52, North River, New York for a Mediterranean cruise on January 10 1931. The cruise would take two months and would represent an unsuccessful effort to make money in the off-season. Note the well-wishers bundled up against the frigid gusts along the New York waterfront* (Everett E. Viez Collection).

of cargo, the Compagnie Générale Transatlantique lost 31,000,000 francs in 1930 and the astronomical sum of 369,000,000 francs in 1931. In the face of such a catastrophe no uneconomical unit could have its working life prolonged. The *France*'s last sailing from New York on September 9 1932 was unheralded since her retirement was announced in mid-crossing. On arrival at Le Havre she was laid-up—always a dangerous time for any large ship. On January 7 1933 a small fire occurred on board which the watchmen were able to put out, but her days were numbered. In 1934 she was offered for scrapping and sold to Dunkirk where

she caught fire once more during demolition before the job was completed in 1935. Her successor in the first class mail service was the giant *Normandie* (79,280 tons) which entered service on May 29 1935.

The *France* remains one of the most luxurious examples of French art and industry ever to put to sea. She represents the splendid pinnacle of the shipbuilders' art in France before World War 1 and, as such, warrants attention in any history of the North Atlantic. She was the only French four-funnel liner and a magnificent vessel throughout her two decades of service.

The last four-funnelled passenger liners did not make their debut until the 1920s, but their story, to all intents and purposes, begins on April 13 1909. On that day Sir Donald Currie, chairman of the Union-Castle Mail Steamship Company, died at Sidmouth. Sir Donald had, for years, been a powerful force in South African shipping, having founded the Castle Line in 1872. Twenty-eight years later, he masterminded the amalgamation of the Castle Line with the Union Line, creating the premier steamship service between the United Kingdom and South Africa. With Sir Donald's death, however, the company came upon rather troubled times, including negotiations with the South African government for a new mail contract. It was about this time that the Royal Mail Steam Packet Company group, headed by Sir Owen Philipps, was in the process of buying up nearly every available steamship line, including Pacific Steam Navigation, Lamport & Holt, Nelson and Elder Dempster. It came as little surprise that the Royal Mail group snatched up the Union-Castle Line in April 1912.

It did not take the new management long to set about a major rehabilitation programme, the first part of which involved several new steamers for the African East Coast service. But it was the mail service in which Sir Owen (later Lord Kylsant) ws most interested, and it was here that he planned his most dramatic move: a pair of steamers far larger than any yet seen on the Cape service and of a totally new design. The plan called for ships that would make an immediate and lasting impression on travellers and shippers alike, and it was left to the brilliant Belfast shipbuilder Lord Pirrie to carry it out. It was not an unexpected choice, for Sir Owen had long maintained close personal and business ties with him, and the new ships were to be the first of a generation of Union-Castle liners built by Harland and Wolff.

Marine architects went to work on the new ships and produced a type totally new to the Cape service. The plan called for two identical turbine-driven ships of 19,023 gross tons, 661 feet in overall length with a beam of 72.5 feet. The hull design, basically traditional, introduced the cruiser stern to South African operations. But despite a tonnage nearly double that previously seen on the Cape service, it was the four-funnelled profile which caused the most stir. This was still the era when a ship's size was apt to be judged by the number of funnels. Yet from an aesthetic point of view, the funnels left something to be desired, for there were many complaints that they were too thin. Were it not for the visual impact that was intended, two funnels would have done nicely.

Initially, the names *Amroth Castle* and *Windsor Castle* were chosen for the pair, but *Arundel Castle* was later substituted for the former. A minor controversy developed over the name *Windsor Castle* for there was already a 40-ton wooden steamboat of the same name in service on the Severn. Union-Castle officials were most anxious to use this name for their new liner, so after much dickering, the owners of the little steamer were persuaded to relinquish the name.

Harland and Wolff began work on the *Arundel Castle* on November 6 1915, but the Belfast yard had so much work already on its books that it handed over the *Windsor Castle*'s contract to John Brown and Company, Clydebank. World War 1 was already well under way by this time, and it is not surprising that consideration was given on several occasions to completing the *Arundel Castle* in an austerity form as a transport or auxiliary cruiser. Work on the *Windsor Castle* was held off until after the war. Subsequently the *Arundel Castle* was completed as a passenger liner and launched on September 11 1919, six years after

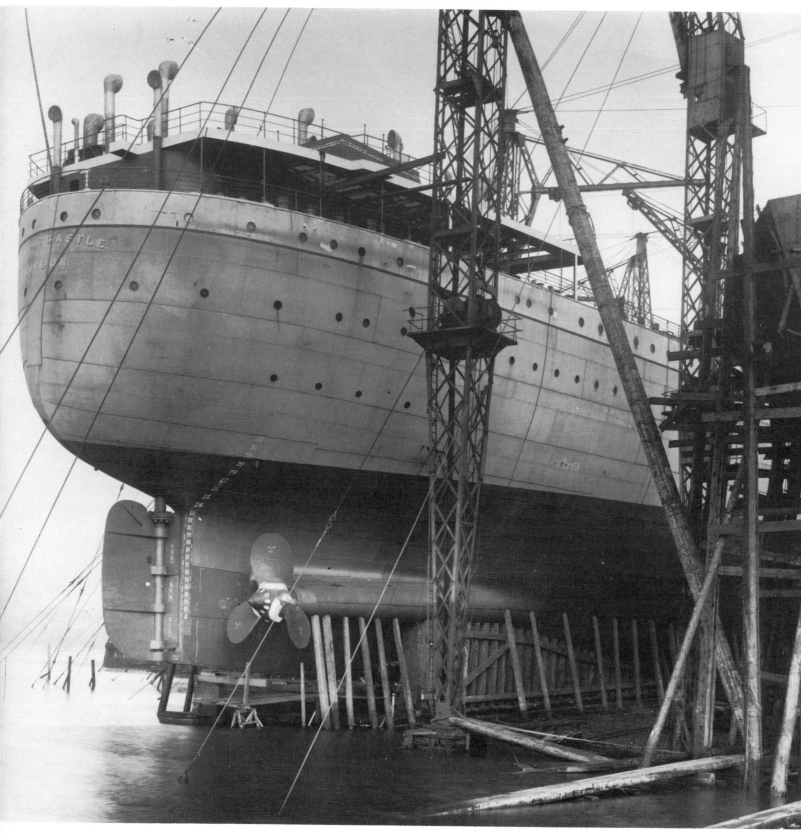

Opposite *A detailed view of the* Windsor Castle*'s stern prior to launching. This view shows the cruiser stern design which the two four-stackers introduced to the Cape service* (Scottish Records Office).

Right *The date is March 9 1921. The place is John Brown's shipyard. HRH The Prince of Wales doffs his hat to the crowd, having just named the* Windsor Castle. *This is believed to have been the first time a member of the Royal Family participated in the naming of a merchant vessel* (Union Castle Line).

Below right *HRH The Prince of Wales has just named the* Windsor Castle *and the ship is seen here sliding down the ways into the Clyde. Clydebank shipwrights were critical of the liner's design, but could not get Union Castle officials to alter the plans* (Scottish Records Office).

first being conceived. The launch of the *Windsor Castle* followed on March 9 1921 and was quite an affair. Prior to that occasion Royalty had been associated only with warship launchings, but the honour of naming the new Cape liner went to HRH The Prince of Wales, later to become Edward VIII. As a result the *Windsor Castle* became the first British passenger ship to be launched by a member of the Royal Family and began a tradition that has persisted to the present day. But all this pomp and fanfare notwithstanding, criticisms of the ships began to surface.

There were many complaints that in terms of plan and propulsion, the new liners were already outdated. For one thing, they were coal burners in an era when almost every other modern vessel used oil. The turbines consumed vast quantities of coal and provided very poor backing power, an affliction common to many early turbine steamers. On trials it was discovered that both new ships showed an annoying tendency to drag aft and were exceptionally difficult to steer. Finally, there was considerable griping because the four smoke uptakes cut through virtually every important public room. 'From a naval architectural point of view,' says George Young, marine editor of *The Cape Times*, 'the pair were abortions.'* The four funneled profile was also something of an anachronism in the early 1920s. One prominent official of John Brown's later revealed that shipyard engineers were so dissatisfied with the plans provided them that they tried in vain to get Union-Castle to alter their ship's design to bring her more in line with the times. As far as the propulsion was concerned, it was just about the best that could be had when the ships were planned in 1914, but was considerably outdated by the time they appeared. Both steamers were twin-screw, with low pressure and

* *Salt in my Blood,* George Young (J.F. Midgley, 1975), p.55.

Left *The first class dining rooms were identical on the* Windsor Castle *and* Arundel Castle. *They were located amidships on the main deck and could seat 196 persons. The style was Georgian, the furniture Chippendale* (Union Castle Line).

Centre left *The first class lounge on the Union Castle four-stackers was located forward on the promenade deck and epitomised the comfortable accommodation of the two ships. Note the many fans used in the warmer Southern climate* (Union Castle Line).

Bottom left *A 17th century style giving the impression of a Tudor mansion was utilised for the first class smoke room on the* Arundel Castle *and* Windsor Castle. *The light wood panelling and leather upholstery were popular among passengers* (Union Castle Line).·

high pressure turbines designed to produce a maximum speed of 17 knots, although they averaged between 15 and 16 knots on their long voyages. They were also voracious coal eaters, consuming about 4,000 tons per voyage. Eleven single and double-ended boilers supplied the steam and it is surprising that Union-Castle resisted suggestions to revise the plan and install the more efficient oil-fired water tube boilers when completion of the ships was delayed by the war.

One facet of the ships' design that evoked considerable comment was the gantry davit concept that was supposed to launch all 12 boats piled in a cluster aft of the fourth funnel on either side of the ship within 20 minutes. One former crewman, William R. Woodhouse, writes that 'in an emergency (they) never would have been launched; it took hours to get them out'.* The concept, like that on White Star's *Britannic,* appears to have been prompted by the sinking of the *Titanic,* but was never put to the test and was ultimately removed during rebuilding in 1937.

Despite the various criticisms of the ships' machinery, the accommodation was highly regarded by passengers, although they too had a complaint. All first class staterooms had a two-inch gap at the top of the bulkheads between rooms. This was done to allow adequate circulation of air in the warmer climates, but it was frowned upon by passengers primarily because of the lack of privacy and because light could leak into the rooms at night. From a safety point of view, it is difficult to understand why such an arrangement was permitted because of the natural draught it would have provided should there have been a fire. Nevertheless, the accommodation offered amenities hitherto unseen on the Cape

* Letter from W.R. Woodhouse to J.H. Shaum, Jr, July 11 1975.

An overhead view of the Windsor Castle *in the late stages of fitting-out at John Brown's early in 1922. Although conceived with the great transatlantic liners in mind, this picture graphically portrays the diminutive dimensions of the ship and her rather cluttered decks. An indication of just how small the funnels were can be had by noting the men standing on deck* (Scottish Records Office).

service: suites of rooms, private bathrooms, many single-berth cabins and comfortable beds. The suites-de-luxe were on the upper deck and consisted of a sitting room, bedroom, bathroom and maids' room. These rooms also featured real beds instead of berths. The public rooms have been described as cheerful and represented a vast improvement over anything previously seen in the South African trade. The first class lounge, for instance, was panelled in oak and furnished in the Louis XVI style. The Georgian style was chosen for the first class dining saloon, the furniture being early Chippendale. In the first class smoking room, one could find a 17th century style reminiscent of a Tudor mansion. Passengers in second and third class also fared rather well, public rooms in these classes being well lit and finished in mahogany panelling.

First into service was the *Arundel Castle*, which left Southampton on her maiden voyage on April 22 1921, arriving in Cape Town on May 9. She edged out the White Star *Ceramic* as the largest liner serving South Africa and was enthusiastically received. The *Windsor Castle* entered service in March 1922 and about the only items to tell the two apart were the derricks against the bridge front of the *Arundel Castle*. At that time the schedule called for the mailships to depart from Southampton at 4 pm on Friday, with a stop on Tuesday at Madeira to land mail and an arrival at Cape Town 13 days later. After discharging passengers and cargo, it was another day's steaming to Mossel Bay and Algoa Bay to drop off cargo before winding up the voyage in Durban where both passengers and cargo were unloaded. During a five day layover, the ship was re-stored, coaled and took on cargo and passengers. Normally the outward bound cargo consisted of Royal Mail and general cargo, while the return trip saw the holds filled with fruit and cowhides. Homeward bound, it was usually straight through to Southampton after stopping at the various South African ports with no call at Madeira.

The two main mailships may have proved themselves popular among passengers, but they certainly did not endear themselves to harbour pilots. Once again the design was blamed; this time it was the turbines' inability to respond quickly and provide sufficient astern power. Add to that the poor steering qualities and exposed harbours, and it is easy to see why pilots did not look forward to their appearance in South African waters. Most pilots had to ask for full speed astern minutes before they actually needed it because of the lengthy lapse of time before the astern turbines could produce adequate power.

A scene repeated with clockwork regularity during the 38-year career of the Arundel Castle. *With Table Mountain forming a magnificent backdrop, the liner manoeuvres in Cape Town harbour* (John H. Shaum, Jr, Collection).

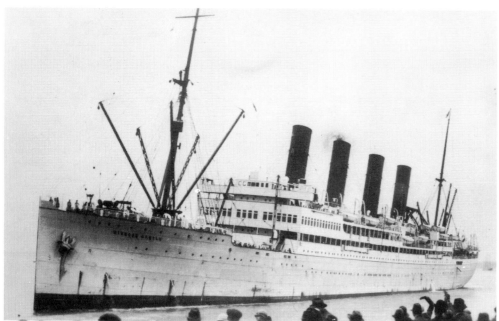

Virtually identical sister ships despite being built at separate yards, the Arundel Castle *and* Windsor Castle *could only be distinguished by the ventilators on the* Arundel Castle's *bridge front. Note their absence on the* Windsor Castle (John H. Shaum, Jr, Collection).

Here is a starboard quarter view of the Arundel Castle *in which can be seen the array of lifeboats behind the fourth funnel. This photograph may have been taken on her trials* (Union Castle Line).

For the most part, the careers of the *Arundel Castle* and *Windsor Castle* were unspectacular as they steamed back and forth at speeds not much in excess of the *Briton* which came out in 1898. In 1925 the *Arundel Castle* made news when, in the midst of a lengthy seamans' strike, she managed to run from Cape Town to Southampton with an array of passengers including college students, a clergyman and even an opera singer, labouring in her boiler rooms to help get her home. Unbelievably, she arrived in port only eight hours behind schedule. A similar situation ensued ten years later when the *Windsor Castle* was despatched to Lobito to pick up Prince George who had just completed a Royal visit to Angola. The detour meant that the ship had to try and make up time, no mean task considering there was no real reserve of speed. As a result, passengers turned out in large numbers to assist the exhausted stokers in pouring coal into the hungry furnaces hoping to add a knot to the ship's speed. The Prince himself even fell to the task of shovelling coal in the vessel's steaming stokehold.

All went generally well through the 1920s and into the early 1930s, but problems were brewing. The Royal Mail group had, by this time, managed to gain control of about one-sixth of the world's passenger ship tonnage, but was bending beneath the strain. It was having problems repaying government loans and had literally bitten off more than it could chew with the acquisition of the White Star Line from the International Mercantile Marine company. With the advent of the Depression, the giant Royal Mail organisation caved in in 1931, allowing the Union Castle Line and the other group members to resume independent management. The following year, Robertson Fyffe Gibb, a longtime employee of the Union-Castle Line, assumed the chairmanship. If anyone could be counted on to bring the company to the forefront of British shipping concerns, he could. At about the same time, the South African government, somewhat unexpectedly, entered into an agreement with the Italians for a subsidised service between Mediterranean ports and the Cape. This new agreement was primarily an effort by the South African government to tap new markets for its produce in Southern Europe, but it can also be interpreted as an attempt to bring new life to the somewhat complacent operation of the mail service by Union-Castle. The Italian liners placed on the Cape service were the 21,000-tonners *Giulio Cesare* and *Duilio,* a pair of magnificent 19-knot liners that could easily outstrip the best Union Castle had to offer. The British company *had* to do something.

Under the leadership of Robertson Fyffe Gibb, the company put into operation quite the most ambitious tonnage programme in its history. First to appear were the splendid 25,000-ton *Stirling Castle* and *Athlone Castle* in 1936. At about the same time, a new mail contract was signed calling for a reduction in the Southampton-Cape Town voyage from 17 to 13½ days and requiring a service speed of 19 knots. The two new ships, plus a third on the drawing board, could meet these requirements, but the older existing vessels could not.

The solution decided upon was to rebuild five mailships, including the *Arundel Castle* and *Windsor Castle.* In order to add three knots to their speed, it would be necessary to *double* the power and lengthen the hulls to obtain the proper form. First to return to Belfast for the work was the *Arundel Castle* which was withdrawn from service early in 1937. For more than nine months, shipyard workers laboured, tearing out the old engines and boilers, lengthening the bow by 15 feet and radically altering the ship's appearance. The old turbines were discarded in favour of newer, more efficient ones, the nine double-ended Scotch boilers came out in favour of four oil-fired water tube type which took up less space and required only two smoke flues. This meant two large funnels in place of the four thin ones, large stacks that had a fine rake to them and added greatly to the ship's appearance. The hull redesign gave the liner a sharply raked prow, and combined with the other changes, increased her gross tonnage to 19,118. The gantry davits aft were removed, providing additional deck space, and in the eyes of many the ship not only took on a much more graceful appearance, but became the finest looking unit ever owned by Union Castle. In addition to the obvious propulsion and cosmetic revisions, there were other changes as well. The most noteworthy as far as passengers were concerned was the elimination of third class in favour of a new tourist class.

Following her extensive reconstruction at Belfast the *Arundel Castle* began her trials on September 20 1937 and met the speed requirement of 19 knots by half a knot. But in order to do this, she was run at top speed and still consumed a rather large amount of fuel. That annoying drag aft was also still present. When the *Windsor Castle* returned several months later, she made 21 knots and didn't drag quite as badly, but then again she was always a shade faster and a little easier to handle. Everyone was pleased, for with the reconstruction of the other liners, the Union-Castle now had a top-notch fleet, and could look to the future with optimism. But it was December 1938 before the new schedule went into effect and by then there was little opportunity for optimism.

Most of the Union-Castle fleet was snatched up early in World War 2 for service as armed merchant cruisers, troopships or hospital ships. The *Arundel Castle* and *Windsor Castle* both became troopers and often operated in worldwide convoy service. The *Arundel Castle* was in one of the first convoys to get through the Mediterranean, although she was unsuccessfully attacked on at least one occasion by glider bombers and torpedo bombers. This same ship also participated in the North African and Sicilian landings and saw service in convoys to Durban, Suez and even US ports.

Early in the war the *Windsor Castle* went through a harrowing experience which was just a prelude for worse to come. The vessel was proceeding toward England on November 4 1940 and was off the Irish coast when she was attacked by a four-engined Focke Wulf FW 200. Four bombs were dropped near the liner, but the plane had trouble moving in for the kill because of the fierce fight put up by her anti-aircraft gunners. The battle was so intense that German propagandists announced the ship had been crippled by a near-miss and severely damaged by a direct hit. There was some truth to the latter statement as exemplified in a purser's matter-of-fact announcement to passengers in the lounge: 'The captain's compliments. He wishes to advise you there is an unexploded 500 lb bomb in the first class smoking room, and will you all please go to the stern of the ship.'* So the passengers, 90 in all, evacuated to the tourist areas of the vessel and although many volunteers offered to try and dump the bomb overboard, the Admiralty instructed the ship to try and make port with the projectile where it was. After more than 30 hours the *Windsor Castle* docked at Greenock, disembarking some *very* relieved passengers! The bomb, very much 'alive', was removed safely from the ship, and she was returned to service shortly thereafter.

But later on the *Windsor Castle*'s luck ran out. March 23 1943 found her in convoy about 110 miles north-west of Algiers heading for the Tunisian battlefront. Aboard were more than 2,000 British troops. It was a beautiful moonlit night when, around 2.30 am, a German torpedo bomber suddenly appeared. At first the liner's crew throught the aircraft was friendly, but at a range of less than 100 yards, the plane dropped a

torpedo at the *Windsor Castle* which took a direct hit. Immediately the engine room and two holds flooded and within 20 minutes Captain John C. Brown gave the order to abandon ship. Captain Brown had high praise for the behaviour of the troops and crew: 'Although the ship was sinking they stood there like troops on parade until finally the destroyers came alongside and took them off.'* The evacuation proceeded quickly and easily and all but Captain Brown and 35 crewmen were transferred to nearby naval craft. The commander hoped the damaged liner could be towed to port, but by daybreak the situation had worsened and the crew members reluctantly left the ship. The *Windsor Castle,* however, remained afloat all day and by 5 pm additional naval vessels had arrived to begin the tow to Gibraltar. There was renewed hope among Captain Brown and the others that the ship might be saved after all, so along with a naval party, he returned to her to arrange the tow. But it was too late. The stricken liner began settling fast by the stern, forcing the group to hastily abandon ship. Captain Brown was the last to leave, sliding down a rope on to the deck of a destroyer. Shortly before 5.30 the *Windsor Castle*'s bow rose high above the sea and she slipped quickly from sight. Three seamen, out of more than 2,000 persons aboard, lost their lives. 'She had always been a dignified ship,' remarked Captain Brown, 'and her end was dignified too.'†

Eighteen months later, her sister ship *Arundel Castle* achieved fame for an entirely different reason. She was chosen to make several voyages under diplomatic immunity to exchange prisoners with the Germans. Her first repatriation voyage was in September 1944 when she carried 800 German prisoners of war to Gothenburg in return for 1,025 Allied prisoners. The *Arundel Castle* returned to Liverpool on September 16 1944 to a tumultuous welcome including salutes from nearby vessels, a Spitfire dipping in salute, military bands and huge crowds. The King and Queen also sent a warm message of greeting to the returning soldiers, the first of six shiploads of repatriates. A second diplomatic mission came in January 1945 when the liner again exchanged German prisoners for Allied captives, this time by way of Marseilles and Lisbon. By the time the war ended, the *Arundel Castle* had steamed more than 500,000 miles and carried more than 200,000 troops. Her longest single voyage took place late

* Unidentified newspaper clipping in the collection of J.H. Shaum, Jr.

* *The Glasgow Herald,* July 20 1945.

† *The Cape Times,* July 20 1945.

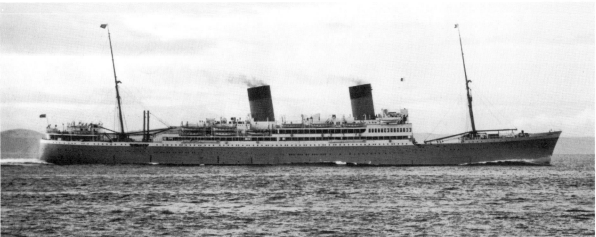

Top *Admiralty officials designated the* Windsor Castle *as a troopship as early as 1938. She is seen here early in her career as a troopship before armament could be installed* (National Maritime Museum).

Above *If there were ever any doubts as to whether the* Windsor Castle *looked better as a four-stacker or two-stacker, this photograph should dispel those doubts. She is seen here on trials following the 1937 refit* (Harland & Wolff Ltd).

Below *The* Arundel Castle *is seen preparing to depart from Cape Town. Two tugs manoeuvre into position to help head her out to sea* (Union Castle Line).

Left *Naval vessels stand by, awaiting the final plunge of the* Windsor Castle. *Her stern already out of sight, the transport is sinking rapidly and will be gone in a matter of minutes* (Union Castle Line).

Centre left *The Union Jack, denoting diplomatic immunity, is emblazoned on the side of the* Arundel Castle, *seen here on a repatriation voyage from Sweden on September 16 1944. Aboard were 1,025 prisoners-of-war* (Stewart Bale Ltd).

Bottom left *Judging from the radar screen atop the* Arundel Castle's *bridge, this photograph must date from the post-war years. A group of well-wishers waits on the Cape Town dock as the liner manoeuvres in the harbour* (National Maritime Museum).

Right *Table Bay is left behind forever as the* Arundel Castle, *dressed fore and aft, departs Cape Town on her final voyage as a mailship. Notice the cars and people along the bulkhead. She was given a tremendous send-off by the South Africans whom she had served so well for so many years* (Union Castle Line).

in 1945 when she travelled for 160 days, covering 45,225 miles.

When the war finally ended, most of the fleet returned to Union-Castle ownership, but not the *Arundel Castle*. The South African government was embarking on a campaign to lure skilled immigrants to the area and approached Union-Castle about providing transportation. Along with the *Carnarvon Castle* and *Winchester Castle,* the former four-stacker was pressed into an austerity immigration service. Since there was no time for renovation following trooping duties, this turned out to be a most unglamorous operation. The three vessels were employed in this fashion from June 1947 to May 1949 and, between them, carried 32,000 settlers to Africa. But before being returned to private ownership, the *Arundel Castle* was required once again for troopship duties, this time to the Middle East. Finally in September 1949 she was handed back to her owners with the hearty thanks of the government, the last Union-Castle liner to be returned after the war.

The vessel was taken to her builder's yard at Belfast for reconditioning and extensive modernisation, a procedure that took nearly a year to complete. During the reconversion many alterations and improvements were made to her accommodation and when she finally resumed service, it was as a two-class ship with space for first and tourist class passengers. The *Arundel Castle*'s first postwar sailing as a mailship began on September 21 1950 from Southampton, and although she was now nearly 30 years old and by far the oldest unit of the fleet, she remained enormously popular, often carrying capacity loads.

A passenger on one of her early postwar voyages was Ray Catterall of Lancashire who was making his first long-distance sea voyage. He was completely captivated by the old lady. 'The *Arundel Castle* had fine passenger accommodation . . . her first class lounge had the atmosphere of a room in some large English country house', he recalls. 'That first voyage on the *Arundel Castle* held some sort of magic which is hard to define. She appeared a very happy ship, and though quite old, the majority of her crew spoke of her in terms of affection quite unlike any liner I have been on since. To put it in a nutshell, she had atmosphere, and . . . some quite large and famous ships can lack this basic ingredient.'*

During the 1950s a number of newer Union-Castle liners appeared to expand the service and take over from the older ships. During this same period, the Union-Castle Line came under the ownership of the Clan Line. Nevertheless the *Arundel Castle* remained in service for most of the decade, not bowing out until 1958 to the new 27,109-ton *Pendennis Castle*, the first new mailship to appear under the new ownership.

The *Arundel Castle*'s demise after so long and honourable a career brought forth a tremendous outpouring of emotion when it was announced she would be sold for scrap. Her final departure from Southampton as a mailship came on November 6 1958 with calls at all the usual ports. At

each, she received a huge send-off, with thousands of people turning out to say goodbye and flotillas of small craft escorting her out to sea. The biggest farewell came when she departed Cape Town for the last time on December 5. More than 10,000 people packed the shoreline to see her off as she headed out of Table Bay, followed by a procession of tugs, like herself, dressed overall for the occasion. Overhead, aircraft dipped in salute as the old mail liner passed out of Cape Town for the final time. She had made more than 200 voyages in her long career, covering some 3,000,000 miles.

The *Arundel Castle* arrived back in Southampton on December 19 and furled her house flag for the final time. Having been sold to Chiap Hua Manufactury Company of Hong Kong for scrapping, the liner sailed away to her doom on December 30 1958. At length, and without incident, she arrived at Gin Drinker's Bay, Hong Kong, for demolition. She was the largest vessel broken up at the Far East port to that date and it took more than a year to demolish her.

The last of the four-stackers to go, she was never the largest, fastest or most luxurious. Despite many shortcomings, she nevertheless epitomised the four-stacker era through her ability to offer reliable, comfortable service both in war and peace.

It was an era whose like will never be seen again, an era when majesty truly went to sea.

* Letter from Ray Catterall to J.H. Shaum, Jr, July 21 1975.

Acknowledgements

A book such as this, of necessity, requires substantial research and the utilisation of relatively new and hitherto unseen material. The gathering of material for *Majesty at Sea* could not have been accomplished without the assistance of a great many people.

In particular, many individuals, both in the United States and Great Britain aided in this project. It might be truthfully said that without the assistance of Everett E. Viez of Boynton Beach, Florida and John Blake of Hull, Massachusetts, this book would not have been possible. Both gentlemen lent unstintingly of their splendid photographic collections and are due a hearty thanks from the authors. Similarly, artists Ken Marschall of Redondo Beach, California, and Edward W. Bearman of West Alldis, Wisconsin, are due thanks for the use of their paintings as is C. Leslie Oursler of Manchester, Maryland. Alan Hedgley, public affairs manager of Harland & Wolff Ltd, provided much useful material as did G. Bentley of Thomas W. Ward Ltd. Without the assistance of Conrad Milster, Jr, of Brooklyn, New York, technical information on vessels' engines would be sorely lacking. Thanks are also tendered to the following individuals who provided information from their collections as well as helpful suggestions: N.R.P. Bonsor, John Maxtone-Graham, L.A. Haslett, Ray Catterall, George Young, Dr and Mrs E.K. Haviland, Alexander Leich, Robert G. Herbert and author Walter Lord who proposed that the work be submitted to Patrick Stephens Ltd.

The authors wish to thank the staffs of the following American and Canadian institutions: The Library of Congress, Prints and Photos Division; US Department of the Navy, History Division and Naval Photographic Center; National Archives; University of Baltimore Library (particularly Laura Brown and James Foster); Delaware State College Library; Audio-Visual Department, Delaware State College; Hagley Museum; Mystic Seaport; Peabody Museum; South Street Seaport; The Mariners Museum; the Nova Scotia Museum; the Museum of the City of New York; and the Libraries Division of the State of Delaware.

We also wish to thank the staffs of the following British institutions: The British Library; The Public Record Office; Institute of Historical Research; National Maritime Museum; Imperial War Museum; London House; The Archives, University of Glasgow; Scottish Record Office; Stewart Bale Ltd; and the *Illustrated London News*. Among maritime and naval societies the assistance of the World Ship Society, Steamship Historical Society of America, United States Naval Institute, Belgian Nautical Research Association and Society for Nautical Research was deeply appreciated at various times.

Very special thanks go to Joanna Simms for technical advice and assistance in photographic matters, and to Martha Shaum for statistical matters. Martha Shaum and Debbie Flayhart sustained the authors during the production of the work over a very long period of time since both ladies had the misfortune to 'marry' the book!

In the course of such a project a great many people are called upon for assistance and it is likely that someone is bound to be overlooked in the final analysis. This is an error of omission rather than commission and regrets are extended to anyone who may have been left out.

Index